MAP

Showing the line of Boundary

between

THE UNITED STATES & BRITISH POSSESSIONS

From the point where the 49th Parallel of North Latitude strikes the Western Coast of the Continent "to the middle of the channel which separates the Continent from Vancouver's Island and thence Southerly through the middle of said channel" &c. to Fuca's Straits, in accordance with Treaty of June 15th, 1846.

Scale of Statute Miles.

The Pig War

Standoff at Griffin Bay

by

Michael Vouri

griffin bay bookstore

Inquiries should be sent to Griffin Bay Bookstore
P. O. Box 1669, Friday Harbor, WA 98250

Library of Congress Catalog number 98-072748

The Pig War / by Michael Vouri

ISBN 0-9634562-5-3

FIRST EDITION, 1999
2 4 6 8 10 9 7 5 3

Cover photo: H. M. S. *Satellite*. British Columbia Archives
Cover design & author photo: Susan Eyerly

Contents

Acknowledgments

Despite the word "War" in the title of this book, the story is about peace.

Historians of the British Empire and American Manifest Destiny in the mid-Nineteenth Century can list many reasons why these nations chose not to fight over the San Juan Island in 1859. Most of them are discussed in this volume. However, it is the central idea that peace was chosen over war that charms visitors to the San Juan Island National Historical Park and inspires teachers to bring their classes on field trips.

Weighty issues of the day aside, war did not break out on San Juan Island because: Royal Navy Rear Admiral R. Lambert Baynes remembered the War of 1812 when his decks "ran with blood;" Captain Geoffrey Phipps Hornby had seen the hospital ships of the Crimean War; and U.S.Army Lieutenant General Winfield Scott had led men in battle from Lundy's Lane in the War of 1812 to the assault on Chupultepec Castle in Mexico. These are the men who refused to consider shedding blood over a tiny archipelago, then in the middle of nowhere; warriors with convictions, and most critically, imaginations.

I would like to acknowledge and thank the following friends and colleagues for helping me tell this story: former San Juan Island National Historical Park Superintendent Robert E. Scott and Chief Ranger Bill Gleason for bringing me to San Juan Island NHP; historian and author Dr. Keith Murray for writing the first scholarly history about the Pig War, and urging me to do the same; George Thomas and John Olbrantz formerly director and deputy director of the Whatcom Museum of History and Art in

Bellingham, for the assignment of curating "George Pickett and the Frontier Army Experience," the 1994-95 exhibition that started this whole process; my friend and editor, Lane Morgan; MacMan, Bruce Conway, for his extra care in helping prepare the manuscript; historian and George Pickett expert Dr. Richard Selcer for reading and offering criticisms of several chapters, helping me out with primary sources and laughing at my bad jokes; historian and Pickett biographer Dr. Lesley Gordon for her time, generosity and quality document photocopies; former newspaper editor and dear friend Dick Beardsley for telling me it was way too long; Pig War historian and park volunteer Bud Rodewald of San Juan Island for many conversations about the incident; Michael Upton, Her Majesty's Consul General for Seattle and the Pacific Northwest, for providing a stack of document copies from the British Foreign and Commonwealth Office; my predecessor at San Juan Island NHP, Detlef Wieck (now at Klondike NHP in Seattle), for valuable observations and opinions that guided my research; and most of all to my publisher and partner Susan Eyerly of Griffin Bay Bookstore for her love, support and considerable investment in this project.

—San Juan Island, April 19, 1999.

The Cast of Characters

(Alphabetical Order)

The Americans

Ellis Barnes - Whatcom County Sheriff
James Buchanan - Secretary of State (1846), President (1859)
Archibald Campbell - U.S. boundary Commissioner
Lieutenant Colonel Silas Casey - Deputy commander, 9th Infantry
Lewis Cass - Secretary of State (1859)
Henry R. Crosbie - Whatcom County Civil Magistrate
William Cullen - Whatcom County Commissioner
Lyman Cutlar - San Juan island settler who shot pig
W.R. Drinkard - Acting Secretary of War
Isaac N. Ebey - U.S. Customs Collector (1854-55)
John Floyd - Secretary of War (1859)
Second Lieutenant James Forsyth. — Pickett's deputy
Charles Gholson - Governor, Washington Territory
Captain Granville O. Haller - Fort Townsend commander
General William S. Harney –Department of Oregon commander
Paul K. Hubbs, Jr. – Deputy Customs Collector (1859)
Captain Lewis Cass Hunt – Replaced Pickett on San Juan Island
W.L. Marcy - Secretary of State (1855)
Charles McKay – San Juan Island settler

Captain George E. Pickett – Co. D, 9th Infantry commander
Captain Alfred Pleasonton – Harney's acting adjutant general
Second Lieutenant Henry Martyn Robert – Corps of Engineers
Lieutenant General Winfield Scott – U.S.Army commander.
Isaac I. Stevens - Governor, Washington Territory (1854)
Henry Webber - Deputy Customs Collector (1854)

The British

Rear Admiral R. Lambert Baynes - Pacific Station commander
Captain George Bazalgette - English Camp commander
A.G. Dallas – Governor, Hudson's Bay Company 1859
John DeCourcy - British Civil Magistrate
Captain Michael DeCourcy - Acting Pacific Station commander
James Douglas - Governor, Vancouver Island/British Columbia
Charles Griffin - Hudson's Bay Company agent
Captain Geoffrey Phipps Hornby - H.M.S. *Tribune* commander
Lord Lyons - British Ambassador in Washington, D.C.
Captain James Prevost - H.M.S. *Satellite* commander
Captain George Richards - H.M.S. *Plumper* commander
Lord John Russell - British Foreign Secretary
James Sangster - British Customs Inspector
George Simpson – Governor, Hudson's Bay Company

CHAPTER 1

Pickett has Landed

Charles Griffin probably heard it before he saw it. There was no mistaking that sound at mid-nineteenth century. Steamers could be detected from miles away, the great cylinders panting and clanking over the flat, gray inland seas with the steady thump of bass drums. As he later noted in his journal it was between 8 and 9 p.m., Tuesday, July 26, 1859. It had been a beautiful evening, typical of the island in midsummer. A southwest breeze made the prairie grasses shimmer in a golden reflection of the silver waters of the Strait of Juan de Fuca below the headlands a quarter mile from his cabin porch. Looking south across the strait, the snow-capped Olympic mountains rose from a bank of clouds, effacing a sky beginning to turn salmon, while directly west, Victoria was locked in a haze of wood smoke from slash being burned to make room for the rapidly growing British colony.

It had been nearly six years since Vancouver Island Governor James Douglas had dispatched Griffin to San Juan Island. His orders were to establish Belle Vue Farm, a unit of the Hudson's Bay Company's subsidiary Puget Sound Agricultural Company. The governor, who then also ran the Hudson's Bay post at Victoria, hoped the farm would entrench Great Britain's claim to the island. An ambiguity in the language of the Oregon Treaty of 1846, which set the international boundary between the United States and Great Britain at the Forty-ninth Parallel, had placed the San Juan Islands in limbo. Both nations claimed them and thirteen years later the dispute remained unresolved.

In this, his first management opportunity with the company, Griffin had done well by any standard. His flocks had grown from 1,350 to nearly 4,500 sheep, and he could take satisfaction in the eighty acres of fenced truck gardens, cleared roads, and the eight tidy cabins that composed the farm compound. It had not always been easy. He'd had to be constantly vigilant about rapidly changing weather, marauding Indians, and most especially, rapacious Yankees from the mainland. In their haste to solidify the American claim to the islands, they would stop at nothing to threaten his business. First it had been customs collectors from Port Townsend, then tax collectors from Whatcom County, and now his prairies were being overrun by squatters, one of whom the month before had shot one of his prize boars and threatened to shoot Griffin himself if he again "trespassed" on the American's "property." Griffin expected a magistrate to arrive soon from Victoria aboard the H.M.S. *Satellite*, a 21-gun steam corvette, to deal with that fellow and the other squatters who had grown increasingly belligerent. That was probably the steamer he heard. It would be long dark before it docked, so he went to bed.

The next morning Griffin awoke to the news—probably from one of his herdsmen— that the ship was not the *Satellite*. It was an American warship—the U.S. Propeller *Massachusetts*. Griffin left his cabin and hiked up the rough track from the farm, over the ridge and down to what is now called Griffin Bay. He took care to steer clear of several other squatter cabins. From the crest of the ridge the bay formed a broad crescent, defining the southern end of the island from Cattle Point to Bald Mountain, giving on to Lopez Island to the east across the San Juan Channel. To the north were the rugged fingers of Orcas Island and the white cone of Mount Baker rising from the North Cascades, fifty miles distant on the mainland. The *Massachusetts* was anchored a few hundred yards off his dock. The black-hulled steamer was used by the U.S.Army to ferry troops and provisions about Puget Sound. Anchored a few hundred yards away from her was the *Shubrick*, a U.S. lighthouse tender that also had arrived the day before, presumably seeking anchorage for the evening.

It was not the first time Griffin had seen U.S. warships.They'd come several times before, in fact the *Massachusetts* had stopped by briefly earlier in the month. But they usually were smaller wind-powered revenue cutters bearing customs agents or, on two occasions, small detachments of soldiers in pursuit of Indian raiders. Clunker though she was—she could only make three knots wide open and was in constant need of repair—the *Massachusetts* still mounted eight 32-pound naval guns on her decks and could carry a company or more of soldiers. And Griffin had not been aware of any recent raids, either by local Indians or the bands generally labeled as "Northerners" from Queen Charlotte Islands or Russian America. What he did know was that on the American Independence Day three weeks before the American squatters had stepped a flagpole in the yard of the so-called U.S. customs house and run up the stars and stripes. That had prompted Griffin, in turn, to fly the Union Jack from his company pole. At the time he did not believe there was anything to worry about. Patriotic posturing was usually harmless. But the Yankee flag was still flying five days later, attracting the attention of Brigadier General William Selby Harney, the commander of the U.S. Army's Department of Oregon, headquartered at Fort Vancouver. The general had been aboard this same *Massachusetts* on his way back from a visit with Governor Douglas in Victoria. The general had stepped ashore, huddled with the American deputy customs collector, Paul K. Hubbs, Jr., and several others, and then walked to the very ridge where he now stood and observed the HBC farm. But that had apparently been the end of it. After a stay of barely twenty minutes, the general left for Fort Steilacoom.

Now here was the *Massachusetts* again, and Griffin could

see long boats from both vessels approaching the shore bearing men in blue, lumber, tents, and what appeared to be field guns. Cannon! Griffin cautiously made his way down the hill and watched from his wharf as the soldiers spilled out of the boats and began stacking their cargo on the beach. Choosing not to make contact with the soldiers until he had more information, he turned for home.

Unbeknownst to Griffin, Hubbs had been roused the night before by a sharp rap on his cabin door. He opened it to find a U.S. Army sergeant in full regalia: blue frock coat with dazzling gold buttons and shoulder scales, dark blue trousers with a sky blue stripe running down each leg, a sword slung from a shoulder strap and a black slouch hat with the brim turned up on one side, garnished by a black ostrich plume. This was First Sergeant William Smith of Company D, Ninth Infantry, late of Fort Bellingham, the unit commanded by Hubbs's Indian war comrade, Captain George E. Pickett. Smith told Hubbs that the company was scheduled to land the next morning to establish a camp. The purpose? Why, to protect the American settlers from the British, of course. The captain already was on beach. Would Hubbs come along and help them locate a camp site? Hubbs hurriedly dressed and followed the sergeant along the gravel beach. The dark silhouette of the *Massachusetts* rode at anchor out in the bay, while ahead on the beach in the twilight Hubbs saw a clutch of men gathered near a long boat. One of them left the group and approached him. It was a Lieutenant Howard, "a fiery Southerner," who immediately offered a flask of brandy and escorted Hubbs to his commanding officer. Thirty-four years-old, slight of build with curly brown hair that extended to his shoulders beneath his regulation kepi, Pickett was well-known as a Mexican War hero who was utterly fearless and could take a drink and play the banjo with the best of them. Hubbs had sat at many a campfire with the Virginian during the White River campaign in 1856. Only weeks before, Hubbs had rowed to Fort Bellingham to complain to his old friend about the treatment American settlers on San Juan were receiving at the hands of the Hudson's Bay Company. Presumably, Pickett had told General Harney and now here was the result. The men smoked and drank while the Virginian laid out his plans for Hubbs. At last, justice would come to San Juan Island.

One man in the area who was not surprised by the *Massachusetts's* arrival was U.S. Boundary Commissioner Archibald Campbell, aboard *Shubrick* . He had received a dispatch a few days earlier from Harney's acting adjutant, Captain Alfred Pleasonton, advising him that Pickett was going to San Juan to head off Indian attacks. Campbell had been given no hint (he later claimed) that the soldiers' stay was meant to be permanent. Having spent more than a year arguing to the point of exhaustion with his British counterpart over the ownership of the islands, Campbell had come to San Juan to see for himself why the British were so insistent about keeping it. He had spent a pleasant afternoon hiking along the bay and taking shots at the small black-tailed deer that emerged from the woods in surprising numbers to nibble at the prairie grasses. He thought nothing of the *Massachusetts's* arrival until he saw the mounds of stores being shuttled to the beach the following morning. It looked as though Pickett meant to stay. Had the dispute been settled without his knowledge? And if so, how had he been left out of the loop? Worse, if the dispute had not been settled, he could well imagine the British reaction to what could only be construed as a provocative act.

There would be hell to pay, and it had been a long time coming.

CHAPTER 2

The Quest for Wealth: Sources of Trouble

For nearly fifty years, the United States and Great Britain contended over the international boundary in the Oregon Country, more than a half million square miles comprising the present states of Washington, Oregon and Idaho, portions of Montana and Wyoming , and the province of British Columbia.

Further complicating matters were tremendous distances between West Coast outposts and the home governments in Washington, D.C., and London, which resulted in serious breakdowns in communications. Local officials groped through the murky regions of foreign policy, interpreting and enforcing treaties and attendant provisos according to instructions that changed with each new government. With the transcontinental telegraph still several years away, steamships often crossed paths bearing dispatches containing conflicting information. Policies enforced had to be undone. Confrontations escalated–or vice versa–before reports reached their readers.

Through it all, the governments of Great Britain and the United States never stopped talking. A peaceful settlement, in lieu of a "disastrous difficulty" (as Royal Navy Captain Geoffrey Phipps Hornby stated it), was always the goal. Bellicosity was the exception rather than the rule. Perhaps it was due to a spirit of Christian brotherhood and a sincere desire to avoid bloodshed. Perhaps it was because the two nations, more than 75 years removed from the Revolutionary War, remained closely tied through language and institutions. No doubt, the hard reality of economic interest, despite a lot of pontificating over questions of "honor," was probably the greatest motivator. Great Britain in the first half of the nineteenth century was more concerned with free trade and commercial growth than she was in paying the high price of empire.

The competition between Great Britain and the United States over the Oregon Country—or "that pine swamp," as the British Lord Aberdeen termed it—really can be traced back to the Nootka Convention of 1790, a document that was to carry heavy freight over the next sixty years.

After Captain James Cook noted in his log the high prices sea otter pelts commanded in China, merchant captains from both nations began dropping anchor in Nootka Sound, about midway up the west coast of Vancouver Island. This did not set well with Imperial Spain, which in 1788 dispatched Captain Estaban Martinez to reassert Spanish claims to the region—based upon a Spanish voyage of exploration in 1774 and a sixteenth-century papal bull granting Spain most of the Western Hemisphere. Thus arose the first conflict between contending European nations in the Pacific Northwest.

Martinez approached his work with a relish. The Spaniard confiscated three English ships in Nootka Sound, clapping two of the crews in irons and dispatching the other crew back to Macao in the hold of an American ship. The Americans—namely the Bostonian Captains Robert Gray and John Kendrick—were left alone, probably because they did not appear to be a threat.

When the British found out what Martinez had done, they called their ambassador home from Spain and squared away the fleet for war. They also sought a diplomatic advantage, and that came with the French Revolution when the Spanish crown lost its closest ally, King Louis XVI. The Spanish fleet was not prepared to take on Great Britain alone, thus the Nootka Convention.

Stripping away the verbiage, it basically allowed for the first joint occupation of the Oregon Country. It also could be interpreted that whoever occupied the lands and made something of them became the rightful owner. At least that was the way the Americans saw it. The brand-new Yankee government of George Washington, specifically his Secretary of State, Thomas Jefferson, took note. The British interpretation was different. In their eyes, Spain had given up and the Northwest Coast was theirs. Thus was another seed sown.

Across the Pacific, Robert Gray departed Macao flush with proceeds from fur sales, sailed round the Cape of Good Hope, and completed the first circumnavigation of the globe by an American skipper. He had only seven weeks to rest from this three-year voyage before he was again dispatched to make more money for his owners. He spent a year trading and charting in the Northwest, wintered in Macao, then returned to the Northwest for more trading. By then the British had sent another ship to make certain the Spanish lived up to the convention and to further the explorations made by Cook. The expedition composed of two ships, *Discovery* and *Chatham*, was under the command of a Cook lieutenant, Captain George Vancouver. The Yanks and the Brits spotted each other on April 28, 1792.

British and American explorer/traders in the Pacific Northwest operated with a degree of comity, except where a territorial claim was at stake. Call it loyalty to the Anglo-Saxon race, the comfort of a common tongue thousands of miles from home, or the simple matter of having a lot in common—they got along. This was first evidenced by the initial encounter between Gray and Vancouver off the Olympic Peninsula, just south of the Strait of Juan de Fuca. They coasted along together for several days exchanging information about their travels. Vancouver wanted to know how thoroughly Gray had explored the Strait. Gray sought to verify what he earlier spotted about 200 miles south and had taken to be Bruno de Heceta's presumed great river, Bahia Asuncion. Vancouver had discounted the Spaniard's assumptions. He was more interested in the Strait of Juan de Fuca, which finally had been charted, but barely explored, by the British merchant Captain Charles Barkley in 1786.

Later, when Gray confirmed the existence of the river and named it for his ship, *Columbia,* he generously made copies of his charts for Vancouver and Heceta. A chagrined Vancouver followed up in 1793 by sending the *Chatham*, under Broughton, over the bar and up river as far as Washougal (east of today's Vancouver). Because his ship had made a far deeper penetration of the river (Gray only went about thirty-six miles), Vancouver felt justified in claiming the territory for His Britannic Majesty. Meanwhile, while Gray was busy making money, Vancouver was making charts—extensive ones—of the entire Puget Sound basin and the complete coastline of Vancouver Island, as well as the navigable channel that ran from the Strait of Juan de Fuca between the mainland and a cluster of islands and islets to the Gulf of Georgia. The channel was called Vancouver's Channel in honor of the explorer, but eventually would become accepted by its Spanish name, the one it carries today—Rosario Strait. [1]

The Spaniards were still around. Captains Bodega y Quadra, Lopez de Haro, Malaspina, Quimper and others continued to explore and chart water passages in what they still considered New Spain. Some of the Spanish names would become lost footnotes in history—such as the poetic Bahia de Gaston, today known as Bellingham Bay. (The Anglo name was given by the politically astute Vancouver for the head of stores for the British Admiralty.) Other Spanish names stuck, among these San Juan, Orcas and Lopez islands and most importantly for Americans, the Haro Strait, a wide, easily navigable channel that ran between that same cluster of islands and Vancouver's Island.

CHAPTER 3

Manifest Destiny & Joint Occupation

The 1790s were a time of ferment for the young United States, not least in the mind of Secretary of State Thomas Jefferson. While he was aware of Vancouver's and Gray's voyages to the Pacific Northwest, it was the overland explorations of the Northwest Company's Alexander Mackenzie, culminating with the Scotsman's arrival on the Pacific via the Bella Coola River in 1793, that moved Jefferson to propose U.S.-sponsored expeditions.The apparently vast, bountiful and virtually untouched continent stretching to the Pacific Ocean was the canvas upon which he would paint his vision of a yeoman democracy, expanding to meet each new challenge.

Jefferson's plans had to wait until his own presidency, when a combination of international events—primarily Napolean's rise and fall and their effects on Spain—dropped the massive Louisiana Territory into his lap. A transcontinental expedition already was in the planning stages when the terms of the sale were being negotiated in 1803. It proceeded on May 14, 1804, under the leadership of Meriwether Lewis and William Clark.

It took two years for Lewis and Clark to make the round trip via the continental divide from St. Louis to the mouth of the Columbia River. But their efforts gave the United States another claim to the Oregon Country to add to Gray's. These claims were underscored in 1810 when the fur merchant John Jacob Astor sent missions overland and by sea to establish a fur post at the mouth of the Columbia.The Montreal-based Northwest Company, getting wind of Astor's doings, also dispatched a mission to the Columbia under astronomer/explorer David Thompson.

Much to Thompson's surprise, the Yankees got there first when Astor's bark *Tonquin* crossed the bar and established Fort Astoria. But the world caught up with Fort Astoria by 1813, when British trapper and trader John George McTavish appeared at the fort's gate one day and informed the occupants that Great Britain and the United States were at war. The H.M.S. *Racoon*, Captain William Black, was in the area, McTavish said, so it would be best if they surrendered the fort to him before anyone got hurt.

Ever seeking profit in adversity, the Astorians put the fort up for sale instead. Down came the stars and stripes and up went the Union Jack without a shot being fired.

After the war, the British government, weary of contending with the rapidly expanding United States, awarded Fort Astoria to the U.S. and acceded to the joint occupation of the Oregon Country with the Anglo-American Convention of 1818. This included the establishment of the international border on the 49th parallel between the Lake of the Woods in Minnesota and the Rocky (or Stony) Mountains. Although the British had wanted a Columbia River boundary, the Americans balked, which prompted British Foreign Secretary Castleraugh to give ground, believing the overture "...an additional motive to cultivate (in the Americans) the arts of peace."

Thus, it was decided that the largely undeveloped land from the Rocky Mountains to the Pacific, north of the 42nd parallel (California-Oregon border) and south of the Russian possessions (the 54th parallel or Southeast Alaska) would be shared. The agreement would be subject to renewal in 1827, unless it was determined that one nation had legitimately settled the area–possession being nine-tenths of the law.

The Hudson's Bay Company (HBC) bought out the Northwest Company in 1821 and quickly took the lead by establishing a network of fur trading posts on tributaries of the Columbia and along the Northwest Coast of British Columbia. Fort Vancouver, about sixty miles up the Columbia from Fort Astoria, became the primary post in the region, dominating the fur trade and administering agricultural colonies that provided foodstuffs for its outposts and for the Russian-America Company in exchange for furs. This alarmed the still largely agrarian Americans, who by the mid-1820s were beginning to think about organizing agricultural colonies of their own south of the Columbia.

What they could not establish in fact, the Americans tried to do on paper. In 1825, Secretary of State Albert Gallantin proposed that the 49th parallel divide British and American possessions across the continent, but the Hudson's Bay Company would have none of it. The Columbia was the main highway into their vast inland fur empire, and the company viewed it as a private canal. Therefore the British government countered the American proposal by again suggesting a border tracing the Columbia River from the 49th parallel south, then west to the Columbia River bar. The Americans would get the Olympic Peninsula, which would grant them access to Puget Sound, plus free navigation rights on the Columbia. The Americans said no and joint occupation continued.

Working in the field to make the British offer a foregone conclusion, Hudson's Bay Company Governor George Simpson systematically continued to undercut Yankee sea captains and fur traders from the Columbia to Alaska. First it was with the Indians, and then with the Russian America company, as the HBC swapped dimension lumber and food products for prime otter and beaver pelts at good prices. From the early 1830s Simpson realized that the HBC would have to diversify if it was to maintain its economic stranglehold on the Oregon Country. He focused on three extraction industries — timber, fishing, farming — that formed the nucleus of the region's economy well into the late twentieth century. To direct the company's farm activities, he established the subsidiary Puget Sound Agricultural Company with sites at Forts Nisqually and Vancouver, as well as a plantation near the Cowlitz River landing in today's southwestern Washington. [1]

Now American immigrants trying to subsist as farmers anywhere near HBC facilities were in the same fix as the sea captains. The HBC could produce more for less. The Americans were effectively stymied, and those who managed to hold on in the area developed a bitterness for the company that would never be forgotten.

However, while the door to Yankee settlement may have seemed shut tight, a sizable crack remained. At Fort Vancouver, Factor Dr. John McLoughlin had a heart, to his eventual undoing and the undoing of his company south of the 49th parallel. Fort Vancouver was the regional center for supplies, news, medical care, and interesting company, and McLoughlin helped the American settlers who began to trickle in. This alarmed Simpson, who never liked the Fort Vancouver site because ships frequently sank crossing the Columbia River bar. By 1841 the American missionary movement embraced the Oregon Country, found the backing of Congress, and began to actively market settlement. It had become America's "Manifest Destiny" to extend democracy from coast to coast. The visionary hoopla was fueled by practical considerations. The Panic of 1837 spurred many farm families west to beat low prices. Oregon was a second chance. McLoughlin helped them out with low interest loans, tools, and information. The dramatic results were typical of the patterns of American westward settlement that began with the first penetration of the Appalachians.

Western historian Ray Allen Billington believed that the British were only too happy to settle for the 49th parallel by 1846 for a couple of reasons. In *Westward Expansion*, he noted that the Walker Tariff, passed by the U.S. Congress and signed into law by President James Knox Polk in 1846, lowered duties on British manufactured goods. Britain repealed its protectionist Corn Laws the same year, opening British markets to U.S. farm crops from the West and Southeast. British business interests were quite naturally delighted by this turn of events and would have brought great pressure to bear on any foreign policy measure that might provoke hostilities with the United States. "(The tariff) mollified English opinion, long opposed to American high protection, and aided the government in its policy of compromise," Billington wrote.

Second, U.S. immigration into Oregon by land and sea had accelerated by startling proportions by 1845. A thousand people had arrived in 1843 alone and another 1,500 would settle in 1844. This was enough to prompt Missouri Senator Thomas Hart Benton to declare, "Let the emigrants go on; and carry their rifles.... Thirty thousand rifles in Oregon will annihilate the Hudson's Bay Company, drive them off our continent."

The British were less impressed by rifles than they were with the exponential growth in Yankee settlement. "Where there had been only 300 Americans in 1840, now there were 8,000 in the country, most settling south of the Columbia in the fertile Willamette Valley," Billington observed.[2]

The incoming farmers helped drive out the fur trade, and by 1842 George Simpson decided to move the HBC's main Oregon Country post away from the aggressive Yankees and the Columbia River bar to a more accommodating site on Vancouver Island. Under the leadership of James Douglas the new fort was established in 1843 in an excellent natural harbor on the southern end of the island and named Fort Victoria. In five years, the once thriving factory and trading hub at Fort Vancouver would be reduced to a modest trading post that received two shipments of goods per year.

"That meant since the British already were evacuating the

area in dispute, British diplomacy could now yield gracefully and without the sacrifice of any important economic interest," Billington wrote.

Simpson, who wasn't much interested in diplomacy, disparaged the Americans on his way out the door as "worthless and lawless characters of every description."

And so the bitterness between the company and the American settlers cut both ways. Despite company policies, HBC employees, especially James Douglas, would never get over being sold out by their own government and being shoved out of the Columbia River valley.[3]

CHAPTER 4

The Treaty of Oregon: A Table Set for Trouble

The Oregon Treaty of 1846 gave the United States undisputed possession of the Pacific Northwest south of the 49th parallel, extending the boundary to the "middle of the channel which separates the continent from Vancouver's Island..." The treaty settled the larger boundary question, but its wording left unclear who owned San Juan Island. The seemingly endless diplomatic juggling that went on before a settlement was reached left both nations so desperate to get on with business that they were willing to overlook niggling details— such as the ownership of the San Juan Islands.

When the British proposed to settle the Oregon question once and for all in 1842, hoping against hope that the boundary might trace the Columbia River, they were well aware that such a boundary would deny the Americans a deep-water port in the region, a prospect that would be totally unacceptable to the U.S. Government.

The British also knew that the as-yet-unpublished findings of the United States Exploring Expedition – which, under the command of U.S. Navy Lieutenant Charles Wilkes, had in 1841 charted a large stretch of the Oregon Country, including the San Juan Islands – already were circulating in the corridors of power. Wilkes had written that the Columbia River bar "rendered the entrance of that river impracticable for large vessels during nine months of the year; and that the only harbor available along the whole coast was at the 'Strait of Juan de Fuca,' three degrees north of the Columbia, and of course within that portion of the territory which, according to any compromise of the Disputed Boundary, would belong exclusively to Great Britain."

By August 1844, President John Tyler's second Secretary of State, John Calhoun, proposed a compromise of the 49th parallel. If the British accepted, he wrote, the U.S. might be willing to cede Vancouver Island and guarantee free navigation of the Strait of Juan de Fuca and other channels and inlets running south of the line. Instead, in late 1844, Britain countered with a proposal to submit the question to binding arbitration. Calhoun refused and it was back to square.

James Knox Polk was subsequently elected president on the crest of highly inflammatory campaign dialogue ("54-40 or Fight"), which favored setting the boundary north of the Queen Charlotte Islands. Reality had yet to set in by the time of his inaugural address, which was so bellicose it prompted the British to alert the Royal Navy to enforce British rights wherever and whenever threatened on the Northwest Coast:

> You will hold temperate, but firm language to members of the Government and to all those with whom you converse. We are still ready to adhere to the principle of equitable compromise; but we are perfectly determined to concede nothing to force or menace, and are fully prepared to maintain our rights. [1]

The Royal Navy already had been active throughout the election year, showing flag along the coast, and sending the 18-gun sloop H.M.S. *Modeste* up the Columbia in July 1844.

In Washington City, the ever-tactful James Buchanan was appointed Polk's Secretary of State and despite Polk's posturing he was determined to settle the Oregon Question peaceably. On July 12, 1845, Buchanan submitted a proposal to the British, outlining what the United States would be willing to consider. It was backed by a windy summary, rehashing Calhoun's arguments going back to the Nootka Convention. He then offered the same compromise of the 49th parallel, providing that Britain accommodate free ports on Vancouver Island.

The British rejected the proposal, pointing out that it contained nothing about free navigation of the Columbia and that Britain already was entitled to all of Vancouver Island. Buchanan replied in August with another lengthy history lesson, this one reaching back to the myth-laden voyage of Juan de Fuca, or Apostolos Valerianos the Greek, on behalf of Spain in 1592 and to the account of that voyage as noted in Samuel Purchas's "The Pilgrims" in 1625, not to mention a personal interview with Fuca by Michael Lok in Venice in 1596. He then withdrew the offer of the 49th.

Finally, on May 20, 1846, the U.S. resorted to brinksmanship, announcing that it intended to "put an end" to the Convention of 1827, which would effectively terminate the joint occupation. The British ambassador in Washington, Richard Pakenham, was grudgingly urged by his government to renew his efforts at a settlement. Foreign Secretary Lord Aberdeen opined that the British government had been conciliatory to the extreme: "Can it truly be said that the Government of the United States have advanced to meet us in the path of mutual concession?"

Aberdeen instructed Pakenham to propose to the U.S. that the 49th be the boundary from the "Rocky Mountains to the seacoast; and from thence in a southerly direction through the centre of King George's Sound and the Straits of Juan de Fuca to the Pacific Ocean, leaving the whole of Vancouver's Island, with its ports and harbors, in possession of Great Britain."

The Columbia River was to remain "free and open" to the Hudson's Bay Company and to subjects of Great Britain trading with the company. The HBC also would be permitted to retain Fort Vancouver and other stations south of the 49th. The HBC subsidiary, Puget Sound Agricultural Company, would be allowed to remain in business south of the 49th or be fairly compensated. The treaty was drafted at the British Foreign Office and was accepted by the U.S. as written.

The final, ambiguous passage concerning the water boundary read:

> From the point on the forty-ninth parallel of north latitude where the boundary laid down in existing treaties and conventions between the United States and Great Britain terminates, the line of boundary between the territories of the United States and those of Her Britannic Majesty shall be continued westward along the said forty-ninth parallel of north latitude to the middle of the channel which separates the continent from Vancouver's Island; and thence southerly through the middle of the said channel, and of Fuca's Straits to the Pacific Ocean; provided however, that the navigation of the whole of said channel and Straits south of the forty-ninth parallel of north latitude remain free and open to both parties. [2]

Sir John H. Pelly, governor of the HBC, read the passage in its draft form. Hudson's Bay officials knew there were two channels, not one, cutting south from the Gulf of Georgia. On May 16 he complained to Lord Aberdeen about the ambiguity, noting that it could have been avoided had the people who actually knew the area been consulted.

The treaty language, he pointed out, should read: "...to the centre of the Gulf of Georgia in that latitude; *and from that point south along the track of Vancouver* (today's Rosario Strait) till it meets a line drawn from the sea to the centre of the Straits of San Juan de Fuca, and from that point to the sea." The San Juan Islands should, without question, belong to Great Britain and specifically to the HBC, according to Pelly, who attached a map to clarify matters. [3]

The map Pelly sent along incorporated data from maps published by George Vancouver in 1798 and an 1846 map, based on Vancouver's atlas, crafted by Charles Pruess, a German cartographer traveling with American explorer John C. Fremont. The maps reveal the islands as vaguely familiar masses blocking the Strait of Georgia from which irregular passages noodle their way to the Strait of Juan de Fuca. While the Preuss map clearly labels the "Canal de Arro," the passage highlighted by a red line denoting the "true" north-south route — or "Vancouver's track" — is Vancouver's Strait, or Rosario Strait, as it is known today. [4]

Buchanan also expressed alarm when he read Article 1. He wrote on June 6, 1846, to Louis McLane, the American minister in London, that the article did not "provide that the line shall pass through the Canal de Arro (Haro) as stated in your Despatch. This would probably be the fair construction."

Buchanan's observation and Pelly's protests were ignored and the Treaty of Oregon was signed with minor adjustments by both nations on June 15. It was ratified by the Senate on June 18, and Parliament followed suit.

However, either Congress and Parliament were unable to focus their attention on such an obscure part of the world or both governments were in a hurry to conclude the agreement and cool the growing crisis in the Northwest before it started to affect business.

The British government changed in June and Lord Palmerston became Foreign Minister. Palmerston was considered more hard-nosed when it came to foreign policy, a trait cited more than once as another reason why the treaty was concluded in a hurry.

After studying the treaty, Palmerston approached Pelly on July 30, requesting clarification of certain geographical details. Pelly again drew attention to the passage identifying the "channel" running between Vancouver Island and the mainland. He wrote that "...there are numerous islands, and, I believe, passages between them. I know there is one close round Vancouver's Island; but I believe the largest to be the one Vancouver sailed through, and coloured red in the tracing, and I think this is the one that should be the boundary."

In February 1847, George Simpson went to Washington to suggest a commission to adjust certain points in the treaty. He wrote:

> There are several channels separating the mainland from Vancouver's island (occasioned by islands); it is therefore very desirable that which is to form the line of demarcation should be determined, otherwise the sovereignty of those channel islands may very well soon become a source of dispute between British and American subjects. [5]

Pakenham dutifully submitted Simpson's observations to his government. Two British survey ships were at that instant exploring the area in question, he was told. The geography was still "imperfectly known" and adjustments should wait on the results of those surveys. Unfortunately the two ships, H.M.S. *Pandora* and H.M.S. *Herald*, never made it beyond the entrance to the Strait of Haro, therefore the territory remained unknown to the powers that be.

Pakenham was soon replaced in Washington by John Crampton, who was given instructions to approach the U.S. and suggest that each nation provide an officer of "scientific attainment and conciliatory character" to mark and survey the area and come up with a water boundary satisfactory to both nations. The word "channel" was key in reaching an accord. The final treaty said nothing about "Vancouver's track." The Foreign Ministry pointed out that in most treaties "channel" meant a "deep and navigable" channel. Presumably this characterized the one charted by Vancouver. If this was the one adopted, the government presumed no "difficulty" would arise. And while it was true that adoption of this waterway would attach the island to Great Britain it was doubted the U.S. would protest for "...these islets are of little or no value..."

Buchanan replied that in his view the British proposal sounded fair, but should be based on further study of the area by boundary survey crews. He took "channel" to mean the "main navigable channel" wherever situated. But he confessed that he had never examined Vancouver's charts, and while he was not prepared to contest the British claim, he declined to adopt the view without additional research and geographical evidence. Crampton then officially proposed a joint boundary commission to make the final determination.

On July 31, 1848, U.S. Ambassador George Bancroft forwarded to Palmerston the charts of Lieutenant Wilkes, who in addition to writing his observations of the Columbia River bar had extensively surveyed Puget Sound and other coastal waters, including the San Juan Island group. Most of the names he gave to the islands were of War of 1812 naval heroes, ships and battles. Shaw, Decatur and Waldron islands, plus Mount Constitution and Mount Erie, remain Wilkes's lasting legacy.

Most importantly, however, Wilkes's charts quite clearly show the San Juan Islands situated in the Strait of Georgia. The Haro Strait is labeled *Canal de Haro*, while Rosario (Vancouver's) Strait is labeled *Ringgold Strait*. Why this map was circulating among the inner circles of Washington but was not used in boundary negotiations remains a mystery. It was certainly clear to Bancroft that, indeed, the Haro Strait appeared to be the proper "channel." However, this was yesterday's news by then to Palmerston. The San Juan Islands were flyspecks on the great canvas of empire. Palmerston thanked Bancroft for the information and that was the last anyone in the halls of power had to say about the issue until December 1852 when local disputes began to percolate.

For Hudson's Bay Company factor and Vancouver Island Colony Governor James Douglas there was never any doubt as to the proper ownership of the islands. To his dying day he maintained the San Juans were the logical extension of Vancouver Island.

He was willing to stake his life and the lives of his countrymen on it.

CHAPTER 5

The San Juan Sheep War

"San Juan is a fertile and beautiful island, with a large extent of open prairie land; but were it barren and rocky, and intrinsically worthless, it is of the *utmost* value to Great Britain, commanding as it does the channel of communications between Vancouver Island and British Columbia...in my opinion, it matters not if all the other islands between San Juan and the Continent pass to the United States, but San Juan is invaluable to our possession; it clearly is ours, both in right and in equity, and to yield it to the United States would be to depreciate our contiguous territory to an extent that someday might prove fatal to Her Majesty's possessions in this quarter of the globe." [1]

-James Prevost (July 23, 1859)

And so the protests of a few businessmen and bean-counting diplomats were shunted aside, the Treaty of Oregon was concluded and it was business as usual again between the two governments. The view among the powerful was that the confusion over a few little islands on the other side of the world would work itself out.

And why should the Americans care? They were stomping Mexico and would soon take possession of the entire American southwest.

The key word above is "equity." Captain James Prevost, RN, commander of the steam corvette, H.M.S. *Satellite*, never wavered on the San Juan question in his role as water boundary commissioner for the British government. Set geographical arguments aside and he would still believe the San Juans were unquestionably British because that is what James Douglas believed.

With the brief exception of the crisis period in mid-1859 when the Royal Navy intervened, James Douglas *was* the British government north of the 49th parallel from the founding of Fort Victoria until he retired in 1864. Vancouver Island had been conveyed to the Hudson's Bay Company by Royal Grant on January 13, 1849, which put the "Company of Adventurers" in the colony business. Hoping to match the tide of American immigration, the government told HBC to provide a suitable climate for British settlers. This required a major change in thinking.

Heretofore, the company had discouraged settlers because they were bad for business. They moved to the hinterlands, got sick, went broke, or were slaughtered by Indians. That meant the company had to spend good money to heal them, bail them out, buy them boat tickets home, or hire soldiers to protect the survivors.

If Douglas wasn't miffed enough by this prospect, the British government tweaked him further by sending someone else to be governor; someone who might figure he could tell Douglas what to do. That lasted less than a year. On September 1, 1851, James Douglas was Chief Factor of Fort Victoria and governor of the crown colony.

Born August 15, 1803, in British Guinea, of a Scottish father and an African-Caribbean mother, James Douglas left home to make his fortune at age sixteen, catching on first with the old Northwest Company in 1819. When Northwest merged with the HBC in 1821, Douglas stayed on. He arrived at Fort Vancouver in

1830, where he was made clerk, but in a few years he rose to become John McLoughlin's assistant, acting in his stead when McLoughlin went to England for a year in 1838. He became chief factor at Fort Vancouver in 1846 and then moved to become chief factor at Fort Victoria, a post he'd founded in 1843. He was appointed agent of the Puget Sound Agricultural Company affiliate in 1849. From the beginning, he considered the San Juans "a dependency of Vancouver's Island."

In many of his missives justifying the British claims to the island, the governor's principal argument was that HBC agents had claimed the island in July 1845 by placing an engraved wooden tablet on Mt. Finlayson ("an eminence near the Southeast point of the island"). Douglas was to flatly maintain years later that this act took place prior to 1846, when the royal grant permitted the HBC to establish facilities anywhere in the Oregon Country between Russian America and the California border. Then in 1851, on authorization of his predecessor, Governor James Blanshard, he established a seasonal fish salting station on the southern end of San Juan Island and took formal possession of all the islands for the British government.

By late 1853 with the formation of Washington Territory and the expected arrival of an aggressive young governor and Mexican War hero, Isaac Stevens, Douglas knew more Americans would move north of the Columbia and snap up new lands in the Puget Sound basin. Stevens already was on record in his belief that while American settlers, focusing on agriculture, represented civilization and progress, the HBC's preoccupation with trade made them little different from Indians. (The governor obviously had not been paying attention to the company's diversified markets.) Stevens had not been in the territory a month when he sent letters to Peter Skene Ogden, who ran what remained of Fort Vancouver, and Dr. William Tolmie, the Puget Sound Agricultural Company head at Fort Nisqually. The letters essentially contained the U.S. blueprint for jettisoning the HBC from the mainland south of the 49th parallel. The companies had to stop trading with the

Indians and get ready to be "bought out" at a fair price.

The prospects looked familiar to Douglas. The Americans would push up to the 49th and those who knew anything about agriculture would grab the islands barren of trees but rich in topsoil. The American customs collector, Isaac Neff Ebey, already had claimed a prime homestead on Whidbey Island. The San Juans with their acres of virgin prairie beckoned. Douglas pointed out to the colonial office that the San Juans could "maintain a large population" because of the extent of timber, arable farmland, and fisheries.

In November 1853, Douglas decided to act. He wrote to the Duke of Newcastle that it was his intention to "assert the sovereignty of her majesty the Queen to all the islands of the Arro Archipelago" lying west of Cypress Island. If Washington and London were not prepared to settle on Rosario as the boundary, Douglas would do it unilaterally. To support his action, Douglas went on to observe (erroneously) that the Rosario Strait was the only navigable channel for sailing ships from the Strait of Juan de Fuca to the Georgia Strait. This was the channel to which the Americans agreed in the treaty, as the document also guaranteed British navigation rights. Douglas cited the 1848 edition Preuss map to demonstrate his point. Preuss still had not consulted Wilkes's charts and had indicated Rosario as the sole channel and boundary. Douglas magnanimously proposed that the channel be open to both nations and free of collection of duties. Duties required on either shore would be paid on Vancouver Island or Olympia. Newcastle did not reply to this document; therefore Douglas took it upon himself to enforce Britain's claims, while discouraging American activity.

His first target was R. W. Cussans, an American citizen who had located a tract of land on Lopez Island, made $1,500 in improvements, and then cut and squared 30,000 board feet of lumber. As Captain James Alden of the U.S. Surveying Steamer *Active* reported on October 31, 1853, Cussans was "compelled" to apply for a license with Douglas and then ordered to clear customs in

Victoria with the timber. The license was issued for six months from July 25, 1853. Cussans was to pay ten pence sterling for each 50 cubic feet of lumber. On September 11 Cussans completed an affidavit for Alden swearing that he had occupied the land assuming it was U.S. territory. He also swore that he had never given security for the payment of any dues to the British government. Douglas responded that Cussans had claimed he was a British subject at the time of application.

Alden added in his dispatch that Douglas's choice of Rosario as the preferred channel was puzzling in that "there is a channel much nearer home, better in almost every respect, and, to them, far more convenient. I mean the Canal de Haro." Alden probably knew the San Juan waters better than any U.S. Navy officer on the coast since he had been a junior lieutenant on Wilkes survey of the islands in 1841. [2]

Douglas was quite proud of himself after his ejection of Cussans:

> I have succeeded in defeating every attempt made to preoccupy the Arro Archipelago through the agency of American squatters, so that those islands will still remain a de facto dependency of Vancouver island *unoccupied* by any whites except a fishing station which was established some years ago by HBC on the island of San Juan.[3]

This was not entirely truthful. For even as he was penning the above dispatch Douglas finally decided to take his crown colony mandate seriously and open San Juan Island to British settlement. There was a problem, however. He had been so successful discouraging colonists, no was around to take him up on it. But Douglas refused to take the blame. Instead he wrote another dispatch lamenting that British settlers were scarce because he was not authorized to grant free land as the Americans were doing.

Douglas's settlement plans were not to be denied. After all, he was also chief factor of Fort Victoria. With a stroke of his pen, he cemented British presence in the San Juans by establishing a branch of the Puget Sound Agricultural Company on the island's southern end. On December 15, 1853, a group of Kanaka (Hawaiian) herdsmen, led by freshly appointed chief agent Charles John Griffin, turned loose 1,350 sheep to graze on a sweeping prairie that gave onto the Strait of Juan de Fuca. Griffin also brought along seed for crops and farmyard animals, including several Berkshire boars. Gazing at the magnificent Olympic Mountains directly across the strait. Griffin appropriately called his prairie home "Belle Vue Farm." He also established sheep stations at three other points on the island, including Oak Prairie (today's San Juan Valley), another valley just south of Roche Harbor, and a clearing above a sheltered bay on the island's east side (Friday Harbor).

Douglas did not bother to advise his government that a corporation and not British subjects had settled the island.

In April 1854 Douglas's worst fears were realized when he heard through the grapevine that Isaac Neff Ebey, in his capacity as U.S. customs collector based at Port Townsend, had, without advising Governor Stevens, threatened seizure of British property on San Juan Island to collect duties. In Ebey's view, the San Juans were American possessions and not a duty-free zone. In a swiftly written dispatch, Douglas told his home government that he had no military forces at his disposal, but even if he did he would not use them. Instead he appointed Belle Vue Farm agent Griffin Justice of the Peace for the District of San Juan Island, at no pay. The American tax collector would be treated as a common offender if he attempted to enforce his jurisdiction. Thus commenced the first standoff on San Juan Island.

Ebey twice visited the island, the first time on April 21, when he handed Griffin the duties bill and told the agent that he should pay it because the sheep "...were liable to seizure" for being smuggled into the territory. On May 3, Ebey returned to collect, landing in an open boat about 6:30 p.m. He dispatched an Indian to Griffin with an invitation to visit him in a tent he was sharing with Henry Webber, his assistant. Griffin paid the call and "...after several minutes spent in conversing on commonplace subjects, I at once put the question to Colonel Ebey, 'What is the purport of your visit.'" Before Ebey could answer, Griffin warned the American of the penalties for molesting property or disturbing the peace.; to which Ebey replied, "I have done nothing."

Griffin returned to his cabin and noted in his journal, "I paid them a visit without gleaning anything of importance from them." He next dispatched a messenger aboard the *Otter*, another Hudson's Bay Company steamer, to advise Douglas. [4]

Douglas steamed to the island the following morning, accompanied by British customs inspector James Sangster. Standing offshore, Douglas through his spyglass could see that Ebey's modest party hardly constituted an invasion force and decided not to land. Instead he called Griffin to the ship and was informed that Ebey had encamped and seemed intent on remaining, probably to collect duties. Douglas must have considered this an empty gesture on Ebey's part because he decided to return to Victoria. Sangster was ordered ashore with a Union Jack flag, which he was directed to run up the Belle Vue flagpole.

Sangster then approached Ebey, who was again asked to state his intentions. The American replied, "I am thinking of putting an inspector on this island (Webber)." Sangster warned Ebey that if he did so Webber would be arrested. Ebey was cavalier. If and when he formally commissioned Webber and the British arrested him, he hoped Webber would be treated well when he was hauled off to Victoria.

The gauntlet was thrown down the next day when Ebey and Webber banged on Griffin's cabin door. When Griffin appeared, Ebey read a proclamation naming Webber assistant collector of customs on San Juan Island. Ebey left soon thereafter and Webber pitched his tent "immediately" behind Griffin's cabin, garnishing the act by running up an American flag. That did it for Griffin. The next morning he issued a warrant for Webber's arrest and directed a Constable "Holland" (likely a Kanaka herdsman) to serve the warrant and bring back prisoner. Sangster went along to observe.

But Webber was armed and belligerent.

> On the constable reading the warrant, and when in the act of raising his hand to arrest Mr. Webber, this gentleman instantaneously presented a revolver pistol at the breast of the constable, telling him if he touched him he would most certainly fire, giving as reason at the time that he did not consider the constable's office legal, as he was given to understand he, the constable, had not been sworn in before a bench of magistrates, and if he or any other man or men attempted to arrest him he should fire, and otherwise protect himself as long as a ball remained in any one of his pistols; he had two brace of pistols hung about his waste and breast, and a knife thrust in his boot at the knee. [5]

Sangster and the constable ran and got six men but Webber was determined as ever to resist. The constable returned to Griffin and asked if he could arm himself, but Griffin, abhorring violence, said no and ordered his men, Sangster included, to leave Webber alone with his knife and pistols. Griffin was disgusted. "...Such a farce! If this is what is called law, then it plainly is rum law." [6]

After all that, Webber and Sangster left the next day, Webber to purchase supplies and report to Ebey, Sangster presumably to tell all to Douglas.

Webber returned, apparently to stay, on May 10. Opting for

the high road, Douglas advised Griffin to leave the American alone so long as he minded his own business and did not attempt to confiscate or molest property. Webber also was to be treated not as a U.S. Government agent, but a private person "entitled to protection by Her Majesty's Government and subject to those same laws." If the American attempted to carry out customs duties he was to be arrested. If he resisted arrest he would be held accountable in the Queen's courts.

Webber was likewise directed by Ebey not to collect, but to peacefully keep tabs on HBC property, for which he would be paid a rate of $5 a day. Webber was only too happy to comply and remained where he was at Belle Vue Farm, where, in what was to become a tradition among contending government officials on San Juan Island, he soon became fast friends with his neighbor, Charles Griffin.

While friendship blossomed, letters were being penned quickly (but delivered too slowly for the pace of events) between Ebey and Douglas and their respective governments. Douglas complained about American effrontery while Ebey, in a dispatch to his boss, Secretary of the Treasury James Guthrie, accused the HBC of violating U.S. revenue laws. His position that the San Juans belonged to the United States was shared but for diplomatic reasons not enforced by Governor Stevens. If Webber was detained, Ebey stated, he would simply replace him with another agent and appeal to the territorial government for help in obtaining Webber's release.

The British Foreign Office was not amused by Ebey's international boundary interpretation, nor Webber's sourdough antics. In July they asked the U.S. Government in Washington, D.C. to "make inquiries" and order local officials to cease and desist.

Secretary of State William Marcy first wrote to Guthrie, advising him that a commission would soon meet to decide the boundary. But he did not disabuse Ebey's opinion on American title. Far from it. In fact, he told Guthrie that U.S. authorities should continue to "hold possession" of the islands.

The colonial office was sending the same message to Douglas concerning the disputed isles: "...In conveying to the approval of HM Govt. of your proceedings with respect to the sovereignty of the islands in the Canal de Arro, I have to authorize you to continue to treat those islands as part of the British Dominions." [7]

This was a dispatch that would be ingrained in Douglas's mind for the next five years. But he still believed the reaction of his government had not been strong enough. Crampton, the British minister in Washington, cautioned Douglas not to "push matters to extremities, unless we are compelled to do so..." The governor found this advisory "...an unfortunate admission, showing a lamentable want of information on the question at issue, and yet it is a fact that may greatly embarrass her Majesty's Government."

Ever the peacemaker, Secretary Marcy in late July wrote a soothing semi-apology to the British, stating that Governor Stevens (then in Washington D.C. on business) told him that he had no reason to collect customs duties from the HBC. Displaying a sure grasp of the pulse of his territory and the character of his officials, Stevens told Marcy that while Ebey had probably posted an agent on the island, the agent likely had not been directed to make collections. In almost the same breath the governor suggested that the U.S. Army garrison at Fort Steilacoom be moved to Port Townsend, about twenty miles across the strait from San Juan Island.

By early 1855 the issue was academic as northern Indian raids drove the Americans, including Webber, away from the islands. Douglas, however, was still smarting from the Webber incident and was sensitive to any American act around the islands, no matter the purpose. In October 1854, for example, he reported that a U.S. Revenue cutter mounting six guns and commanded by U.S. naval officers was lurking in the area. "They appear resolved to gain forcible possession of the *disputed* territory, and I hardly know how to prevent them," he wrote.

The ship probably was nearby, but more with an eye to thwarting northern Indian raids, which had hit Whatcom, Whidbey and points south throughout the year. The Northerners had been raiding into the Strait of Georgia and Puget Sound basin since Fort Victoria opened in 1843. They came in swift, high-prowed canoes, hitting Coast Salish and white communities alike without warning, taking slaves from the Indians, firearms, pots, and anything else not nailed downed from the whites. They also were not averse to lopping off heads and carting them home as trophies. They spooked white settlers so much that military posts would soon be established at Bellingham Bay, just east of the islands, as well as at Port Townsend.

However, Northerners never attacked HBC posts for fear of immediate reprisal.

The British had coined the term "forest diplomacy," whereby civilian posses or British warships found the village of the offending parties and burned it to the ground if the miscreants were not swiftly turned over to justice. This may explain why Webber and Charles Griffin became such close neighbors. [8]

It was Americans who troubled Douglas most of the time now. In January 1855, the governor wrote that he had "never been free from alarms." He complained about American newspapers; and also about acting U.S. Territorial Governor Mason for landing on San Juan Island with troops from Fort Steilacoom in pursuit of northern Indians. These officials had with them "a large train of lawless followers." If that wasn't bad enough, U.S. Revenue cutters were continually threatening to enforce duties and now the fledgling government of Whatcom County of all things, was attempting to collect so-called "back taxes" on the HBC operation at Belle Vue Farm.

Whatcom County in those days embraced most of Northwest Washington from the Cascades to the San Juans. But its few white settlers lived in two small villages lying on either side of a waterfall giving on to Bellingham Bay, about twenty miles east of San Juan Island. No matter that the communities had barely forty citizens, a complete county government had been elected, appointed, and hired, which accounted for just about all of its citizenry. One of these was County Commissioner William Cullen, an Irish-born agent of the Puget Sound Mining Company, the San Francisco-based coal mining operation on the bay. Cullen was determined that San Juan Island was rightfully in the orbit of the county and thus the HBC operation had to pay its due. Being an Irishman full of cradle-spawned hatred for the English, he approached the issue with relish.

Starting in October 1854, Sheriff Ellis Barnes four times visited the island and ordered Griffin to pay $80.33 in back taxes or face a sheriff's sale. The sale would be conducted on the beach under his very nose. Griffin told him to get lost. Barnes posted tax sale notices in December and proceeded to the beach (presumably Grandma's Cove, which is just below the Belle Vue Farm site) to open an auction. No one appeared to purchase the sheep, Barnes went away and Griffin felt confident that he had seen the last of the sheriff. He was wrong.

An "armed party" composed of Cullen, Barnes, coal company manager (and county judge) Edmund Fitzhugh and five other prospective "bidders" in three rowboats dipped through unseasonably calm waters and landed on the beach on March 30, 1855. By some accounts it took them the better part of two nights and one day to reach the island. Again they ordered Griffin to pay, and when he refused they left. But they sailed off only a short distance and returned in the wee hours. The next several hours were spent rounding up sheep, building a makeshift pen on the beach and conducting a starlight auction. This time more than forty breeding rams were "sold," Cullen the instigator buying ten or twelve for his personal use at fifty cents to one dollar a head. But the Americans did not bring boats to match their ambitions. In desperation they commandeered an Indian canoe and tried to coax the rams into it. The result was predictable. Deputies were butted, the canoe foundered and several rams galloped across the black prairie with Americans in stumbling pursuit. [9]

Somehow Griffin missed the racket. He got up as usual at

dawn and left his cabin to check on one of the herds. He hadn't been out long when he was approached by an Indian boy bearing a hastily scrawled note from one of his herdsmen. The Americans had penned and sold forty-nine breeding rams, thirty-four of which had already been driven down to the beach. Another twenty-four sheep also were sold, sight unseen, he was advised, presumably to be snatched later "...I imagine by stealth."

Griffin rounded up several Kanakas and ran to the makeshift pen. After releasing the remaining fifteen animals, he scrambled down the bluff to the beach to stop the Americans. The boats already were pulling away with the thirty-four rams aboard. Griffin and one man beat through the surf to the gunwales and attempted to untie the cords securing the animals. Three of the frustrated Americans, all armed, turned and pushed the HBC men away. Griffin and his assistant made another attempt, whereupon "..one of them drew from his belt a Revolver Pistol, which the moment I saw I expostulated with them, telling them I could not possibly contend against such a force...Seeing no other recourse I immediately left the spot. They as quickly left in two boats and one canoe." [10]

The American Sumas *Vidette* saw it differently. In its eyewitness version, the sheep buyers were leading the rams to the beach when "Griffin charged down the hill accompanied by about twenty Kanakas, who were armed with knives, and ordered that the sheep be cut loose. Dramatically, Sheriff Barnes ordered his men to protect the property 'in the name of the United States.' Since Barnes's men were armed with revolvers, the Kanakas retired and shortly afterward six of them in a canoe, started across the channel for Victoria."

One of the Americans spotted what he thought to be the *Beaver*, clearing the harbor at Victoria seven miles off.

> We did not wish to be taken prisoners and lie in jail until the boundary question could be settled by the two governments; we loaded about one-half of

> the sheep into our boats and "lit out." We were all worn out from loss of sleep and hard work, the tide was running very strong against us, our boats were heavily loaded, but we bent to the oars and like Wellington at Waterloo, prayed for 'night or Blucher to come to our relief... [11]

Griffin bent to the oars himself to report in Victoria the "theft" of thirty-four breeding rams.

Douglas immediately complained to Governor Stevens, who once again learned of a San Juan action after the fact. Stevens disapproved of the ram auction but felt compelled to back Americans in asserting their rights south of the 49th parallel, disputed islands or not. Douglas next reported the incident to the Foreign Office. Again, he neglected to define what he meant by "British property." The wronged party was Charles Griffin, a British subject "who had been menaced with violence and put in danger of his life," not the Hudson's Bay Company.

All in all, Douglas termed it "an exceedingly annoying affair" and expressed regret that the HBC could not muster the wherewithal to apprehend the Americans, even though the *Beaver*, the Hudson's Bay Company's legendary steamer, gave chase. While the Americans were armed with six-shooter revolvers, the HBC men had single-shot, smoothbore Northwest Trade guns. Douglas reported forty-five rams stolen, although eleven "escaped" during the loading carnival.

It was July before British Ambassador Crampton made a claim on the United States on behalf of the HBC. According to his figures the Americans owed: £650 for 34 rams; £650:13 for 267 ewes and 142 lambs; £500 for the hire of the *Beaver*; and £1,000 for incidental losses for a grand total of £2,990:13 — altogether about $15,000. [12]

All items of claim, aside from the rams, were attacked as "fraudulent and unfounded" by the writer of the account in the House documents.

Douglas was not satisfied and wrote yet another letter of complaint to Lord John Russell, again neglecting to say the wronged party was the HBC. Now he was called on it. Russell reminded Douglas that in November 1853 he had stated that the San Juan Islands should remain a "de facto" dependency of Vancouver Island, unoccupied by any whites except the fishing station. But the attached report from Griffin indicated a major agricultural operation on the island. The two statements did not add up and Douglas and the HBC were chided for masking their activities, and then asking for compensation as private citizens rather than as a corporation with a charter for colonization.

Douglas apologized profusely in his next correspondence, admitting that he had "omitted to give information on certain points." [13]

On the American side, Secretary of State Marcy responded to the affair by instructing Isaac Stevens to lay off:

> The President has instructed me to say to you that the officers of the territory should abstain from all acts, on the disputed grounds, which are calculated to provoke any conflict, so far as it can be done without implying the concession to the authorities of Great Britain of an exclusive right over the premises.The title ought to be settled before either party should attempt to exclude the other by force or exercise complete and exclusive sovereign rights with the fairly disputed limits. Application will be made to the British government to interpose with its local authorities on the Northern borders of our territory to abstain from like acts of exclusive ownership, with an explicit understanding that any forbearance on either side to assert the rights respectively claimed shall not be to any concession to the adverse party. [14]

He followed this with a letter to Crampton on July 17, confessing to "some apprehension that collision may take place between our citizens and British subjects in regard to the occupation of the disputed points along the line between Washington Territory and the British Possession on the north of it." [15]

He assured the ambassador that he would notify Stevens to use discretion, adding that he hoped the British would write a similar missive to Douglas. Crampton agreed and said he had dispatched copies of the letter to the Governor General of British North America, to George Simpson of HBC and by October, to Douglas.

The so-called "Marcy Letter" was thenceforth carried in the vest pocket of every British official in the old Oregon Country to be used as a club against any overreaching Yankee. However, while this "hands-off" message was recognized as the continuing policy of the U.S., Douglas did not feel bound to it, insisting to the end that the San Juans were British possessions and the U.S. had no rights nor legal claim to them.

The Royal Navy agreed in spirit with Douglas. The Pacific Station commander in 1855 was Rear Admiral H.W. Bruce. In his view the "serious difficulty" in the Northwest was "owing to the grasping spirit and habits of the neighboring Americans..." The Admiralty urged caution, primarily because the U.S., at least in spirit, supported the Russians in the Crimea. Nevertheless, Bruce was advised in 1856 to move his ships from Central America to Vancouver Island to secure British interests in case American filibusters made a move on British possessions. [16]

If it accomplished anything other than satisfying County Commissioner Cullen's bloodlust, the Barnes incident prompted the U.S. Congress finally to move on appropriating money to pay for a boundary commission, which the British had proposed as far back as 1848. The money was allocated on August 11, 1856, whereupon Archibald Campbell was appointed commissioner, with a chief astronomer and surveyor to assist him in marking the boundary between the Rocky Mountains and the Pacific.

The respective commissioners by agreement were supposed to exchange their instructions. However, British commissioner Captain James Prevost's orders included a caveat not intended for Campbell's eyes. He had been directed by his government to press for the Rosario Strait, and failing that, to seek another channel within the archipelago that might conform to the language of the treaty.

Prevost was advised that possession of the islands by the British Crown "...must contribute very much to the quiet possession of Vancouver's Island, and her Majesty's Government therefore desire that you should use your utmost efforts to induce the American commissioner to assent to the view which Her Majesty's Government have taken of the case." [17]

The Englishman's position had been spelled out for him by his government before a single measurement had been taken. Marcy's marching orders to Campbell were hardly less partisan, but they were not withheld from the British. When Campbell finally saw the secret verbiage two years later he decided that the water boundary proceedings had been prejudiced from the start.

The primary British argument for Rosario Strait was that it ran directly south from the 49th parallel through the Strait of Georgia, thus satisfying the language if not the spirit of the Treaty of Oregon. As early as 1846, British warships regularly used the Rosario Strait over the Haro Strait as a matter of policy, hoping to reinforce the British claim. The American position, as postulated by Campbell, was that if one drew a line directly south from the middle of the Strait of Georgia, it would run directly through the Haro Strait.

Prevost also was told to push for an accommodation on Point Roberts, that strange comma of land that dips below the 49th parallel from the British Columbia mainland into U.S. territorial waters. Most importantly for the British, "quiet possession" of Vancouver's Island was to be maintained, which Prevost interpreted as keeping the Americans away from Victoria's back porch, i.e. San Juan Island. That aim was reflected in all that passed from his lips or flowed from his pen over the next three years. San Juan would form a "wall of defence," he wrote, protecting Vancouver Island and the R.N. anchorage at Esquimalt.

The United States Board of Engineers in 1858 likewise concluded that "by establishing a military and naval station at Griffin Bay, on the southeastern shore of San Juan Island, she shall be able to overlook those inner waters equally with Great Britain from Esquimalt Harbor, and thus counterbalance the preponderance she is seeking to establish."

Prevost and Campbell met six times between June and December 1857, and to no one's surprise could not agree on a water boundary. Looking for a way to end dispute and continue to guard Victoria's flank, Prevost in November 1857 proposed President's and San Juan channels – soon to be called the "Middle Channel" – which divide San Juan Island and its satellites from Orcas and Shaw islands. This would award all the islands except San Juan to the United States.

Campbell declined.

Those who knew anything about the dynamics of Douglas, Isaac Stevens, or the land-hungry American miners trickling down from the diggings up the Fraser River Valley knew the climate was ripe for major trouble.

For while letters were being written and surveys taken, the U. S. Revenue agents continued keeping book on the goings on at Belle Vue Farm. Between 1855 and 1859, taxes were assessed (but not collected) on the HBC. As of May 20, 1859, the HBC had 4,500 sheep, 40 cattle, 5 yoke of oxen, 35 horses and 40 hogs, plus 80 fenced acres under cultivation with oats, peas, and potatoes. Griffin had nineteen employees, three of whom were naturalized American citizens who actually voted in the territorial election. There were altogether twenty-nine settlers.

No Americans settled on the island until several frustrated miners drifted over from the Fraser River diggings between the summer of 1858 and January 1859. Indian fears had heretofore kept them away. For example, in April 1858 Deputy Collector of Customs Paul K. Hubbs, Jr., was shot at by a party of Clallams from the Olympic Peninsula encamped on the island. Captain Granville O. Haller, commander of Co. I. Fourth Infantry at Fort Townsend crossed the strait with a small guard to "capture the offenders." Griffin had helped Hubbs escape and was pleased to see Haller and his men. The Clallam fled.

Then in late February 1859, Griffin wrote Douglas that a party of Americans from Victoria had been there over a ten-day period surveying and laying out land in hopes of establishing preemption claims pending a U.S. takeover of the islands. The surveying was directed by a Capt. C. L. Denman and Mr. Gelette. Griffin reported he had heard Denman talking about bringing lumber because he wanted to buy "Webber's house" and furnish it.

Douglas already knew of the enterprise and wrote the colonial office that he was continuing to regard San Juan Island as a dependency of Vancouver Island as per his instructions of September 21, 1854, and he had appointed Griffin Justice of the Peace. Griffin's occupation until recently had been "general and complete" as well as undisturbed by Americans. However, Douglas now feared that as a result of the surveys the "whole island will soon be occupied by a squatter population of American citizens if they do not receive an immediate check."

> ...This movement has, I have no doubt, been commenced by some designing person exciting and working upon the minds of the ignorant masses with the view of hastening the settlement of the Boundary Question and fortifying the claims of the United States Government. The course is one full of danger, and I fear that HM Govt. would not approve of my adopting measures for the summary and forcible ejection of squatters, while the sovereignty remains avowedly in dispute; at the same time circumstances may call for decisive action. [18]

Douglas had no hopes that the governor of Washington Territory would help. Even so, he proposed that Americans and British join together in ejecting squatters until the boundary was settled. All in all, he was prepared to protect British interests. A couple of months later Douglas received a dispatch from Colonial Secretary Lord Lytton. He was astonished to read that Lytton not only shared his views, but had stressed that possession of the San Juan Islands was "essential to British interests." The governor was ordered to "warn off" squatters attempting to settle on British Dominions on San Juan Island and maintain British rights by exercise of "civil power."

By taking this position the crown was courting the very trouble it sought to avoid; for the territorial government in Olympia could likewise view the HBC as an "alien squatter." Even more critical, the colonial secretary's instructions ignored the Marcy agreement of 1855.

Whose laws would be obeyed?

On May 12, Lord Robert Lyons, the new British ambassador in Washington, D.C., contacted Secretary of State Lewis Cass. Pending the results of the ongoing boundary survey, U.S. citizens should be restrained from settling on San Juan Island, Lyons wrote. No mention was made of the HBC sheep farm as the only British interest nor of how Americans could cause a local "collision." [19]

Charles Griffin's railback pig had the answer to that.

CHAPTER 6

The Pig Incident

Lyman Cutlar warned Charles Griffin several times about the pig. Actually, it was a Berkshire boar, and contrary to local folklore, no record exists that it was ever a prize animal worth $100, a truly enormous sum in 1859. The name is more romantic than the animal, as Berkshire boars were more commonly known as "railbacks" and they were (and continue to be) renowned for rooting. They were not all that rare on the frontier.

So much myth that has grown up around this incident that visitors to San Juan Island National Historical Park continue to ask: "Who ate the pig?" And they wonder why two great nations would be willing to go to war over such an absurdity.

The facts are a Kentuckian named Lyman Cutlar came to San Juan Island in April 1859, or so he said in a sworn deposition later that year after all the hubbub died down. Pioneer memory has him being twenty-nine, a failed miner looking for an easy stake on which to live with his Indian wife and child, though no record exists of that either. He stated he claimed the standard 160-acre homestead under preemption laws, but none applied on the islands at that time. His opposite, Charles Griffin, maintained that Cutlar was squatting on more like a third of an acre. Squatting is a derogatory expression used by those who own a lot of land to describe those who want to scratch out a living on a little piece of it.

The "farm" was in the path of Griffin's main sheep-run that led to other grazing lands that dotted the island from the home prairie to Roche Harbor on the northern end. According to several descriptions, it was a humble place with a garden that, as Griffin stated, was "imperfectly enclosed" by a crude fence. Most accounts describe the fence as having three sides. Whether it was a triangular enclosure or was attached to Cutlar's cabin, we'll never know. Accounts given forty to fifty years after the fact have Cutlar rowing forty miles to and from Port Townsend across the Strait of Juan de Fuca to buy seed potatoes. He then had to lug them up the hill from today's Grandma's Cove to about a mile and half from Belle Vue Farm before putting them in the ground.

Cutlar was not the only Yankee trying Griffin's patience. Others had taken advantage of the work of the self-proclaimed American surveyors in Victoria and were squatting about the prairies where Griffin grazed his sheep or encamped on Griffin Bay.

Griffin was growing more exasperated and he told Douglas so:

> There are now upwards of 16 squatters who have recently come and established themselves on various parts of the island, all claiming to be Citizens of the United States and they have one and all taken up claims and making improvements/a log cabin and a potato patch/ on the most valuable prairies I have in possession of my herdsmen and stock. [1]

One settler had the temerity to land twenty or more head of cattle, the agent added.

Griffin was raising sheep, which required ample acreage to be profitable and now those lands were being carved up by a bunch of no-account miners trying to scratch out a subsistence until something better came along. The simple fact was that the Americans were trespassers. The governor was going to have to do something about it.

That was Griffin's view in so many words. As for the facts, all we have are letters from Griffin and A.G. Dallas and a sworn affidavit from Cutlar.

Because of Cutlar's three-sided fence, Griffin's cattle and pigs had "free access" to the potato patch. "One of the pigs, a very valuable boar, he shot this morning at some distance outside of this same patch and complains the animal was destroying this crop," Griffin stated in letter to Governor Douglas, written that very day. [2] His Belle Vue journal account was more succinct: "An American shot one of my pigs for tresspassing!!!" [3]

Cutlar came to Griffin to confess the shooting and proceeded to offer "a remuneration which was so insignificant it only adds insult to injury, and likewise used the most insulting and threatening language and openly declared that he would shoot my cattle if they trespassed near his place."

Griffin wrote that Cutlar also said he "would just as soon shoot me as he would a hog if I trespassed on his claim," which prompted Griffin to retort that Cutlar had no right to squat on the island, "much less in the centre of the most valuable sheep run I have on the island." [4]

Cutlar responded that he had received assurances from American authorities in Washington Territory that he and all other Americans squatting or taking up claims on San Juan Island would be protected and their claims recognized as being established on American soil.

Lyman Cutlar gave his own account on September 7, 1859, in the Whatcom County courthouse. He also wrote a letter to U.S. Deputy Collector of Customs Paul K. Hubbs, Jr. Here is the gist of both documents: [5]

Cutlar claimed he repeatedly drove off Griffin's "black Boar" and that the company was aware of it. He shot the hog on June 15, 1859, after being awakened by the laughter of Jacob, a Kanakan herdsman —or as Cutlar termed him, "a colard man"— in Griffin's employ. Cutlar followed the Hawaiian's gaze and saw the hog "up to his old game." Maddened by "...the independence of the Negro, knowing as he did my previous loss," Cutlar rushed into his cabin, reemerged with his rifle and shot the hog.[6] After awhile he felt badly about it and went to see Griffin. He told Griffin that he shot the pig in a "moment of irritation" and then offered to replace the animal or have Griffin select three men to determine a fair price. That's when Griffin told him the animal was worth $100.[7]

"Mr. Griffin flew in a passion and said it is no more than I expected," Cutlar said, "for you Americans are a nuisance on the island and you have no business here and I shall write Mr. Douglas and have you removed."

Cutlar replied, "I came here to settle for shooting your hog, not to argue the right of Americans on the island for I consider it American soil."

That evening (some say it was the next day) Griffin went to Cutlar's place with Dr. William Tolmie, founder of the Puget Sound Agricultural Company; Vancouver Council Member Donald Fraser; and Alexander Grant Dallas, governor of the Hudson's Bay Company west of the Rockies and Douglas's son-in-law. Dallas did the talking, according to Cutlar.

In a very "supercilious" manner Dallas asked Cutlar "how he dared to do it." Cutlar replied that he dared to do whatever he wanted and had no cause to feel guilty. He thought he was being virtuous by confessing the act and offering to pay. The animal was so "worthless," the American added, that Griffin would not have missed it anyway. Dallas reminded Cutlar that he was on British soil and if he did not pay $100 he would have to go with them to Victoria. According to Cutlar, Dallas then said that the *Beaver* was awaiting them with a "possy" on board.

Cutlar snorted that he would not pay $100 for an animal that was not worth $10. If they brought their posse he would have his friends resist them. "I then told Mr. Dallas to crack his whip and left them," Cutlar wrote. As they rode off, Cutlar said they shouted back, "You will have to answer for this hereafter."

Dallas remembered it differently when he wrote Brigadier

General William Selby Harney, commander of the U.S. Army Department of Oregon, on May 10, 1860. [8]

According to Dallas, he and his associates (Tolmie and Fraser) dropped in on Griffin in the afternoon of June 15. Dallas told Harney that they traveled to San Juan that day on the *Beaver* and found Griffin still seething. [9] They may have suggested a soothing horseback ride or perhaps it was "let's go up there and scare the bastard away." No one wrote it down. In any case:

"We took the opportunity in passing Cutlar's hut or tent to call on him. No demand of $100 or any sum of money was made upon him, nor did I threaten to apprehend him and take him to Victoria. On the contrary, I stated distinctly that I was a private individual and could not interfere with him," Dallas wrote. He next said that Cutlar threatened to shoot any other HBC animal that passed his way.

"What has been dignified by the name of his farm consisted of a very small patch of potatoes, partially fenced on three sides and entirely open on the fourth," Dallas wrote. Even though it would be a virtual impossibility to keep more than five thousand head of sheep and other ranging farm animals out of such a flimsy cantonment, he claimed, the hog was not shot in the patch, but in the woods bordering Cutlar's property.

He closed by insisting that no threats were made by either party and that the Hudson's Bay Company had shown remarkable forbearance, all things considered.

Which brings us to Hubbs, the deputy collector of customs. He was probably the first person Cutlar told about the incident—the man who baited the lion with his blow-by-blow account to Harney.

Hubbs was a Tennessean with a genteel background. His father, Paul K. Hubbs, Sr., was a lawyer, former plantation owner, and a friend of Andrew Jackson, who once appointed him ambassador to the court of Louis Philippe of France. The entire family was pulled west by the California Gold Rush. Following a bitter family dispute, which involved young Paul's loyalty to a mining camp rowdy named "Texas Jack," Hubbs abandoned the gold fields first for Honolulu, then Fort Vancouver. From there he drifted north to live, he claimed, among the Haida. He said he even participated in their raids on other groups—acts which usually involved taking slaves and chopping off heads—before coming south in 1855-56 to fight for Washington Territory against the Klickitats and Nisqually in the White River War. The war availed him the opportunity to rub elbows with a lot of important people, which, combined with a considerable verbal ability, resulted in his being appointed deputy collector of customs on San Juan Island in April 1857. The younger Hubbs must have made peace with the family because Paul K. Hubbs, Sr., lived in Port Townsend at the time of the pig incident. The elder Hubbs was to become a political force in Washington Territory, being elected to the legislature and to the Board of Regents of the new University of Washington. [10]

As the ranking (and only) U.S. official on the island, the younger Hubbs took it upon himself to fire off on June 23 a dispatch to his boss, Customs Collector Morris H. Frost. In the letter, actually dated June 2 — *before* the incident—Hubbs complained vigorously about the Hudson's Bay Company, whose actions were "odious and intolerable." He frantically urged that either the boundary dispute be quickly settled or that "a large military force" be landed to protect American settlers.

Curiously enough, when Hubbs gave his affidavit at the Whatcom County Courthouse the same day that Cutlar gave his, he gave only the bare facts with no embellishment. The deputy collector of customs swore, under oath, that he only told Harney what Cutlar told him and proceeded to offer a dispassionate account much as a newspaper reporter would cover a city council meeting.

Hubbs later recalled that he rowed more than twenty miles to Fort Bellingham. There he met with his old White River War buddy, Captain George Edward Pickett, the post commander, and told him Cutlar's story. Pickett assured Hubbs that he would relate the incident in detail when Harney inspected the fort in early July. [11]

Hubbs is the only one who wrote about this meeting, more than thirty years after the fact. The only other person who could have called his account into question was Pickett's then-second lieutenant at Fort Bellingham, James Forsyth. But in 1892 when Hubbs wrote his version, Forsyth, a brigadier general, was still trying to explain why his troops killed 150 Sioux men, women, and children at the "Battle" of Wounded Knee two years earlier. [12]

Hubbs said that Pickett was true to his word, but no record exists that Pickett ever told Harney about the pig incident. Harney always claimed that July 9, the day he visited San Juan Island, was the first he'd heard of the pig.

Meanwhile, the Americans on San Juan Island decided a show of support was in order for Lyman Cutlar. The former miners among them were probably bitter over their treatment around the upper Fraser River diggings. Unlike American gold strikes, where miners filed claims for exclusive rights, claims on British lands were reserved for the crown. Douglas stringently followed this rule and then forced the miners to pay a monthly fee. He also prohibited American retailers or ship owners from doing business in British territory. This incensed former Governor Isaac Stevens, now a delegate for the territory to the U.S. House of Representatives. When the gold strike turned out to be marginal, Stevens and the miners gave up, but they did not forget.

The American settlers on San Juan Island decided to show national solidarity by throwing an old-fashioned flag-raising party on the Fourth of July. Charles McKay in 1908 still remembered the celebration that preceded Harney's visit. All fourteen Americans gathered at Hubbs's log cabin, about 100 yards on the rise above Belle Vue Farm.

"...We passed a resolution that each one of us had to make a speech," McKay recalled. In the course of the speechmaking a Welshman among the Americans, and no lover of things English, pointed out that the squatters should be independent of Great

Britain. [13]

Hubbs also vividly remembered the ceremony, but with considerably more detail, both in his 1892 Seattle *Post-Intelligencer* story and again in the Friday Harbor newspaper in 1909, a year before his death. The pole they erected in front of his cabin was fifty-five feet high, he remembered, and the flag soared to the masthead amidst "showers of bullets, and not withstanding its ducking and dodging was struck in its starry night, but 'got there all the same.'"

The Americans decided to leave the flag where it was—presumably near the site of the future redoubt, where it could be viewed by Charles Griffin and hopefully fellow Americans pushing up the strait.

Griffin took note and promptly raised the Union Jack over his cabin.

So what really happened? Whose account is correct? Hubbs's story of what transpired between Griffin, Dallas and Cutlar is unreliable given his lukewarm affidavit and the exaggerations evident in his newspaper articles. A.G. Dallas obfuscated by neglecting to tell Harney that Griffin demanded $100 for the pig. He also lied when he wrote Harney that he had given scant notice to the affair when on August 5, at the height of the crisis, he had written a stormy letter to Douglas howling for blood. In the end, it is hard to believe that Dallas could walk away without satisfaction. He probably did threaten Cutlar. [14]

Wherever the truth lies, Dallas's words were heavy enough to alarm and excite the other Americans on the island – particularly Hubbs.

CHAPTER 7

William Selby Harney

Contrary to much that has been written by some twentieth-century historians, William Selby Harney was not a complete idiot. In fact, he was a skilled frontier army officer. He quelled an Indian uprising, attempted to hammer out a just peace, and did such a good job of it he was actually called out of retirement to offer advice to William Tecumseh Sherman—a man who seldom sought anyone's counsel. Nor was he completely uncultivated. He learned French, married a French woman, and lived abroad for a time.

Harney's problem was an active imagination, occasionally bordering on paranoia. He also had a propensity for focusing on nits and gnats best left to his chiefs of staff or lower ranking line officers. He hated taking orders from superior officers because he believed he had no superiors. He occasionally lied to achieve his ends.

There could not have been a Pig War without him.

William Selby Harney was born August 22, 1800, in Haysboro, Tennessee. He was directly commissioned a second lieutenant in the First Infantry in 1818 (as opposed to attending West Point), thanks to the intercession of Andrew Jackson, who was Harney's patron as long as he lived. The influence of Old Hickory manifested itself time and again in Harney's stormy career. Jackson harbored a hatred for the British resulting from a trauma suffered as a boy during the Revolutionary War when a British officer slashed him for not cleaning his boots. Jackson subsequently smashed the British at New Orleans during the War of 1812, and spared no effort to check them on the southeastern frontier, at times without the permission of his government. Harney took notes and soon formed his own pathological hatred for all things British. [1]

Harney was more than six feet tall with blue eyes and red hair that eventually turned silver. As a young man he had "tremendous physical strength and endurance," according to Jefferson Davis, who as a young West Point graduate served with Harney on the plains. Davis particularly recalled Harney being a fleet runner who on many occasions bested the Indians in races. In fact, Harney once chased a dog that was tearing up his garden a mile and half before catching and beating it. [2]

However, from the start he demonstrated a knack for getting into trouble. At his first post—Fort Warren, Mass., near Boston—he brashly "took command" of the post when his commanding officer was away. He was court-martialed but, thanks to his powerful patron, was acquitted.

He next campaigned against the Winnebagos in 1827, and then against the Sauk and Fox in the Black Hawk War of 1831. He firmly believed the Black Hawk War was justified because the Indians did not follow the letter of the law, even though the law was unjust.

> Throughout his professional life he employed the same reasoning, citing the letter of the law against any individual who disagreed with him. In an army composed of officers jealous and distrustful of each other, Harney was not above using the court martial

as a means of revenge against his professional adversaries.[3]

When the Second Dragoons were created May 1836 in response to the Seminole uprising, then-Major Harney connived with by-then President Jackson to wrest the lieutenant colonelcy of the unit from the man to whom it already had been assigned. He justified these machinations by developing a reputation for dash and daring, which often resulted in the reckless endangerment of his men. Colonel Stephen Watts Kearny of the rival First Dragoons wrote of him:

> You know the opinion I have of Colonel Harney, that he has no more brains than a Greyhound. Yet, I consider that by his stupidity and repair in action, he has done more to inject the Indians with a fear of us and the desperate state of their cause, than all the other commanders. [4]

This was borne out in July 1839 when Harney and another small contingent were attacked and eleven of his dragoons were killed. He managed to escape with his slave and eight soldiers, vowing revenge. He was good on his word. Almost two years to the day he caught up with this same group of raiders, killing four of them and hanging five more after a kangaroo court.

He was in Texas fighting Comanches when the Mexican War broke out in 1846. General Zachary Taylor—too far away to oversee all matters on his own—gave Harney wide discretionary powers to protect the frontier and enlist volunteers if needed. This Harney did and more, taking it upon himself to raise an "invasion army" with seven volunteer units plus a band of Delaware Indians. Without authorization, he crossed the border, defeated a small Mexican force and occupied the town of Presidio. That's when General John E. Wool ordered him back. Harney disputed the order and took his sweet time—five full days—before returning, leaving behind a company of volunteers who were eventually defeated by the Mexicans.

Harney's behavior exhibited "extreme imbecility and manifest incapacity," wrote Wool in a report to U.S. Army commander, Lieutenant General Winfield Scott. [5]

Scott took note. When he decided in early 1847 that he needed the Second Dragoons for his push from Vera Cruz to Mexico City, he gave command of the regiment to another officer and ordered Harney to remain behind. Harney protested to his Democratic patrons in Washington, among them President James Knox Polk, another Tennessean who was called "Young Hickory" during his election campaign. Harney also refused to obey the order, which resulted in a court martial. The court martial board was lenient—they thought Harney was merely displaying patriotic zeal. They let him off with a reprimand and permitted him to go to Vera Cruz anyway, much to the mortification of Scott.

Never known for bipartisanship, Polk wrote that Scott had "arbitrarily and without cause" throttled

> ...One of the most gallant and best officers in the service. He was not under any charges of any kind. He was, however, a Democrat in politics, was one of General Jackson's personal friends, and was appointed by him. I can conceive of no reason but this for the arbitrary and tyrannical conduct of General Scott in doing such gross injustice to this gallant officer. [6]

The president went on to write that Democrats had been unjustly punished by Whig officers in not only Scott's camps but Taylor's as well, and he was quite ready to check Scott's "tyrannical" course. He decided to send a letter ordering Harney's reinstatement even before hearing the results of the court martial board. Polk closed by writing: "...I am resolved that Col. Harney shall not be sacrificed to propitiate the personal and political malice of Gen. Scott..."

For all of this vinegar, Harney was just the officer Scott needed to lead his cavalry in Mexico. Harney continued to disobey orders, attacking without authorization Mexican positions outside of Vera Cruz. Scott stormed, but victory took Harney off the hook. He then performed heroically at Cerro Gordo—an entrenched Mexican position about halfway to Mexico City—using his dragoons as shock troops to dislodge Mexican infantry. The action won for him a brevet rank of brigadier general.

He went on to excel in several other minor engagements, though he did not have a prominent role in the assault on Mexico City, as that was primarily an operation for infantry and artillery forces. What he did do was hang a group of Irish-American deserters, who, unsatisfied of their lot with the U.S. Army and lacking confidence in the ultimate victory, went over to the Mexicans. With great flair Harney arranged to have the deserters trussed and positioned on the gallows so that they were facing Chapultepec castle in the distance. They were advised that when the U.S. flag appeared over Chapultepec, signaling victory, the traps would be sprung one after another, which is exactly what happened. The man who ran the flag up the pole, at least according to legend, was First Lieutenant George Pickett of the Eighth Infantry. [7]

The upshot of Harney's Mexican service, especially the court martial and the snipes from Scott's staff, was a bitterness toward officers whom he perceived to be his tormentors. This, coupled with the Democrat-Whig factionalism, eventually would permeate the officer corps and undermine morale throughout the service. The results were resignations by some of the best officers, among them George McClellan, U. S. Grant, William Tecumseh Sherman, Thomas "Stonewall" Jackson, and Braxton Bragg. With few skills to attempt anything else, the Harneys and the Picketts stuck around.

Harney was reassigned to Texas and the Second Dragoons after the war, where he helped establish a line of border forts from the Oklahoma panhandle to the Rio Grande. One of these was Fort Gates, where Pickett would spend several years and lose his first wife in childbirth. There is no hard documentary evidence that the men had anything other than a casual relationship in Texas. Harney certainly was not a Pickett patron at that time.

Harney went to France with his wife of twenty years in 1854, but returned the next year to join the fight against the Brule Sioux on the northern plains. The war broke out when an inexperienced lieutenant named Hugh Fleming allowed his second in command to ride into an Sioux camp with a platoon of soldiers and a mountain howitzer to arrest an Indian for stealing a cow. The soldiers and the Sioux chief, Conquering Bear, were killed. [8]

Before leaving on the Brule campaign, Harney was said to have remarked: "By God, I'm for battle—not peace," an utterance that came to haunt him a few years later. In September 1855, his combined infantry and cavalry forces attacked Little Thunder's camp in a pincer movement at Blue Water Creek. The attack, relentless pursuit and slaughter of refugees was characterized by a ferociousness that earned him the name "Mad Bear" from the Teton Sioux. Other nicknames from the Indians included "The Butcher," "The Hornet," and "The Big Chief Who Swears."

He was an early proponent of winter campaigning against the Indians (when they were most vulnerable), a tactic that would be adopted by Phil Sheridan and executed by George Custer, Nelson Miles, and others after the Civil War. However, like Miles, Harney could be magnanimous in victory. Despite his ruthlessness in combat, he possessed a genuine empathy for the plight of the Plains Indians, as he was demonstrate in his later years. He drafted his own peace treaty and cowed the Brules into signing it, only to have it derailed by the Department of Indian Affairs. The department had recently come under the aegis of the civilian Department of the Interior. Being a man of his time, Harney did not view Indians as equals, but he thought it unseemly to cheat a defeated people who owned nothing but the clothes on their backs. He suspended the activities of one crooked agent and sent him packing back to Washington. The agent whined to Indian Affairs Commissioner George W. Manypenny, who conspired with Congress to have Harney's treaty rejected. Harney believed the idea of civilians trying to administrate Indian policy was doomed to failure. He believed a strong, but just hand—free of the corruption of Indian agents—was a better way to go, and he made his opinions widely known.

But before a major confrontation arose Harney was sent to Kansas, where he supervised the general elections and kept the peace in that troubled state. In 1858 he was promoted to brigadier general—a general officer died which opened a slot—and out of his job as commander of the Second Dragoons. He was given the newly created Department of Oregon, where the War Department hoped he could use his skills to bring a quick end to the rising of the tribes in eastern Washington Territory.

The Department of Oregon had been split off from the once-massive Department of the Pacific, recently under the command of his old nemesis, John E. Wool. Harney's chunk now encompassed present-day Washington, Idaho, Oregon, and parts of Montana and Wyoming. Spokanes, Palouses, Yakimas, and other Northern Plains groups in today's eastern Washington state still seethed over Isaac Stevens's whirlwind treaties and had risen in revolt. The murders of two miners brought the army. In May 1858, the Indians ambushed a 164-man contingent under Lieutenant Colonel Edward Steptoe. The combined cavalry and infantry abandoned their artillery—anathema for any commander—and skulked through the Indian lines that night to save their scalps.

Before Harney cleared the Isthmus of Panama, regular army units led by Ninth Infantry commander Colonel George Wright and Major Robert Garnett defeated the Indians in running battles in eastern and central Washington respectively. Harney arrived in time to make the peace with the help of the Jesuit Father Joseph de Smet. He also reopened the Walla Walla Valley to resettlement and set about making improvements to roads and river crossings.

However, without a serious challenge to occupy his mind, Harney lapsed into old patterns, imagining intrigue and insubordination where none existed. The junior officers at Vancouver Barracks bore the brunt of his wrath, frequently being placed under arrest for minor infractions. The commander of the U.S. Army intervened on the side of the junior officer in one case, pronouncing Harney's act "not discipline, but vengeance!"

It was in this frame of mind that William Selby Harney undertook his inspections of the northern forts in July 1859.

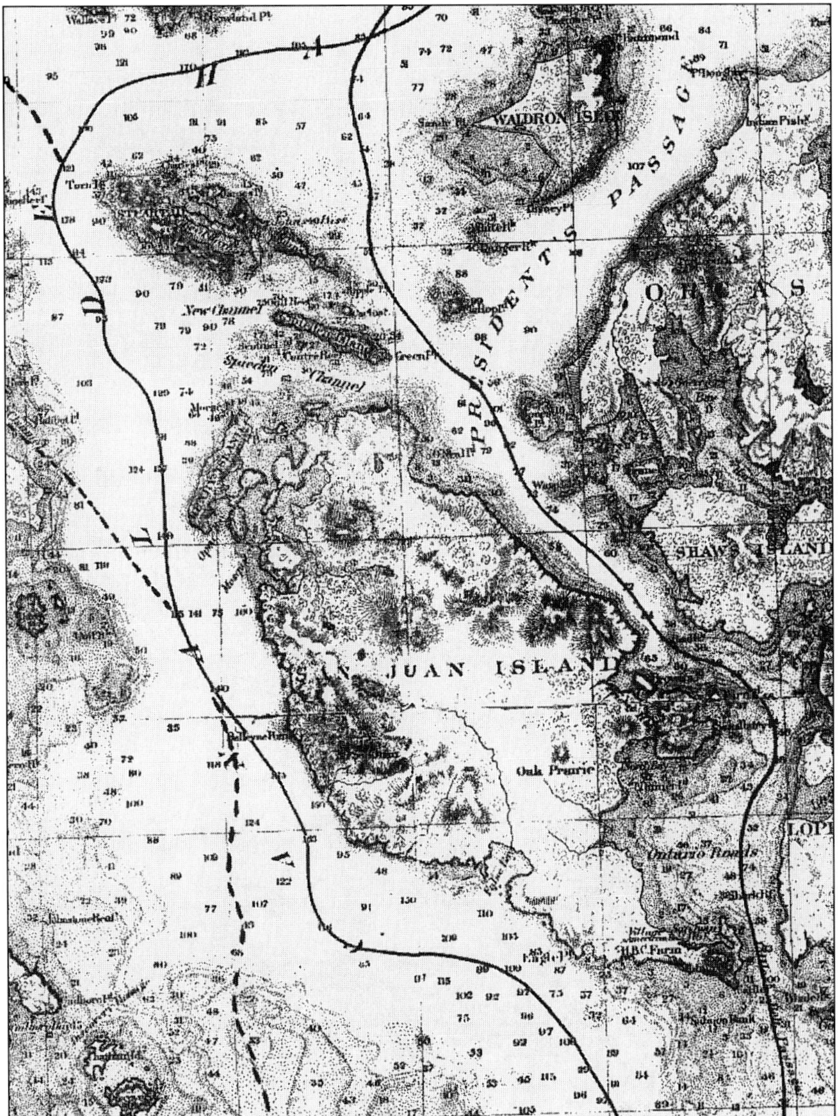

Detail of San Juan Island from 1846 map titled *United States & British Possessions.*

James Knox Polk
San Juan Island NHP

James Buchanan
San Juan Island NHP

"WHAT? YOU YOUNG YANKEE-NOODLE, STRIKE YOUR OWN FATHER!"

Political cartoon from *Punch*
San Juan Island NHP

Alexander Grant Dallas
San Juan Island NHP

Charles Griffin
San Juan Island NHP

James Madison Alden sketch of Belle Vue Farm 1859
San Juan Island NHP

Captain George E. Pickett
Library of Congress

General William S. Harney
San Juan Island NHP

James Madison Alden's view of Griffin Bay in October 1859.
San Juan Island NHP

On October 29, 1859, a Royal Navy officer stationed aboard the H.M.S. *Satellite* came ashore and used his new Daguerreotype kit to capture these images of the growing American encampment near Belle Vue Farm. Note the conical Sibley tents (above) on the parade ground and the new dress uniforms worn by Third Artillery soldiers (below). Both photos San Juan Island NHP

Captain Geoffrey Phipps Hornby, RN

Governor James Douglas

The 31-gun steam frigate H.M.S. *Tribune*, under Hornby's command, was dispatched by Douglas to chase Pickett off San Juan Island. All photos British Columbia Archives

The H.M.S. *Satellite* (top) was the largest in her class in the Royal Navy and a modern weapon compared to the H.M.S. *Ganges* (above), the flagship of Pacific Station commander, Rear Admiral R. Lambert Baynes. The old ship was nearly useless in inland waters, but her 74 guns were considered a threat by the Americans. British Columbia Archives; Baynes, National Maritime Museum, Greenwich

Early garden being created at English Camp, probably in late spring, 1860. Note the commissary under construction in upper left. British Columbia Archives.

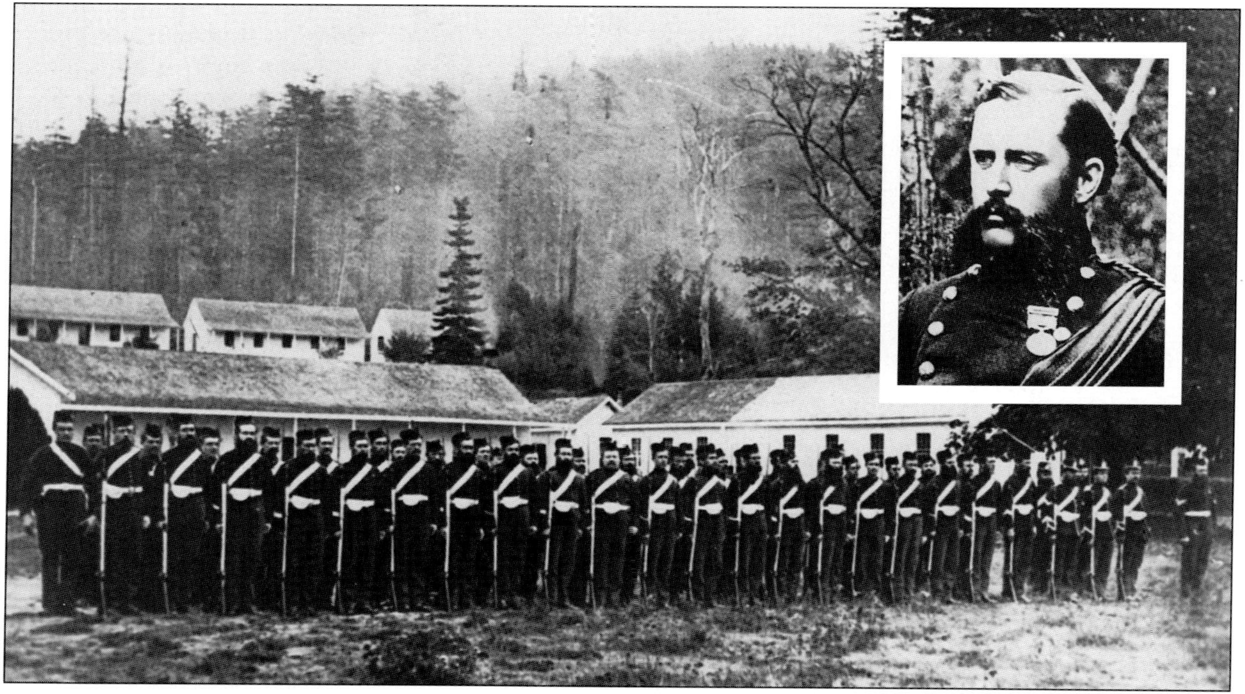

British Royal Marines pose in formation at English Camp in the late 1860s. The camp's first commander, Captain George Bazalgette, is shown in inset. British Columbia Archives

This early 1860s photograph of the Garrison Bay shoreline shows the Royal Marine camp taking shape with the commissary (storehouse) on the left and the guardhouse on the far right. The guardhouse was patterned after the one at the American camp. British Columbia Archives

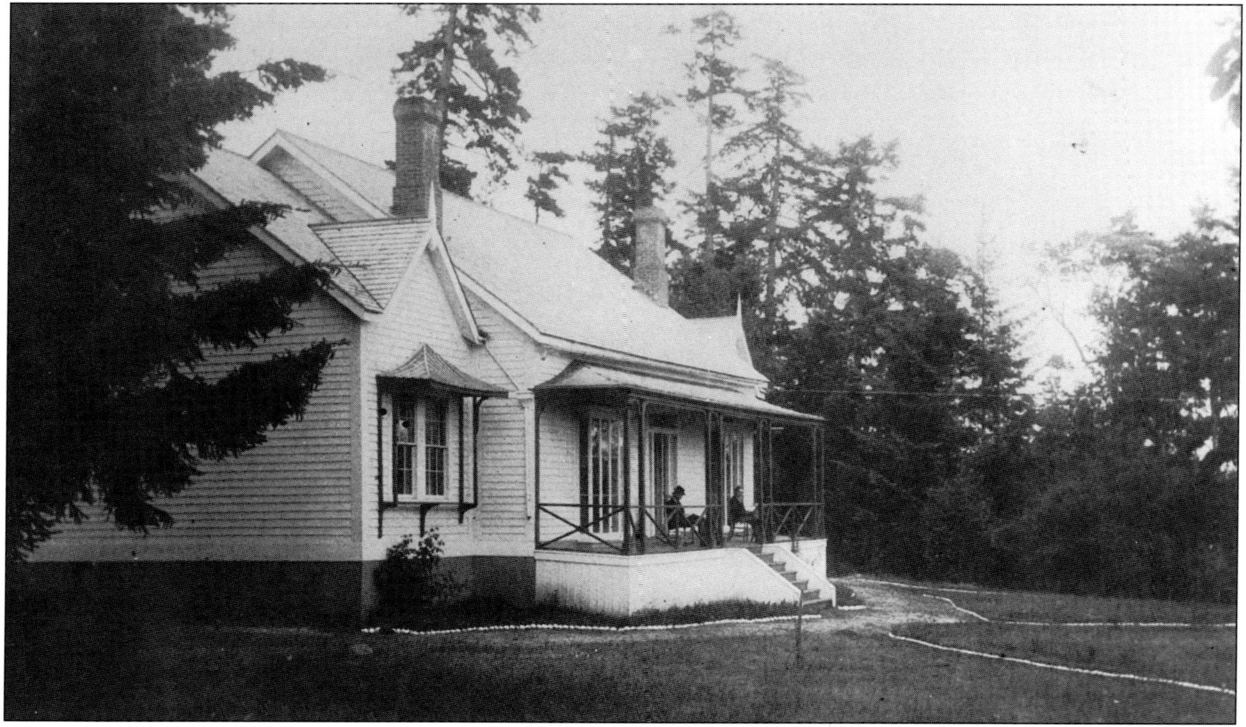

Early view of Commandant's residence at English Camp. Note the tennis court. British Columbia Archives.

American Camp as it appeared during the joint occupation in the late 1860s. The guardhouse was brought to San Juan Island from Fort Bellingham by George Pickett. The officers' quarters at upper left still stands within a white picket fence reconstructed by the National Park Service. San Juan Island NHP

Kaiser Wilhelm I
San Juan Island NHP

General Winfield Scott
San Juan Island NHP

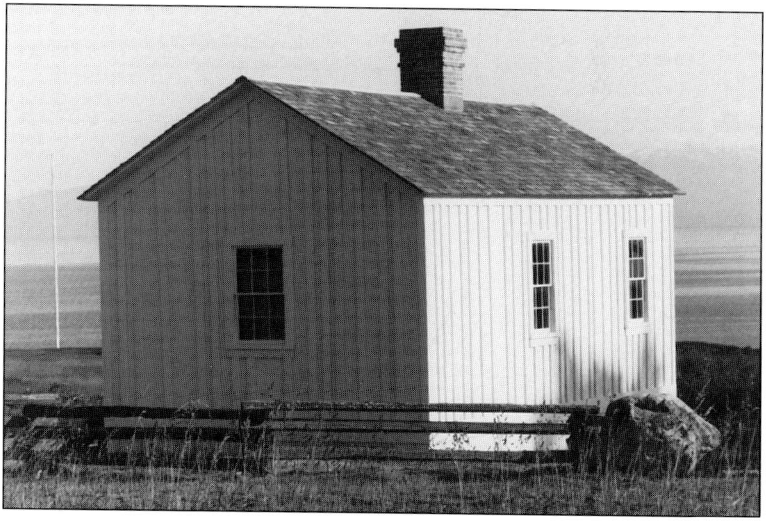

The original laundress quarters braves the winds at American Camp today above the Belle Vue Farm site. Susan Eyerly photo

The Blockhouse still stands at English Camp. The lower portion is replaced every few years because of tidal action. Susan Eyerly photo

The English Camp Parade Ground today. Compare this photo with the two historical views on the previous pages. Susan Eyerly photo

Former hospital building at American Camp after the joint occupation. San Juan Island NHP

AUCTION SALE OF PUBLIC BUILDINGS

OFFICE CHIEF QUARTERMASTER,
Department of the Columbia,
PORTLAND, OREGON, October 20, 1875.

There will be sold at Public Auction on TUESDAY and WEDNESDAY, the 23d and 24th days of November, the buildings comprising the late Camps occupied by the American and British forces on San Juan Island, Washington Territory.

THE SALE ON

TUESDAY, NOVEMBER 23, 1875.

At 11 A. M., will be at the Camp occupied by the U. S. Troops and comprises:

One BUILDING 69x20x8 with an Unfinished Addition 40x20x8.
One BUILDING 25x12x6½.
One BUILDING 20x12x7.
One BUILDING with Kitchen 43x18x7.
Quartermaster and Commissary Store Houses, Blacksmith and Carpenter Shops, Hospital, &c.; in all about 25 buildings,

ON THE FOLLOWING DAY

WEDNESDAY, NOV. 24, 1875,

At 11 A. M., the Sale will be at the Camp formerly occupied by the British Troops, and comprises:

One BUILDING 41x29 with Wing 12½x29 and KITCHEN attached 18x20.
One BUILDING 32x13. **One BUILDING 32x36.**
Hospital, Store Houses, Carpenter and Blacksmith Shops, &c., in all about 15 buildings.

The buildings will be sold at each Camp, separately, and must be removed within 30 days after the Sale.

TERMS, CASH U. S. CURRENCY

R. N. BATCHELDER,
Major & Qr. Mr., U. S. A., Chief Qr. Mr.

Above poster was created to promote the auction of the buildings at both camps in 1875. San Juan Island NHP

CHAPTER 8

The Petition

San Juan Island can be especially spectacular in July. The golden prairies on the Strait of Juan de Fuca shimmer in clear marine sunlight, while heavily forested uplands on Griffin Bay give onto saltwater marshes and rocky beaches teeming with shorebirds. Just off the western shore, orca whales engage in the timeless pursuit of salmon. Anyone with time on his hands and access to a steamer would be tempted to drop anchor.

But according to William Selby Harney, it was the American flag on Paul K. Hubbs, Jr.'s pole that caught his eye around noon on Saturday, July 9, 1859, as he steamed up the Strait of Juan de Fuca bound for Admiralty Inlet and Port Townsend aboard the U.S.S. *Massachusetts*.[1]

The general had been on a tour of the Department of Oregon's northern outposts, which included Forts Bellingham and Townsend and the army camp at Semiahmoo on the 49th parallel, headquarters of the British and American boundary commissions. His last stop had been in Victoria on July 8-9, where he personally thanked Governor Douglas for helping American settlers during recent northern Indian raids. Ironically in weeks past Harney had been demonstrating his anglophobia by so harassing the remaining HBC operation at Fort Vancouver that the factor had protested to the home government. But Harney could not visit the area and not pay his respects to a governor who had been so generous and loyal to fellow members of the Anglo-Saxon race. The two apparently discussed a wide range of topics – with the notable exceptions of the boundary dispute, San Juan Island and stray pigs. [2]

According to various accounts, the *Massachusetts* rounded Cattle Point and heaved to a stop off the Hudson's Bay Company dock on Griffin Bay. Charles Griffin checked his watch and made an entry in his journal. It was 1:00 p.m. [3]

Harney was rowed ashore, where he was met on the beach by a contingent of American citizens. Among them was Charles McKay, who, after 1910, would claim the distinction of being the last survivor of Pig War. Like Cutlar he had left the gold fields of the Fraser in 1858 to establish a squatter farm on the island. Hubbs also was along, having been the one who spotted the ship and rushed to run the flag up the pole.

McKay remembered "...seeing such a strange thing as a man of war coming into our harbor, we all went to see him land. So he said 'Are you Americans?'" [4]

"Yes."

"Is that your flag?"

"Yes."

"What are you doing here?"

Hubbs quickly told the story of the "hog scrape," while Harney strode purposefully up the hill from the dock. When the group reached the crest of the rise about where the redoubt would be built, the general spotted Belle Vue Farm and decided to leave. Barely ten minutes had gone by and Hubbs probably knew he would have to talk fast and throw in a little spice to press his case. The party scrambled down the hill, Hubbs at Harney's side chattering away. Did the general know that northern Indians raided the islands last summer and fall, murdering and beheading two Americans on San Juan? It happened right under the noses of the vaunted Royal Navy in Victoria. True, the H.M.S. *Satellite*, the RN's newest and biggest steam corvette (21 guns), had captured and run off several war canoes in the strait in recent months. But it was hardly enough to make a dent.

Speaking of British ships: Did the general know that the *Beaver* brought Mssrs. Dallas, Fraser, and Tolmie of the Hudson's Bay Company to arrest Lyman Cutlar, an American citizen? Did he know that the Hudson's Bay Company considered the Americans "trespassers" on crown lands and planned to run them all off? Hubbs capped his tale by asking Harney to "...send us a company of soldiers to protect us from the Hudson's Bay Company's threats to take us prisoners," according to McKay. [5]

History blurs here. McKay claimed Harney suggested the citizens draft a petition asking for protection from the northern Indians, although no record exists of his involvement. At any rate, Hubbs drafted and submitted the petition to the Americans on the island on July 11. Signed by twenty-two American citizens including Lyman Cutlar, it asked for military protection against Northerners. It then *commended* the Hudson's Bay Company for helping American settlers in time of need, a line that somehow slipped Harney's mind weeks later. According to Henry Crosbie, then the U.S. civil magistrate for Whatcom County, this was the second petition for troops submitted to Harney by the San Juan Americans. The first one, asking for twenty soldiers, was sent in May following a raid by northern Indians on the Smith Island lighthouse, "which the general, with the usual reluctance of military officers to credit the alarms of citizens, withheld." Many of the recent Indian problems were restated in the petition, but oddly enough, nothing was said about the pig incident or threats of the Hudson's Bay Company. This could be taken as strong evidence that the settlers were coached by Harney. After all, marauding Indians offered more justification for placing troops on the island than a dead pig.[6]

Looking back over the years, Hubbs described Harney going back to the *Massachusetts* and firing a salute to the American flag waving over the log cabin. The general then:

> ...dismissed his staff officers, and in private communications the arrangements were made which led

> to the occupation of the island by the United States troops and hastened the long-delayed question of sovereignty which took a Jackson or Harney to consummate. [7]

Hubbs probably meant Old Hickory's illegal march into Florida in 1818, when he captured the Spanish city of Pensacola without the sanction of the president or the U.S. Congress. In the process Jackson hanged two British subjects for "spying." He was the man on horseback doing what politicians seldom had the nerve to do, and Harney was cut of the same cloth, at least in Hubbs' estimation.

Hubbs maintained that Harney promptly steamed back to Fort Bellingham to see Pickett, whereupon the two Southerners plotted strategy. McKay also recalled this side trip, but the ship's log indicates the *Massachusetts* lumbered across to Fort Townsend and thence up Puget Sound. The general returned to Fort Vancouver on July 13 after anchoring at Olympia, where he met with former Governor Isaac Stevens. He then traveled overland to the Cowlitz River landing.

On the 18th Harney dispatched Special Orders No. 72, directing Captain George E. Pickett to abandon Fort Bellingham and occupy San Juan Island.

The next day he wrote the War Department to explain himself. This letter is more revealing of Archibald Campbell's prejudices – not to mention Isaac Stevens's views – than it was of current boundary facts. Ten days earlier at Semiahmoo the commissioner had presumably given the general a briefing on the dispute that likely included his frustrations with the apparent duplicity of Prevost and the British. Harney opened with a rehash of Manifest Destiny, particularly as it applied to the Oregon Country *before* the Treaty of Oregon. The British did not belong on Vancouver Island and environs because they could not attract British settlers, he wrote. Already more Yanks than Brits lived in Victoria and with "pressing necessities of our commerce on this coast" the British would have to give ground. He then stumbled into the realm of sociology, declaring it "common knowledge" that the British were "too exacting" to colonize so close to an American possession. More critical, Vancouver Island was as important in its proximity to the United States as Cuba was to Florida. He echoed the inflated estimations of San Juan Island's strategic value, as expressed by the U.S. Topographical Engineers report filed five years earlier. [8] His description is remarkably similar to British Boundary Commissioner James Prevost's version:

> SJI contains good water, timber and grass and is the most commanding position we posses on that Sound—the most suitable point to prevent the northern Indians from visiting the settlements to the south of it. At the Southeastern end "one of the finest harbors on the coast is to be found, completely sheltered, offering the best location for a naval station on the Pacific Coast. [9]

The general's central reason for dispatching Pickett surfaced when he turned his attention to the settlers' petition and the Hudson's Bay Company. Despite the petition's emphasis on northern Indians, Harney made only passing reference to them, dwelling instead on the pig incident and the harassment of Cutlar. Northern Indians were a problem, but the settlers especially needed protection from the "oppressive interference of the authorities of the Hudson's Bay Company at Victoria...." [10] This was fueled by Hubbs, who revealed the depth of his resentment of the HBC — and offers a hint of his July 19 discussion with Harney — his June 23 letter to U.S. Collector of Customs Morris H. Frost:

> The monopoly of the Hudson's Bay Co. is intolerable & odious to the (American) settlers. Collision is imminent and that of such a character as may produce the most serious result to the two Governments.

> It is in the desire to prevent this and in what I deem a legitimate discharge of my duty that I forward this to you Sir who have some Knowledge of the threatened difficulties that can only be avoided by a settlement of the Boundary question, or if not settled the placing immediately (sic) a large military force to protect the American settlers from being carried off at will of the Hudson's Bay Co., and shut up in the prison of the British Colony somewhat worse than the Dartmoor was in 1813. [11]

Harney was particularly outraged that "...Mr. Dallas, son-in-law of Governor Douglas, came to island in the British sloop-of-war *Satellite*, and threatened to take one of the Americans by force to Victoria, for shooting a pig of the company." Over the next several weeks Harney would persist in claiming a warship brought Dallas to the island to punish Cutlar, despite the fact Hubbs insisted he told Harney it was the *Beaver.* It would become "...a necessary part of Harney's case that a warship brought A.G. Dallas to the island," Historian Hunter Miller wrote. "...without the supposed use of such a vessel of war, arguments based on threats of Dallas would not have been very impressive." Pacific Station records indicated that no warships called at San Juan between May 7 and July 27. [12]

Harney closed his letter by stressing that he dispatched Pickett to San Juan Island to "..prevent a repetition of this outrage." Orders also were sent to Lieutenant Colonel Silas Casey, deputy commander of the 9th Infantry Regiment. Since January 1856 Casey had commanded all U.S. military forces from the Puget Sound to the 49th parallel from his base at Fort Steilacoom, south of today's Tacoma, Washington.

However, Harney did not say that each man received a different version of the order and was not advised of the content of the other. While Pickett was directed to abandon Fort Bellingham and reestablish his company on San Juan Island in a "suitable position near the harbor at the southeastern extremity," Casey was ordered to provide support via the *Massachusetts.* The ship, under lease to the army, would cruise the archipelago and northern sound and with her eight, 32-pound naval guns, turn back any northern Indians heading south. But she would first sail to Bellingham, pick up Company D and drop them at San Juan, then embark Company I, Fourth Infantry at Fort Townsend and stand by in case hostilities broke out with the British.

Much has been made of how Casey, a higher ranking officer, was reduced to a support role for George Pickett, who was given independent command over a vast domain. Most of it comes from *San Juan and Secession*, a paper delivered to the Loyal Legion of Seattle in 1896 by Granville O. Haller. The author was not an unbiased source. In 1859 he was commander of Company I at Fort Townsend, 20 miles across the Strait of Juan de Fuca from San Juan Island. Instead of getting the San Juan command, Haller and company were ordered to abandon their comfortable post, steam about the Sound aboard the *Massachusetts* and render assistance if needed to Pickett, whom Haller outranked by time in grade and brevet and, by the tone of his prose, intensely disliked. His temper already was shortened by the popular phrase, "Haller's Defeat," which in Washington Territory identified the opening engagement of the Indian War of 1855. [13]

Casey's "demotion" also has been cited as key to an intrigue perpetrated by Harney and Pickett, the two Southerners. One source on the incident —albeit a dubious one, as he wasn't within two thousand miles of San Juan Island nor even in the army at the time—was Major General George B. McClellan, Pickett's West Point classmate and lifelong friend. McClellan claimed that Harney and Pickett nobly entered a cabal to start a war with Great Britain in hopes it would unite North and South for a common purpose and thereby head off civil war. Haller later debunked McClellan's theory. In his version Pickett and Harney got together to start a war all right, but with the far darker motive of distracting the North so the South could achieve independence.[14]

No records exist, in either official or private correspondence, to validate these theories.

In fact, Casey was not subordinated to Pickett. The *Massachusetts* and Haller were placed under Casey's command for "better protection and supervision of the waters of Puget Sound." Casey also was given latitude to deviate from the order based upon his considerable military experience. (His textbook on infantry tactics would be used by both sides during the Civil War.)

It was not unusual for a company commander to exercise independent command on the frontier where regiments rarely assembled as units. Pickett merely moved his company from Fort Bellingham to San Juan Island for the purpose of providing direct protection to American citizens–something he had been incapable of doing from Fort Bellingham. If Haller had landed his troops to reinforce Pickett then he would have assumed command by virtue of his rank, as Casey would do two weeks later. Very much aware of this, Pickett refused Haller's help at every turn.

On San Juan Island, Pickett had been ordered to find a site suitable for four to six companies, preferably in a defensible location. However, when he landed his troops the next day, Pickett ordered his tents pitched on about 300 square yards of open hillside directly above the HBC dock on Griffin Bay, flanked by woodlands. The crest of the hill overlooking today's American Camp prairie was directly in his rear, leaving him vulnerable to naval bombardment.

While the camp was going up, Pickett ordered his second lieutenant, James W. Forsyth, to post a proclamation stating the army's intentions. It was this proclamation, more than the landing of troops, that set off James Douglas. The offending passage read:

> III. This being United States territory, no laws other than those of the United States, nor courts, except such as are held by virtue of said laws, will

be recognized or allowed on this island. [15]

The origin of this proviso remains a mystery. Harney, at least on paper, ordered Pickett to protect American citizens and resist all attempts at interference, by "intimidation or force," by British authorities on Vancouver Island. Any grievances the British had with American citizens were to be handled "under our own laws," Harney specified. The order says nothing about assuming jurisdiction over the entire island.

Pickett's proclamation was posted just in time for John DeCourcy to see it when he arrived from Victoria at 6 p.m. that evening aboard the H.M.S. *Satellite.*, according to Charles Griffin's journal. On rowing out to the ship Griffin learned that DeCourcy had replaced him as Justice of the Peace and Stipendiary Magistrate for the District of San Juan.

Douglas, having been apprised of the pig incident and feeling confident about being backed by his government, also decided to take action on San Juan Island. He had engaged DeCourcy nearly a month before because of "complaints of squatters disturbances," which undoubtedly included the pig incident. Douglas also was insistent that DeCourcy travel to San Juan on a warship. DeCourcy's instructions, issued July 23, were to restore possession of squatters' properties to HBC, arraign trespassers and collect bail from them to insure they reported to court in Victoria, and seek assistance from naval and military authorities if necessary. Employment of armed forces was to be a last resort. At all times he was to be " most careful to avoid giving any occasion that might lead to acts of violence." [16]

These instructions were read aloud at the HBC flag post the following day (July 28), but not before DeCourcy approached Pickett's camp at 3 p.m. The Irishman, who proclaimed himself a distant relative of Royal Navy Captain Michael DeCourcy (who did not agree), marched up to the camp perimeter and ordered a guard to point out his commanding officer. Once Pickett had been located, DeCourcy approached and introduced himself in his official capacity.

Pickett knew precisely who DeCourcy was and what he was doing on San Juan. The ubiquitous Hubbs had warned him almost immediately upon landing that Douglas had appointed a new justice of the peace and other "civil officers" to deal with the Americans.

DeCourcy described his initial encounter with Pickett in this July 29 dispatch to Douglas:

> I asked him, 'By what right or for what reason he had landed and occupied this island.' To which he answered that he did not consider that I, or any other person, had the right to ask such a question; but as it was generally known to everyone about, he had no objection to state that he occupied and landed on the island by order of his *Government*. I then informed him that his acts were illegal; that he was trespassing, and that it was my duty to warn him off the premises and island. [17]

Pickett responded by calling over Henry Crosbie, and introducing him as the "Resident Stipendiary Magistrate" of the island for the United States. Crosbie told DeCourcy that he had no authority on the island and would be in for trouble if he attempted to enforce the law, whereupon DeCourcy stomped off to read his commission at the HBC flagpole. He returned to the camp later on and overheard Pickett promise protection "... to any and every American citizen who might wish to squat on this island. He further said that they had a right to squat on every part of the island."

DeCourcy's commission has been open to debate over the years. Captain DeCourcy, the distant cousin and Royal Navy officer soon to play a prominent role in the incident, maintained that Douglas appointed John DeCourcy in anticipation of Pickett's landing. But Douglas claimed he appointed DeCourcy to enforce

British law on San Juan Island because of the unrest caused by the American squatters and then the pig incident. It probably would have better served Douglas to go along with Captain DeCourcy's interpretation. By sticking to his story, Douglas revealed that he fully intended to enforce jurisdiction over the island as Harney charged, which, in essence, validated Pickett's landing as a necessary American counterstroke.

Indeed, Cutlar, in his September 7 affidavit, stated that he believed a process had been issued and that DeCourcy came expressly to arrest him for trespassing on the sheep run. A Captain Gordon of the constabulary came to Cutlar's cabin with a posse on the 29th, Cutlar stated, but that he was not at home because he had spent the night in Pickett's camp. Charles McKay, Hubbs and others had coaxed him to hide and Pickett had promised protection. Cutlar believed that if Pickett and his soldiers had not been there, he would have been taken to Victoria. [18]

Hubbs's recollection is somewhat saltier. Pickett, tongue in cheek, suggested to Crosbie that he issue a warrant for Cutlar's arrest and have Hubbs serve it, after which the two would come to the army camp. Hubbs approached Cutlar's cabin the morning of the 28th and told the miner he was under arrest. Cutlar laughed and replied, "I surrender." Armed with six shooters, Hubbs and Cutlar negotiated a mile and a half of enemy country and en route encountered "Major DeCourcy and two other British officers." A showdown seemed imminent, but the British officers politely stepped aside and let the Americans pass. Hubbs and Cutlar were soon having a whisky and enjoying a laugh with George Pickett and company.

Crosbie reported a few weeks later that a process was not served. But he did believe the HBC and Victoria government intended to evict all American settlers from the sheep runs, which would effectively deny them access to arable farmland. He concluded that "the only inference that can be drawn is had there been no probability of at once an active resistance to the execution of process, the original intention would have been carried out." If John DeCourcy had not arrived, commission in hand, in Pickett's camp, Crosbie wrote, he would have left San Juan Island to Pickett, the squatters and Griffin's sheep. Ironically, as with Webber and Griffin in 1854, Crosbie and DeCourcy would become friends and number among the few involved who maintained effective communication. Each would praise the other's restraint.

While conviviality was brewing ashore, Prevost and his boundary commission counterpart, Archibald Campbell, were exchanging amicable visits in the harbor and somehow avoiding the main topic at hand, at least according to Campbell's later claims.

By contrast, despite his bold talk, Pickett had come away a troubled man from his initial encounters with the British. In a letter dated July 27 to Captain Alfred Pleasonton, Harney's acting adjutant (or administrative officer), Pickett groused that the *Satellite* did not fire the accustomed ceremonial salute on arrival and that DeCourcy and Prevost did not advise him they were coming ashore. The "very great want of courtesy exhibited towards us by these 'Bulls'" threatened his authority and did not set well with his considerable ego. "You know I am a peacable man, but we cannot stand everything." As a result he was going to be firm. "As a matter of course I shall not allow (DeCourcy) to take any official action; should he attempt to exercise any authority, I shall at once inform him that I do not recognize him and prohibit the opening of any court except those authorized by U.S. laws." However, this bold talk was laced with insecurities, as evidenced by this final entreaty to his old Mexican War comrade: "Please my dear *amigo mio*, tell me anything–*entre nous*–that you think ought to be done." [19]

True enough, the situation seemed certain to escalate and Pickett would soon have his mettle tested by the Royal Navy. The performance of his company over the past three years could hardly have inspired confidence.

CHAPTER 9

George Pickett and the Frontier Army

Maria Roberts was alone on her farm when the brig *George Emery* dropped anchor in Bellingham Bay on Aug. 26, 1856. A long boat made for shore, full of armed men in blue uniforms. Company D, Ninth Infantry, Captain George Pickett commanding, had arrived from Fort Steilacoom with all of the gear requisite to establishing an army post— including several head of beef and some milk cows.

The captain approached Maria, removed his hat, introduced himself, and then politely informed her that he was going to evict her from her property, tear down her house and build a fort. She and her husband would be paid for the property, of course, after it had been appraised. [1]

This was the long-promised fort for which a federal survey team had visited the bay and selected the site a year before. It was to serve as a deterrent against northern Indian raids and lend the community the essential perception of solidity required to attract capital and people to dig coal. It also would serve notice of a strong American presence to the British in Victoria and just fifteen miles to the north on the mainland.

Ninth Infantry deputy commander, Lieutenant Colonel Silas

Casey, cut Pickett's orders on August 16, dispatching him to Bellingham Bay and authorizing the fortress on the Roberts Claim. The Post returns for August 1856 indicate Pickett's initial command included First Lieutenant Robert H. Davis, the nephew of Jefferson Davis; Second Lieutenant Hugh B. Fleming, late of the Sioux Wars, and fifty-seven enlisted men. [2]

At this point—through the commotion of soldiers scurrying about setting up a temporary camp and sailors shoving cows overboard to swim to shore—Maria Roberts could have cared less about northern Indians. The U.S. Government was committing thievery here, not the Indians. And she was no shrinking violet either.

This "large, courageous motherly woman of dark complexion" thought nothing of packing a Colt's revolver and hoofing it to town on her own when the Northerners weren't around. With a heavy German accent, she ordered Pickett and his men off her property.

Gentleman (by act of Congress at the very least) that he was, Pickett again courteously informed Maria that she had to leave, that the federal government was claiming the entire plateau—640 total acres—and that she would have to move into town. Nothing doing, she said. Her husband was away and she wasn't going anywhere. She was heavily pregnant and almost due. Unmoved, Pickett next ordered a work party to remove the roof of her home and then had her bodily removed to the edge of her property line. There was nothing left for her do but hike the trail to Whatcom and wait for her husband to return.

Charles Roberts indeed had words with Pickett, but to no avail. Pickett gave the family permission to rebuild their cabin just off federal property on the beach below, where Maria Roberts and her daughter would remain, unmolested, until the federal government finally relinquished the property in 1868.

Who was this Captain George Pickett, with the fancy manners, the English-style accent, and hair that smelled like the women on San Francisco's Barbary Coast? [3]

George Pickett & the Frontier Army

George Edward Pickett was born on January 25, 1825, at Turkey Island Plantation, Virginia, home to one of the Virginia Tidewater's most respected families—the "Fighting Picketts of Fauquier County." When the family fortunes declined following the Panic of 1837, George was sent "out west" to Quincy, Illinois, a Mississippi River town where his maternal uncle, Andrew Johnston, practiced law. It was hoped a little of Uncle Andrew's industry would rub off on the young man, but George was bored with law and spent more time fishing the river and learning to play the banjo than he did with the books.

Johnston eventually arranged with his law partner, U.S. Representative John Stewart, to get George an appointment to West Point. Pickett scraped through the entrance examination and then barely survived the four-year course, managing to graduate fifty-ninth, or dead last, in the illustrious Class of 1846— class that included future stars such as George McClellan, Thomas "Stonewall" Jackson and Ambrose Powell Hill. As always, Pickett was quicker with a song or a prank than he was with mathematics or military thought. Indeed, one classmate called him "...a jolly good fellow with fine natural gifts sadly neglected."

Nevertheless, when war broke out with Mexico almost immediately following graduation, Pickett was a brevet second lieutenant in the Eighth Infantry. His associates included several other Southerners, among them the stolid Captain James Longstreet and First Lieutenant Lewis Armistead, men with whom Pickett's life would be inexorably entwined for the rest of his career.

In the fall of 1847, George distinguished himself during Winfield Scott's campaign against Mexico City. He was promoted to first lieutenant after showing reckless bravery at Churabusco and was made brevet captain for snatching the regimental colors from a wounded Longstreet and carrying them over the wall during the final assault on Chapultepec Castle.

Following the war he went with the Eighth to Fort Gates, Texas, where in 1851 he brought his new bride, childhood neighbor Sally Minge. Sally and a baby son would die in childbirth a year later.

By June 1855, Pickett was ready for a change and got it when he was assigned as a company commander with the new Ninth Infantry regiment, authorized by Congress in March and forming at Fortress Monroe, Virginia. Once in fighting trim, the unit was to be dispatched to Washington Territory to quell the Indian uprisings and establish peace on the frontier.

Pickett's Indian war was limited. In an all-too-common practice of the time, he was detached from his company in November and sent to Florida to sit on court martial duty. There he would remain until the end of March 1856. By the time he arrived, the Ninth had been split. Eight companies went east of the Cascades with regimental commander Colonel George Wright, while Casey took two companies to Fort Steilacoom. There, Casey consolidated his companies with elements of the Fourth Infantry and Third Artillery to fight Puget Sound Indian groups outraged by treaty terms. Pickett arrived in the territory in time to participate in a brief engagement on the White River in the Cascade foothills. A few weeks later Company D was sent to Bellingham Bay.

Chilly mornings heavy with dew, warm afternoons, and spectacular sunsets over the San Juan and Gulf islands characterize Bellingham Bay in mid-September. Occasional light winds blow up from the south, but it's not hard to spend the day outdoors. One can easily imagine Captain Pickett's men doffing their heavy woolen uniform coats, rolling their off-white flannel wool shirts to the elbow, and with forage caps pulled over the eyes, digging, digging, digging in the eternal rhythm of soldiers; digging latrines, digging garbage pits, and most important, digging the trenches into which the palisades would be set.

Through it all hammers barked and whips snapped as horses strained to pull loads up the track from the beach. To help with the finish carpentry, Pickett hired three civilians from Whatcom at $4 per day ($84.83 per month), who worked through the end of the year, after which he kept one on duty through June.

These facts are known to posterity thanks to monthly "Post Returns," documents through which local commanders reported the activities of their posts. Pickett's comments, entered in a looping scrawl, are terse and to the point: "Nineteen on extra duty" (meaning digging or hammering), "Ran out of report forms," "Still need horses." No mention was made of the night Lieutenant Davis challenged Edmund Fitzhugh, who managed the local coal company, to a duel over a card game. It was well known that both men were hotheads and nothing ever came of it. Nor did anyone bother to note the death of the civilian who was attempting to fire his rifle on the Fourth of July. The man was the first to be buried in the post cemetery.[4]

Such was life in the antebellum frontier army.

By the time Fort Bellingham was founded the U.S. Army had become a frontier police force, its units fragmented and scattered across the trans-Mississippi West. The primary mission was to open the way to westward-bound settlers in the form of exploring and mapping the wilderness, building roads and bridges, and fighting, protecting, and then containing Native Americans.

Legislators who stumped for expansion across the continent were less willing to expand the budgets of the army and the newly formed (1849) Department of the Interior. Believing they could keep the peace on the frontier just as efficiently with a "suitable number" of Indian agents than with a bigger army, President Polk and Congress agreed to set the authorized strength of the post-Mexican War Regular Army at 10,000 officers and men. However, as territory was added and more and more settlers hit the trails, reality set in and spurred by the urging of Secretary of War Jefferson Davis, Congress boosted the Army to 18,000 by 1855. Still the Army rarely had enough men to do the job.[5]

The Army's lineup by 1859 consisted of four artillery, ten infantry and five mounted regiments. Regiments were composed of ten companies of 74 private soldiers. A company was led by a captain, followed by two lieutenants and a first sergeant. The unit was then divided into four squads, each headed by a sergeant and a corporal.

The Regulars were primarily led on the company level by West Point graduates such as Pickett, who had proved their mettle in the Mexican War. As time went on, the best of these officers, not to mention the more quality enlisted men, left for greener pastures, in many cases leaving the culls and misfits behind.

No wonder.

An infantryman in 1859 enlisted for five years, starting at $11 a month and rising to $17 a month if he was eventually promoted to sergeant. Officers earned from $25 a month as a second lieutenant to $75 a month for a colonel. Extra pay was allotted for quarters, remote service and food, but overall pay paled in comparison to the civilian world and was certainly less dependable. Throughout his tour as Company D commander one of Pickett's most consistent laments was that his men had not been paid. The paymaster was to call every two months but at times the men were six months or more without money. This left them at the mercy of the post sutler, who dispensed canned goods, beverages, writing paper and other necessaries and sundries on accounts that were collected when the pay arrived. Some soldiers never caught up or were able to save a dime.

Lieutenant Davis became so fed up with the pay, the discipline and military life in general that he resigned his commission, took an Indian wife and made a living hunting deer.

This was probably viewed as a step up in society, as the peacetime army could hardly count on the regard of a grateful nation. Officers such as Davis were adjudged a drain on the public purse, "sustained by a laboring people, fed from the public crib, but doing nothing whatever to support themselves or increase the wealth of the nation." Enlisted men were rated just above dogs on the social ladder, considered too lazy to work for living.[6]

They ate only slightly better than dogs. Daily rations included fresh or salt beef or pork, fresh bread or hardtack, coffee, and fresh or desiccated vegetables. Soldiers serving on the West Coast usually found hardtack alive with weevils and salt meats spoiled as rations were shipped up the coast from San Francisco. Some relief came from truck gardens, which had been authorized in 1851 at the discretion of post commanders. Most commanders considered gardens more trouble than they were worth, except for Pickett, who inherited a thriving patch from the Roberts family. Pickett and his officers expanded the garden and did so well that Fort Bellingham produce was sold as far south as Fort Steilacoom. Enterprising souls who owned their own firearms also could vary the bill of fare by bagging an elk or wild turkey. The company also issued old weapons for hunting expeditions to supplement rations.

Frontier soldiers more often shouldered a pick or shovel than they did a rifle. They felled trees, dug ditches, and performed countless other tasks of drudgery that might ordinarily been pulled by civilians instead of fighting men.

Discipline was grim. The Articles of War gave latitude to regimental court martial boards in dispensing punishment, which included flogging and other forms of torture ranging from confinement by ball and chain or straddling a sawhorse to being suspended on a pole by wrists and thumbs or carrying a 40-pound log around the parade ground. In wartime deserters could be shot or hung, but ordinarily were flogged raw, branded on the hip with a big D, and sent packing.

Punishment was a deterrent only if you were caught. In 1856, the year of Fort Bellingham's founding, 3,223 out of 15,000 U.S. Army regulars deserted. "Of the first 500 men enlisted in the new Tenth Infantry in 1855, 275 deserted before completing their five-year terms," writes historian Robert Utley.

Fort Bellingham's returns reveal the post's first desertion, in September, followed by five more in November, eventually numbering fifty over the fort's three-plus year history It was not uncommon for soldiers to desert in groups, especially in view of the boredom that caused many a soldier to resort to drink. If any statistic runs consistently throughout Fort Bellingham's returns it is the number of men in confinement in the uplands blockhouse.

From December of 1856 through July 1857 the post never had fewer than nine in the guardhouse, with as many as thirteen in irons in June. One reason may be that while Pickett was diffident to the point of obsequiousness with superiors, he could be elitist and vengeful with subordinates. Indeed, when the fledgling community of Whatcom was threatened by northern Indian raids in the Spring of 1857, Edmund Fitzhugh wrote the following to Governor Isaac Stevens: "We might all be killed as we expect no assistance from the Military Post, they having as much as they can do to protect their perimeter, their pickets not being finished and many of the soldiers being in irons in the guardhouse." [7]

U.S. Army Inspector General Colonel Joseph K. F. Mansfield, taking the measure of Company I, Fourth Infantry at Fort Townsend in 1858, attributed disciplinary problems not so much to punitive officers as to taking peasant boys directly off the immigrant ships and dropping them into uniform. The 1860 census reveals that 40 out of the 57 enlisted men in Pickett's company listed Ireland as their country of origin. [8]

It was Wellington's "scum of the earth" dictum all over again.

More than seventy-four soldiers had deserted from that post in three years. This was attributable to poor instruction and lack of discipline at time of recruitment; the vicinity of the posts to gold diggings in Colville and British Columbia; mistreatment at the hands of sergeants; but most of all "the worthless unprincipled character" of many recruits. Fort Townsend had thirteen in irons that December and since the post's last payday there had been eighteen desertions. Six of the deserters told Mansfield they'd been driven away by a cruel first sergeant; and not only that, the food was bad and their clothing pitiful. One soldier was so desperate he deserted while on guard duty, taking his prisoner with him.

"I have to remark that there must be great neglect, or want of attention, at the recruiting depot at Philadelphia, and at the General Depot," Mansfield wrote. [9]

The Fourth had been recruited separately from the Ninth, but there were many similarities. Despite prescribed training periods, the Western troops were uniformly ill-trained for military duties, lacking in discipline and full of defects, acquired as well as congenital. Two Irish recruits—one who could barely walk and the other with a useless right arm—had been enlisted. A German soldier in the guardhouse for desertion could not speak English and required an interpreter. At other posts he'd found soldiers nearsighted, lame, and even left-handed. "Awkward left-handed men are quite common," he wrote. "...I do not think a left handed man should be enlisted. He cannot fire efficiently by the right shoulder in the ranks."

Unfortunately for national security, the right-handers were little better. The troops at both forts had spent so much time carving posts out of the wilderness that they had little time to be soldiers. At Fort Bellingham, for example, "extra duty" meant just that; one dug and hammered and hefted and cultivated the post's abundant truck garden for extra pay, in addition to marching and drilling and standing inspection.

The result was disastrous, especially when Mansfield tested the Fort Bellingham soldiers' marksmanship with the Harper's Ferry musket.

This company ... fired at the target 6'X22" at 200 yards distant, one round per 40 men, and put only one shot in the target," he wrote. "This only showed the want of instruction and practice...Like all posts in this new country the soldiers work more than they drill and they need instruction here as well as other posts in target firing, rifle drills and bayonet exercises."

The skirmishers—theoretically the best shots in the company who would move in advance of the formation during a battle—fared little better when put to the test. Their performance was only "tolerable," Mansfield reported.

The pay was good enough that only "good and active men

and men of good habits should be allowed to enter the service," Mansfield believed. And despite its fifty desertions in three years, Mansfield actually considered the Bellingham company "in a good state of discipline," noting that twenty of the desertions were in San Francisco, long before the troops arrived in Bellingham.[10]

These were the troops and their leaders prepared to face off against the might of the Royal Navy: Bad shots who were more familiar with cultivating cabbages and hammering nails than with drill and who could barely read and write. Either George Pickett was not spending enough time at his own post to realize how unprepared he was, or he was counting on employing the techniques he learned as a youth appearing in amateur theatricals in Quincy and at West Point (he preferred the female roles, incidentally).

In any case, what John DeCourcy, Governor Douglas, and the Royal Navy did not know, certainly would not hurt the Americans. Pickett was obviously prepared to bluff until it was called.

CHAPTER 10

Governor Douglas Responds

James Douglas was aware of Pickett's landing even before the *Satellite* returned to Victoria on the evening of the July 28 with an alarming report from Magistrate John DeCourcy. Telegraph communications were nonexistent in the Pacific Northwest, but steamship traffic had increased dramatically in the past two years. So word of an imminent landing had spread from Semiahmoo to Olympia before Pickett's foot hit the beach.

Headlines in the July 27 Victoria *Colonist* screamed "San Juan Island Invaded By American Troops," the accompanying story replete with details of troops dispatched by General Harney. The Olympia *Pioneer and Democrat* took a decidedly chauvinistic view two days later, observing: "We suppose our neighbors may grumble a little at this summary way of settling the disputed title, but then it is the privilege of John Bull to grumble and the motley crowd of native born British subjects congregated in those new colonies can just grumble away." [1]

The Olympia crowd should have known Douglas better than that. Before the ink was dry on the Treaty of Oregon he had been enforcing Great Britain's claim to the San Juan Islands. First it had been the logger Cussans, then Ebey, Webber and Sheriff Barnes. Nothing could shake him in his belief that the San Juan Islands belonged to the HBC and the Crown. The governor had dealt with Pickett before and he was convinced the captain had no grasp of geography, let alone international law. In December 1856, Lieutenant Fleming from Fort Bellingham appeared on the Victoria docks with a few soldiers, all in uniform and fully equipped. When Douglas stormed to the waterfront demanding an explanation, Fleming, in the name of Captain George Pickett, asked the governor to ferret out and deliver to him some recent deserters from the fort. If the governor did not wish to do it himself, Fleming would do it for him. Douglas had ordered him to leave.[2]

Now in his position of acting vice admiral while the Pacific Station commander, Rear Admiral R. Lambert Baynes, was away Douglas had the authority to act. Even before the latest edition of the *Colonist* appeared urging action, the governor ordered Captain Michael DeCourcy, the ranking naval officer in Baynes's absence, to dispatch at once a warship to San Juan Island. DeCourcy ordered H.M.S. *Tribune*, 31-gun steam frigate, to prepare for sea. He also assigned more royal marines to the ship including one lieutenant, three noncoms and nineteen privates.

The *Tribune's* commander, Captain Geoffrey Phipps Hornby, was to prevent the landing of further armed parties of U.S. soldiers for the purposes of occupation, and also the erection of fortifications. Douglas's orders held a frustrating dichotomy for Hornby. He was to use force if necessary, but not provoke the Americans into a "collision," according to Royal Navy Lieutenant Richard Mayne of the *Plumper*, who claimed to be aboard the *Tribune* when Hornby received his orders.[3]

Hornby was well-suited to the task. The son of Admiral of the Fleet Phipps Hornby, Geoffrey Hornby, at thirty-three, was one of the more highly regarded young officers in the Royal Navy, quiet but firm and an excellent sailor. He was given command of the *Tribune* in London in the spring of 1858 during the height of the Fraser River Gold Rush. As with many English gentlemen of the age, his yearning for adventure took him overland across Europe and Asia before he finally joined his ship in Hong Kong in October. A few weeks later the ship set off on a horrendous

North Pacific crossing, barely making it into Esquimalt Harbor in February 1859. Forty of the crew deserted almost before the anchor dropped. [4]

With the *Tribune* there were now five British warships in the area. The others were the *Ganges, Pylades, Satellite,* and *Plumper* — a total of 167 guns and 1,940 men. The numbers, initially tabulated and presented to Harney by Silas Casey, are impressive at first glance. They have been cited by everyone who has written on the topic, the first being Harney himself who elevated the number of "fighting men" to 2,140.

There are some problems, however.

First, the *Ganges* may have been an 84-gun ship-of-the-line, a "first rate" in Royal Navy parlance. But she was a sailing vessel—the last of her class in the Royal Navy—which made her a lumbering dinosaur in the age of steam. She was probably towed into Esquimalt Harbor and would have been nearly useless in Griffin Bay or anywhere in the interior waters of the San Juans.

Second, the number of fighting men may be grossly inflated. Most of the 1,940 men listed were sailors. Ships' companies were comprised of able seaman, coal stokers, wipers and gunners, not infantry. How many bluejackets could be armed and sent ashore against Pickett's forces is unknown, but had to be limited. Why else would Hornby worry about not having enough men in ensuing days? About 400 marines and royal engineers were scattered on ships and shore stations in and about Vancouver Island and British Columbia. Hornby's initial allocation of infantry was twenty-three marines. He was promised forty-six more marines, plus fifteen royal engineers, which were to be sent to him from New Westminster, British Columbia, on the mainland. While Hornby was unaware that Pickett's men were bad shots and might bolt at the first volley, he did know that a company of infantry with rifled muskets could do a lot of damage.

Hornby left Victoria at 5 p.m., on Friday, July 29, arriving on San Juan Island at 9 p.m. Also on board the *Tribune* were A.G. Dallas and George Hunter Cary, the attorney general for Vancouver

Island, sent at the last minute to monitor John DeCourcy's actions.

Douglas hoped the presence of a first-class British warship, with more on the horizon, would intimidate the Americans and encourage them to leave or at the very least modify their behavior. Such tactics had worked in the past in the Pacific, which the British had dominated since the War of 1812. He also believed that should hostilities break out, it would be easier to deal with Pickett's lone company rather than the bulk of the Ninth and Fourth Infantry and Third Artillery—close to 2,000 soldiers—who had so quickly and skillfully dispatched the Indians in eastern Washington Territory the year before under George Wright.

Hornby steamed out of Esquimalt and beat across Haro Strait toward the rocky west side of San Juan Island. The black frigate, cutting a white wake and trailing smoke through the blue water, skirted the southern end of the island, where from the port side, sailors could view Belle Vue Farm and the long pebble beach that ran to Cattle Point, around which was a flat expanse of Griffin Bay. Even at 9 p.m., it was still light enough for Hornby to spot the inoffensive American lighthouse tender *Shubrick*, riding at anchor with Commissioner Campbell aboard. The commissioner was probably enjoying the sunset in anticipation of a pleasant journey the next day through the islands to his headquarters at Semiahmoo. In late July the sky would be turning lavender, laced with clouds of almost incandescent pink reflected in shimmering silver waters. Panning his glass from ship to shore, Hornby spotted a cluster of white tents clinging to a straw-colored clearing on a hill that rolled gently into the bay. Through the smoke of the cooking fires, his trained eye at once noted the camp was not fortified; not even entrenched! He could easily sweep the hillside with his guns and drive the Americans into the woods on both sides of the clearing. He must have wondered at a man who would establish a camp and not fortify it.

The following July 30 report came from Hornby via the HBC steamer *Beaver* to Captain Michael DeCourcy:

> This morning, I perceive the Americans have formed a camp about 200 yards from the beach, in which they have two howitzers; the ground rises considerably behind the camp, and on either side, at a distance of 300 yards, it is flanked by woods...I am assured that the force at the disposal of the American captain consists of 50 soldiers, with the two howitzers above mentioned, and about the same number of armed civilians; and if they take to the bush, the Magistrate does not see how they could be arrested, at the same time they might be expected to commit serious depredations on the cattle of the Hudson's Bay Company. [5]

Magistrate John DeCourcy planted this seed in Hornby shortly after the *Tribune* dropped anchor, explaining that, as per his instructions of the 23rd, George Pickett, an American, must be warned off Hudson's Bay Company lands or be arrested as a trespasser. If he did not leave, then DeCourcy would have to arrest Pickett and anyone "aiding him in resistance." By now, that "anyone" meant Company D. As a former military man—he was frequently addressed as "Major"—DeCourcy knew he could hardly suppress infantry with a revolver and Griffin's Hawaiian shepherds. The Royal Navy would have to back him up. This stated, DeCourcy confessed that he did not feel justified in asking Hornby to act unless Hornby had a larger force "sufficient, in fact, to line the bush..." He spun a vision of Royal Marines chasing panicky farmers and soldiers through the woods. They would be fools to press the point, he said. They needed more men, or better yet, time to allow matters to cool.

Cary and Dallas also advised the governor on July 30 that the Americans were much stronger than expected; too strong for Hornby to bully at this point. Both men pressed Douglas to dispatch another ship. In the matter of the warrant, Cary recommended issuing a "summons" to Pickett instead. The actual arrest warrant should be postponed until Sunday (July 31). By then, reinforcements should arrive. Might would make right.

Douglas agreed and ordered Capt. Michael DeCourcy to take the steam frigate H.M.S. *Pylades* to San Juan "trusting that the exhibition of an overwhelming force might prevent resistance and the probable effusion of blood."

That's when Royal Navy balked.

As the ranking Royal Navy officer in Victoria at the moment, DeCourcy had received his own report from Hornby. He also had extensive discussions with *Satellite* Captain James Prevost, freshly arrived from the scene and thoroughly dismayed by the actions of George Pickett. DeCourcy realized the incident was moving into deadly ground and had to be stopped. That evening (July 30) he went to the governor to urge restraint, accompanied by Captain G. H. Richards of the *Plumper*. While DeCourcy probably had a sincere desire to avoid bloodshed, he also was moved by practical considerations. His boss, Rear Admiral Baynes, was away. Douglas, as commander-in-chief and vice admiral, was nominally in charge, but DeCourcy still had to answer to Baynes. Baynes was personally as well as professionally committed to the Royal Navy's worldwide policy of nonconfrontation.

"British policy in the mid-Victorian era was one of restraint. Britain was secure at home and abroad," writes historian Barry Gough. "She sought no self-aggrandizement. Naval commanders on foreign stations during this period frequently served as interpreters of the policy of 'minimum intervention.'"

That meant it was up to individual commanders to decide how and why and when to employ force in guarding British commercial and territorial interests.

> Sometimes, as in the San Juan crisis, British citizens at the scene of contention considered these officers overly cautious. But their actions conformed to their government's foreign policy. No officer dared

> to intervene where powerful nations had claims to the same territory unless British rights were in grave danger; if he did so without cause, he would face censorship of Parliament, the Foreign Office, the Admiralty and the British public. [6]

Not so Douglas. He believed the American act was no more than an invasion by freebooters who had to be dealt with in kind. If his policy had prevailed, war would have been inevitable.

No sooner were the captains seated in the Douglas parlor than DeCourcy asked Douglas for "more specific instructions," particularly "when I was to resort to force." The captain said he realized the islands were in dispute and wanted to do all he could to avoid conflict with the United States—especially as it appeared Great Britain could become involved in a European war. Unbeknownst to him, France and Austria , the latter Britain's ally, were at that moment engaged in the Battle of Solferino in northern Italy. France would win, upsetting the balance of power in Europe.

The captains expressed "very strong" reservations about the deployment of British ships against the U.S. troops and suggested "milder measures" at first. The "civil process" of arresting Pickett should be abandoned, they urged, but a detachment of marines could be dispatched and held at ready just in case.The message was clear: Douglas could issue his orders, but the navy was not prepared to obey him.

DeCourcy then recommended a formal meeting between Prevost and U.S. Boundary Commissioner Campbell to divine if the boundary dispute had been settled and the British had not received word. If the boundary had not been settled, then perhaps Campbell would know why the U.S. troops were camped on disputed ground. It is hard to believe Prevost did not already know the answers since he met with Campbell on Griffin Bay on the 27th and 28th, or so Campbell claimed. The American also was adamant about being as mystified as Prevost over the proceedings. Perhaps Campbell assured Prevost that the American troops were there to protect the American squatters from northern Indians, as he had been advised by Alfred Pleasonton a few weeks before. Whatever was said between the two commissioners, Campbell's presence in the harbor during Pickett's landing made him suspect in the minds of the British. [7]

Overwhelmed and perhaps a bit intimidated by the captains' solidarity, Douglas agreed that Pickett's arrest should be postponed or, as he put it, "adjourned." If the warrant had not been served, they were not to serve it; if it had been served it was not to be enforced. He also canceled Hornby's orders to prevent the Americans from landing more troops and from erecting fortifications, and agreed to a meeting between Prevost and Archibald Campbell. Maybe Campbell could influence Harney. Prevost left for Semiahmoo the next morning in hopes of finding his counterpart.

Douglas wanted DeCourcy to go to San Juan Island as well with *Pylades* to supervise events, but not before Monday, August 1. Richards and the *Plumper* meanwhile would go fetch the marines from New Westminster.

On San Juan Island, George Pickett was involved in high drama as was his wont. It began the evening of the 29th when Paul K. Hubbs, Jr.'s "black sea monster" (the *Tribune)* dropped anchor, then turned on her chains until a broadside (about fifteen guns) was trained on Pickett's camp. She then whistled down her boats. Forty years on, Hubbs, compressing several days into one evening, jotted down this stirring dialogue:

> "Captain," said the writer, "this looks uncomfortable."
>
> "Not in the least," was Pickett's reply. "Stay here while I speak to my men."
>
> At that moment a boat landed with several British officers. The most prominent was Captain Hornby, who advanced to the tent and asked for the com-

> manding officer. Half a minute later appeared the hero of Gettysburg, cool and courteous as a French dancing master and never did an officer appear to a greater advantage, for he was now about to be in the element of his glory. The following words took place in the writer's hearing:
>
> Hornby: I have 1,100 men on board to land tonight.
>
> Pickett: Captain, you have a force to land, but if you undertake it, I will fight you as long as I have a man.
>
> Hornby: Very well; I shall land them at once.
>
> Pickett: If you will give me forty-eight hours, till I hear from my commanding officer, my orders may be countermanded. If you do not you must be responsible for the blood that follows.
>
> "Not one minute" was Hornby's reply.
>
> Pickett, turning to the writer, said: "Summon your men and take the hill. Fire one-third at a time at close range. As you fire wheel your men to the left and join me at the road. We'll make a Bunker Hill of it. I will not leave you and don't be afraid of their big guns."[8]

Actually, Pickett did not meet with Hornby until Sunday the 31st, *after* Hornby had received his orders from Prevost not to interfere with the Americans in any way. Nevertheless, the Virginian was plenty worried. The British seemed to be closing in, which made him feel even more isolated and still at loss over what to do next. In a letter dashed off to Casey on the 30th, Pickett wrote:

> From the threatening attitude of affairs at present, I deem it my duty to request the *Massachusetts* may be sent at once to this point. I do not know

> that an actual collision will take place, but it is not comfortable to be lying within range of a couple of war steamers. The *Tribune*!, a 30-gun frigate, is lying broadside to our camp and from present indications everything leads me to suppose that they will attempt to prevent my carrying out my instructions."[9]

He enclosed an exchange of letters between himself and Charles Griffin, who at this late date lodged a written protest and ordered Pickett off the premises, perhaps to lend weight to any actions taken by John DeCourcy. Pickett responded that he was on the island under orders from his *government*. This statement would generate more confusion and uncertainty among Douglas, the Vancouver Council and the Royal Navy. The letter was signed "in haste..."

Pickett may have been anxious, but the Olympia *Pioneer and Democrat* had every confidence in him. A July 29 article boasted: "Captain Pickett is just the man to be put in command. With every attribute of the gentleman, he is a perfect soldier; a man of great prudence and self-command, and with decision, promptitude and energy, he will be equal to any emergency that may arise." The newspaper began referring to San Juan Island as a "Seat of War."[10]

Aboard the *Tribune*, Hornby was using his Sunday to catch up with personal correspondence while awaiting American reinforcements or for Pickett's men to start digging or both. In a July 31 letter to his wife he mused that the "hot-headed Hearney (sic)" had hopes of winning the presidency." Despite the reservations he stated in his letter to Michael DeCourcy, he strutted a bit for his woman. He wanted to "...bundle these fellows off neck and crop," he wrote. But the governor had forced him to follow a "medium" course, urging him to avoid a collision, which would be impossible under the circumstances. The idea of issuing Pickett a summons was as ridiculous to him as it was to John DeCourcy. Here again was another example of a military man believing his hands had been tied by civilian authorities. [11]

But then, almost in midline, Hornby received the urgent communication from Michael DeCourcy, modifying his orders:

> ...I have received fresh order to take no steps against these men at present, or prevent others from landing. ..The object now seems to be to avoid a collision at all hazards until we hear from the American authorities, but I fear if the marines (from New Westminster) are landed, it will inevitably produce one sooner or later. We have had one lucky escape. The Governor told me it would be well if I called on the commanding officer (Pickett) and told him what my orders were. When I called he was away, and before he returned my visit I had received my counter-orders, so I have not the disgust of having blustered, and then been obliged to haul in my horns. [12]

Pickett did visit the *Tribune* later on that day, but not before he was overwhelmed by a swarm of "tourists" and a couple of newspaper editors from Victoria, including one named Amour De Cosmos. They poked around the soldiers' tents and visited the ships in the harbor. De Cosmos claimed to have shared "refreshments" with Pickett himself. Several of the "sovereigns," as Pickett called them, became bellicose a few refreshments down the line, but Pickett later assured adjutant Pleasonton that he had used "a great deal of my peacemaking disposition" to restrain them. [13]

Hornby's impression of the Virginian was not entirely unfavorable. He viewed Pickett as "more quiet than most of his countrymen, but he seems to have just the notion they all have of getting a name by some audacious act." The Englishman also thought Pickett sounded more like "a Devonshire man than a Yankee." Little comes down to us of what was said in the meeting. Hornby wrote that Pickett "...dropped one or two things which may be useful for us to know, and I hope did not get much information out of me."[14] Painfully polite as the encounter may have been, it resolved nothing. Hornby urged Pickett to leave. Pickett refused, and that was that. However, the frigate's big guns and the crispness of the sailors at gun drills must have unnerved the American. When he returned to shore he ordered his men to pull up stakes. They would move across the neck of the peninsula to a new location on South Beach. The level expanse of prairie there would easily accommodate reinforcements if needed...and they were far away from the *Tribune's* guns.

The waters of the Pacific Northwest were in motion on Monday, August 1.

While Pickett saw to the details of moving his camp, the *Massachusetts* with Company I, Fourth Infantry on board was steaming toward San Juan Island. Alarmed by Pickett's letter, Casey honored Pickett's plea for the ship, but was at a loss to offer advice because, as he wrote Pleasonton, he had not been informed of the "tenor of Captain Pickett's instructions."[15]

That afternoon, Prevost, after a fruitless overnight trip to Semiahmoo in search of Campbell, steamed into a harbor full of ships on Griffin Bay. Along with *Tribune* and *Plumper* were the *Massachusetts*, the *Constitution* – an American merchant steamer Pickett had requisitioned to haul stores, not to be confused with Old Ironsides – and the ubiquitous revenue cutter *Jefferson Davis*. Firsthand accounts differ as to the order of arrival. Some have the *Satellite* showing up last, others the *Massachusetts*, while still others claim the *Plumper*, apparently stopping off on route to fetch the Royal Marines and Royal Engineer sappers.

Many of the officers already were on shore, including Haller and the *Plumper's* Richards. Thirty-seven years later Haller wrote that in a heated private meeting with Pickett, he questioned Pickett's actions. Haller said he offered to land his troops, which Pickett refused. Haller then told the Virginian that he was jeopardizing his career by pursuing Harney's agenda; that his actions, though ordered by Harney, were unlawful and provocative and that Pickett was bound to the higher law of U.S. policy. Pickett waved him off and Haller, joined by Richards, visited Belle Vue Farm, where he inspected Griffin's roses and told Lieutenant Colonel Moody of the Royal Engineers what he knew about events in Europe. He flattered himself in 1896 that it was *his briefing* about what had happened at Solferino that swayed the British into a position of restraint.[16]

Two British officers took a different view of Haller's presence on San Juan on August 1. According to David Boyle, first lieutenant on the *Tribune*, the *Massachusetts* steamed into the harbor while Prevost and Hornby were seeking Pickett on shore. The Royal Navy, he wrote, had not yet received the order to stand down from opposing troop landings. Boyle claimed he warned the *Massachusetts* skipper that the British would prevent the Americans from so doing. Haller's troops, more than 120 according to some accounts, disembarked anyway and Boyle was about to beat to quarters when the *Plumper* arrived with the fresh orders. Francis Norman, a sub-lieutenant aboard the *Tribune*, later claimed this disembarkation from the *Massachusetts* illustrated perfidy on Pickett's part. The Virginian had denuded the British quarterdecks by inviting the officers, Hornby and Prevost included, to a picnic at the new Spring Camp site above South Beach. However, even Haller insisted that he went ashore alone and Hornby himself reported to Douglas that U.S. troops had arrived in the harbor on August 1 but left the same day without landing. No U.S. reinforcements were landed until Silas Casey arrived on August 10.[17]

While ashore Prevost, in the absence of Campbell, decided to interrogate Pickett. They had been acquainted since 1857 when the boundary commission teams were organizing at Semiahmoo. Pickett was diffident with Prevost, contending that "he was merely a subordinate carrying out the orders of his superiors." He was there to protect citizens of the United States and to allow U.S. civil powers to enforce the law. He assured Prevost that he and Magistrate Crosbie would approach their duties delicately to avoid "misunderstanding." However, he firmly believed San Juan Island belonged to the U.S., and therefore U.S.Army officers "were perfectly justified in all their acts with regard to it, and that the strictest orders had been given to protect and respect the property of settlers on the island, British or otherwise."

Prevost, in turn, insisted the islands were British: "...and as the line of boundary was still in abeyance, the act of violence committed by landing an armed force without any communications with me, or with British authorities was as discourteous as it was unjustifiable."

If Pickett's company remained, then the British might be forced to land the Royal Marines as a defensive measure, Prevost warned; to which Pickett replied that British subjects and property would be protected and that Crosbie and himself would act with the greatest "caution and latitude."

This is the same man who said, "We'll make a Bunker Hill of it," or so claimed Hubbs. It is hard to believe this George Pickett was part of a "southern cabal" to start a war. He could have been prevaricating, but it seems unlikely.

Pickett then took Prevost by surprise by relating that Crosbie had "held court" and fined Cutlar for shooting the boar. Not only that, the fine would be turned over to the HBC. This must have been connected with Hubbs's "arrest" at Cutlar's cabin. Word got around, for John DeCourcy also reported August 1 that this judgment against Cutlar had taken place the day before. Crosbie himself made no record of the action, nor did Cutlar mention it in his affidavit. [18]

Prevost finished with Pickett, and steamed to Victoria to file his report with Douglas. He arrived at the tail-end of a meeting that included Douglas, Michael DeCourcy, members of the Vancouver Island Council and Lieutenant Colonel John S. Hawkins of the Royal Engineers, the British land boundary commissioner. Still believing that *Pylades* was going to join *Tribune*, Douglas that morning had sent instructions to DeCourcy reminding him that, while he would "deplore" any act the would disrupt the peace, DeCourcy was to enforce Great Britain's claim to the islands. If it was necessary to land the Royal Marines to back that claim then so be it.

Before DeCourcy weighed anchor, Hawkins rapped on his cabin door. The colonel thought the home government should be immediately informed and he volunteered to make the long journey to England. He would have to leave at once to catch the mail packet out of San Francisco for Panama. The two men went to the governor, who liked the idea and immediately summoned the council. The council, led by longtime Douglas associate Roderick Finlayson, approved Hawkins's trip. They also urged Douglas to recall Magistrate John DeCourcy and avoid landing marines, as that might bring on a collision. [19]

The men must have eagerly turned toward the late-arriving Prevost hoping he bore an explanation from Campbell. The captain lamented that he could not locate Campbell, but that he had written a letter for him and dropped it at Semiahmoo– a letter that, from the reaction it received, would have been better left in drawer overnight. [20]

The meeting concluded with the council recommending that all British subjects residing on San Juan Island leave in protest of the American invasion. Hornby was designated the senior naval officer until Michael DeCourcy returned from San Francisco. Before departing DeCourcy asked Douglas to send "specific" instructions to Hornby. Prevost would deliver those instructions and continue his search for Campbell.

Dazzled by another spectacular sunset, those aboard ships on Griffin Bay probably heard the soldiers ashore indulging in the timeless rituals of the campfire, while the soldiers listened for the ships' bells tolling the hours. Sentries and lookouts paced, probably wondering at all the hubbub over a speck of rock in the middle of nowhere, let alone some farmer's infernal pig. Tobacco, whisky and other sundries had been exchanged between the Americans and British shore parties. Almost everyone spoke the same language and seemed nice. Thank goodness no one had started anything yet.

But like soldiers and sailors of any time, anywhere, they knew they were powerless to shape events. They would keep their powder dry, do what they were told, and pray for the protection of a merciful God.

James Douglas and William Selby Harney would do the rest.

CHAPTER 11

"Tut, tut, no, no, the damn fools."

James Douglas must have had a sleepless night, the events of August 1 looping in his head. First the captains worked him over, then the council and Finlayson backed the captains and urged him not to place Royal Marines on the island. How it must have galled him. The Hudson's Bay Company and Great Britain—then one and the same in the Pacific Northwest—had suffered the indignity of being shoved out of Oregon. Douglas had founded this colony, of which the San Juan Islands had always been considered a part. He had acted decisively to save New Caledonia, now called *British* Columbia, during the Fraser River Gold Rush. He was not about to sit back and be overrun again by the Yanks. If Pickett's soldiers remained, he would land the marines as a counterbalance. British claims would be preserved and the clarity of joint martial law would replace the passions and uncertainties of civil law, often enforced on the frontier by self-interested parties.

This "mature reflection" spurred Douglas to reject the council's suggestions and on August 2 he decided to land British troops so "that the occupation at least might be a joint one." He fired off letters to John DeCourcy, the magistrate, and Hornby, advising them of his intentions.

To Hornby, he wrote:

> Circumstances beyond my control and too various for explanation in this form compelled me to assert to the first modification of your orders revoking the authority given you to prevent the landing of U.S. troops and the erection of Military Works by the detachment occupying San Juan Island...I place the fullest reliance on your firmness of temper and discretion and I trust that Captain Pickett will be reasonable and mitigate as much as possible the evils that must necessarily arise out of conflicting jurisdiction of a joint occupation, I hope they will not seek to force a quarrel upon us, in that case, however the sin will rest upon their own heads. I have written DeCourcy (the magistrate) to be cautious and not to push matters in his department to extremes, wishing you well.[1]

That was precisely what concerned Hornby. In an August 1 letter to Captain Michael DeCourcy, he worried that he could not assist the magistrate ashore without avoiding a fight with Pickett. The island was in a state, he reported. Griffin was complaining about soldiers trampling his crops and stampeding his sheep. Tourists were poking about. The smallest spark could ignite a collision in Hornby's view, so landing troops on any pretense would be folly. [2]

DeCourcy was en route to San Francisco by then, so Douglas wrote a second, "informal" letter to Hornby addressing his concerns. The last thing he wanted was to provoke the U.S. soldiers on San Juan, but he could not allow them to harm British subjects or property and sacrifice "the honor and dignity of Her Majesty's Government." Nor was he going to abandon the island to a military occupation and "a Squatter population of American citizens." He urged Hornby to enter into a full and frank communication" with Pickett to avoid hostilities. The occupation was contemptible and violated every agreement between the two nations, but he was willing to dismiss it – if an equal number of Royal Marines set up housekeeping:

> "If the joint occupation were wholly a military one I conceive that peace and good understanding might be preserved provided the officers in command were mutually desirous of maintaining friendly relations, and you might if you saw fit opportunity without weakening our position or committing us in any way propose that the Civil Magistrates should be withdrawn on both sides..."

He stressed five points to justify landing British troops:

1. maintain the integrity of the British claim
2. maintain national honor and dignity
3. maintain control and influence over Indian tribes
4. protect British subjects and property
5. carry out any action which circumstances may hereafter compel you to take. [3]

The last proviso probably made Hornby flinch and may have convinced him of his future course. Douglas attached his formal protest to the U.S. authorities, which stressed that because the islands always had been "undeviatingly" claimed to be in the Crown of Great Britain, he did "formally and solemnly protest against the occupation." It was signed, "By James Douglas of the most honorable Order of the Bath, Governor and Commander-in-Chief in and over the Colony of Vancouver Island and its dependencies, Vice Admiral of the same &c., &c."

On August 2, the *Plumper* arrived on Griffin Bay from New Westminster with forty-six marines and fifteen Royal Engineers,

Colonel Moody commanding. The *Satellite* returned on August 3. By then Hornby had mulled over Douglas's instructions and decided to meet with Pickett at his camp.

Pickett worried Hornby. Nothing he had done thus far had inspired confidence in consistent behavior. He was still puzzled over Pickett's July 31 move across the prairie to the spring above South Beach. It belied military thought and made moot Douglas's orders to stop the erection of fortifications. The Americans, he wrote, "do not seem enclined to strengthen nor have any preparations for intrenching or other defence been made by them, though the camp has been shifted from its first site to one close to the sea on the other side of the island and equally exposed to the fire of Ships, as was their original one." [4]

Pickett, Hornby, Prevost and Richards met in Pickett's tent at South Beach at 2 p.m. on the 3rd. Hornby did all the talking and wasted little time on pleasantries. He wanted to know why, and on whose authority, Pickett occupied the island. Pickett replied "by the general commanding," whose orders came directly from Washington, D.C. He had an "equal desire" with Douglas that a collision be avoided and he was certain U.S. citizens would not provoke one. However, if the British landed, Pickett warned that "...his orders as a Soldier gave him no other discretion but to seize a small force, attack an equal one," and go down fighting if outnumbered." He concluded by observing–probably more cleverly than intended – that the British so outnumbered him that they did not *need* to land. They could achieve their ends by merely standing off shore and the world would not think the less of them. [5]

If Hornby agreed with the last point, he did not say so on paper. He handed Pickett Douglas's formal protest to convey to Harney, explaining that because the United States placed troops and a magistrate on the island, Great Britain could do the same. Magistrates could call on military forces at any time to enforce the law, which would involve considerable risk. He then played Douglas's card. Why not get rid of the magistrates, suspend the courts, and have a joint military occupation, the officers on both sides adjudicating the affairs of their countrymen? Unless Pickett pulled up stakes and vacated the island, no other solution would avoid bloodshed.

It was too much for Pickett to digest on his own. Throughout his military career he had shown a tendency to sniff at authority on the one hand and crave its security on the other. The Virginian said he could not condone a joint military occupation until he received direction from Harney. He asked for time to send a dispatch. Perhaps Hornby should do the same with Douglas, Pickett added. [6]

Hornby's patience reached its limits. Pickett was vacillating while he was showing initiative. He warned Pickett that because his occupation was illegal the onus was on him to avoid "necessary evils" and accept his clearly equitable solution. The marines would land the minute he thought the "honor of the flag" or protection of British rights was at stake. As the meeting broke up and the guests moved to the tent flap, Hornby and Pickett continued to joust over who would bear the responsibility if fighting broke out. If Hornby forced a landing it would be his fault. If Pickett did not allow a landing he would be to blame. As the frustrated Hornby prepared to leave, Pickett stopped him and asked if he would write him a letter offering his interpretation of their conversation and reiterating the British position. Hornby consented and went on his way with Prevost and Richards. [7]

That evening Pickett sent a dispatch to Pleasonton via the *Shubrick.* His correspondence continued to register surprise and chagrin at the British response to his landing. He had been WARNED OFF [his capitals] by the Hudson's Bay Company agent and forced to deal with three captains, though he nobly "thought it better to take the brunt of it." A joint military occupation had been offered, but Pickett "declined anything of the kind." He admitted that the British could land anywhere, anytime they wanted and he could do little to stop them, as his force was a "mere mouthful" for the warships in the bay. He had been as diplomatic as possible under the circumstances, and had put them off by giving them a "pill" to swallow. He also "... endeavored to impress them with the idea that my authority comes directly through you from Washington," he wrote.

The British were not impressed:

> ...(the British) seem to doubt the authority of the general Commanding, and do not wish to acknowledge his right to occupy this island, which they say is in dispute, unless the United States Government have decided the question with Great Britain. I have so far staved them off, by saying that the two governments have without a doubt settled this affair; but this state of affairs cannot last, therefore I must ask that an express be sent to me immediately on my future guidance. I do not think there are moments to waste. [8]

This letter reveals that—far from being one of the principals in a conspiracy, or even a scheme to grab the islands—George Pickett, until his meeting with Hornby, was ignorant of even the most fundamental background of the Treaty of Oregon; thought Harney's orders came from Washington; was shocked that the British doubted the general's authority; and, most troubling, seemed unaware the islands were in dispute. He thought they were U.S. territory!

This was obvious to James Douglas, who told a joint meeting of the colony's Legislative Council and House Assembly that Pickett's act was "originated in error, and been undertaken without the authority of that government." By contrast, Douglas's government, arrest warrants and timber permits aside, had "abstained from exercising exclusive sovereignty over the islands." Finally, ever the executive accustomed to having his orders obeyed, Douglas proclaimed, even as Hornby and Pickett were meeting, that he expected British troops would be landed. [9]

Hornby had other ideas.

British policy weighed heavily on his mind. He also was convinced that Pickett's orders originated with Harney and were not sanctioned by the U.S. government. This was confirmed when Hornby produced his copy of the 1855 "Marcy Letter" (in which the Secretary of State had pledged that U.S. officials would not provoke the British over the San Juan Islands) and Pickett said he had never seen nor heard of the document.

Hornby also was aware of Pacific Station directives, which reflected the British government's policy of nonconfrontation—especially with the rising industrial might of the United States. And he was one of the few players involved who had a realistic idea of the risks. He had heard stories of blood-washed quarterdecks from his father and Admiral Baynes. He had seen for himself hospital ships crammed with the human wreckage of the Crimean War. Even farcical conflicts had real victims.

Above all, he knew Pickett was not bluffing. Anyone so obtuse about the implications of his acts, anyone so clearly unsure of himself, made Hornby's course clear. He would keep the marines aboard ship and await Admiral Baynes. He dipped his pen in a bottle and wrote two letters to Douglas; one an official report justifying his actions, the other more candid and personal.

In the official document he outlined the gist of his conversation with Pickett and then listed, in four points, his reasons for not landing troops. First, the British were powerful enough to blow Pickett from his prairie camp and Pickett knew it, therefore if the British chose not to fight, it was by virtue of restraint and the flag was not "compromised" (essentially Pickett's point); second, remaining on the bay gave them mobile striking power, unlike the Americans who were wed to their camp; third, they could hardly protest the landing of an armed force if they also put one ashore; and finally, because the Americans demeaned themselves, it did not mean the British had to follow suit.

The other letter was more frank and informal.

"It seems undesirable to have an open rupture here, until

they can have heard of and replied to our case at home," Hornby wrote. Pickett and Company D had been on San Juan Island for a week. It would be "undignified" to land the marines after the *Massachusetts* sailed off without landing a single soldier from Haller's company. If the British chose to land, it would have to be with a superior force, which would prompt the Americans to counter. Taking a plunge into political waters – always dangerous for a military man – he stated that Lord Palmerston never had, and never would, enforce the British claim against the U.S. If Washington pressed London to give up the land, London would comply. What a "mess" they would all be in if the government had already done so. [10]

As far as Hornby knew, Pickett's modest force was all there was likely to be on San Juan. Surely the British could afford to be more forbearing in the face of a motley collection of expatriate Irishmen led by a posturing Southerner.

Hornby's letters exhibited insubordination rather than common sense, as far as Douglas was concerned. But the governor could not shape events without military force, which the captains had denied him. His orders from the home government were clear: Hang on to the San Juans. Now his own navy was standing in his way and the legislature and newspapers were calling for his scalp. How it must have galled him to read the following, from the legislature: "The House would therefore inquire why British forces were not landed, to assert our just right to the island in question, and uphold the honor of the country and our Queen." [11]

The enemy *Pioneer and Democrat* proclaimed: "...there are thirty Americans on the island, and they are fairly made set of chaps, not easily scared." Paul K. Hubbs, Jr., was quoted: "The monopoly of the HBC is intolerable and odious to most settlers. Collision is imminent, and of such character as may produce the most serious result to the two governments." [12]

Somewhere along the way, it's uncertain when, because in all his correspondence he never gives a date, Archibald Campbell finally appeared in Pickett's camp. From the first, the commissioner had watched Pickett's doings with a mixture of curiosity and alarm. As far as is known, he still believed Pickett was on San Juan as another futile exercise against the northern Indians, although he was puzzled by the guns, the tents, the lumber for buildings and heavy gun platforms. In the past, a squad of light infantry would slip in aboard a revenue cutter, camp for the night and leave.

The commissioner asked to see Pickett's orders. Pickett produced them, adding proudly that he had not only enforced them to the letter but was determined to hold the island no matter what—which included forbidding the British to land marines! Campbell read the orders and blinked. *"...resist all attempts at interference by the British...by intimidation or force."* Either the world had turned upside down while he was gunkholing, or Pickett was indulging in a dangerous fiction. In an August 14 letter to Harney, Campbell questioned why the British could not land the same as the Americans. They were certainly justified under the terms of the standing agreement between the two nations, but "...I found Captain Pickett had different views, derived from your instructions, which he confidentially showed to me. I perceived that they were susceptible of the interpretation he gave them, though they were not directly mandatory on the subject." 13

Despite his concern, Campbell was reluctant to interfere in what he presumed to be a military matter, especially if fresh orders from the War Department had reached Harney without Campbell's knowledge. He had returned to Semiahmoo on August 1 – missing Prevost by a day – to prepare for an expedition deep into the Cascade Mountains along the 49th parallel. Prevost and the Satellite finally caught up with him at Semiahmoo on August 4.

Prevost already believed he had been deceived. Their gentlemanly disagreement over the proper water boundary—Haro or Rosario—in recent weeks had degenerated into an exchange of petulant letters loaded with double-talk as both men viewed their roles with growing frustration. This was compounded when Campbell accused Prevost of coming to the table armed with the "secret" instruction not to consider the American claim. Is it any wonder that the commissioners did not meet personally to discuss Pickett's landing, but exchanged a series of letters with the *Satellite* anchored in Drayton Bay? [14]

Prevost right off wanted to know if Campbell knew beforehand that troops were going to be landed, and, if so, if the landing had been sanctioned by the U.S. government. If not, he invited Campbell to join him in urging Harney to withdraw the troops not only to avoid war, but to keep from spoiling business opportunities on both sides of the Atlantic. Not to be undone by Campbell's wordiness and exaggeration, Prevost concluded:

> ...that an act so unprecedented in the history of civilized and enlightened nations, and so contrary to that natural courtesy which is due from one great nation to another, cannot be productive of good, and may in the end entail such serious consequences, that I am sure both you and I would deplore to the last hour of our existence any hesitation or neglect on our parts to do all that lies in our power to avert pending evil... [15]

Campbell accused Prevost of overstepping his bounds by asking a boundary colleague about military matters over which he had no control. Not only did Campbell refuse to acknowledge any questions about the landing, he further lambasted Prevost for making threats:

> ...Notwithstanding the apparent air of moderation with which you have clothed your words, there pervades in your whole communication a vein of assumption and an attempt at intimidation by excit-

> ing apprehensions of evil, not well calculated to produce the effect you profess so ardently to desire...[16]

More exchanges followed. Prevost stubbornly demanded answers and accused Campbell of evasion and subterfuge; Campbell denied he was evading anything, since Prevost had no right to question him. On and on it went throughout the 4th and 5th, until they both gave up and complained about each other to their superiors. Prevost was so certain Campbell was in collusion with Harney that he refused to have anything more to do with him. [17]

While the commissioners were hurling barbs, the *Pylades* under Captain Michael DeCourcy was beating against a terrific southwest storm, not uncommon in August off the Washington coast. Even under steam, the ship could not make headway enough to get Colonel Hawkins to San Francisco in time to catch the mail boat to Panama City. DeCourcy decided to head back to Victoria where Hawkins could catch a commercial steamer and pick up the next mail boat when the weather calmed. Running with the wind, DeCourcy spotted a tall ship on the horizon. It was the old H.M.S. *Ganges*, the 84-gun "first rate" with Rear Admiral R. Lambert Baynes on board. DeCourcy ordered a boat and braved the wild seas to consult with Baynes aboard *Ganges*.

At first sight, the Pacific Station commander belied the image of career fighting sailor, who, as a midshipman, had seen action at New Orleans during the War of 1812. He was in his sixties by then, short, slight of build and balding, with his graying hair combed over to hide a shiny pate. He fancied top hats, high collars and elaborate bow ties with his sea uniform—consistent with a well-known and appreciated sense of humor. He had been an admiral since 1855 and in his current job since 1858. Hudson's Bay Company factor Angus McDonald probably summed him up best: "...plain, little, big-hearted, unassuming, lowland Scotsman, lame but full of salt and fresh fun." Nevertheless, the admiral's cool demeanor was in sharp contrast to Douglas or Harney. Most critical to the situation, he had a low threshold for idiotic behavior. He is purported to have said when informed of the crisis, "Tut, tut, no, no, the damn fools." [18]

The *Ganges* dropped anchor in Esquimalt on August 5, whereupon Baynes approved Hornby's course, but it was not until August 13 that he put it in writing. Hornby was commended for avoiding a potentially disastrous situation by refusing to land the marines. Moreover, Baynes agreed with Hornby (and Pickett) that the British claim to the island would not be compromised by the Royal Navy remaining on alert on Griffin Bay rather than forcing the issue ashore. He formally canceled Douglas's orders, and directed Hornby to "strictly avoid all interference" with Pickett's force and "by every means in your power to prevent the risk of collision taking place." As insurance against this possibility, Hornby was ordered not to assist Magistrate John DeCourcy unless it was absolutely necessary. Douglas, in turn, was asked to advise the magistrate not to act against the Americans without consulting Hornby. [19]

Douglas was furious. Hornby was being praised for rank insubordination! He struck off a letter to Baynes, pointing out that, quite the contrary, if his instructions had been "vigorously carried out" by Hornby, the British would have maintained jurisdiction and the U.S. troops would have been withdrawn or reduced in number. And yet, as matters stood, he had no objections to Baynes's orders, as this same course had previously been urged by Captain DeCourcy. [20]

His conciliatory attitude toward Baynes aside, Douglas was still angry enough to dispatch a hot letter to Colonial Secretary Lord Lytton:

> Hornby did not deem it advisable to carry out my instructions...the absence of movement of this kind has not only increased the confidence of the occupying party; and it places me in a difficult position, for so much time having elapsed the carrying

> out of the movement of this period, deprives it of most of its force.

He would have driven them out "...had it not been for the opposition of the civil and military authorities of this Colony." Now he would have to act "as circumstances demand." [21]

Braced for the governor's criticisms, Hornby wrote a letter for the record to Baynes, stating that his forces at that time consisted of sixty-nine marines, fifteen engineers and the ship's company, whom he believed could land and contend with Pickett. However, Baynes could rest assured that he, Hornby, would not do as the Americans had done, "violating" territory under negotiation between the two nations.

Hornby need not have worried. He was later praised for his forbearance in several quarters, including Royal Engineers commander, Colonel Moody. In a letter to British Army General Sir John Fox Burgoyne (a descendent of the Revolutionary War general of the same name), Moody remarked that it was lucky for Great Britain that Hornby was on San Juan. The captain had performed superbly despite the fact that "...the governor wrote a very clever letter indirectly ordering him to land troops, but throwing the responsibility on him. Hornby has far too much 'mother wit' to be caught that way—of course he did not land them."

When Douglas was portrayed as a great peacemaker in the incident some months later, Hornby commented to his wife:

> I hear that Governor Douglas has got much praise in England for keeping peace with the Yankees. That is rather good, when one knows that he would hear of nothing but shooting them all at first and that, after all, peace was only preserved by my not complying with his wishes, as I felt he was all wrong from the first. I got the abuse for saying that San Juan was not more our island than the Americans; and that we should be equally wrong in landing troops there

and now they find out I was right.[22]

And so fighting had been averted. If there was any one moment when Great Britain and the United States could have plunged into war, it was the encounter between Hornby and Pickett on Griffin Bay. They were far removed from their respective seats of power, pushed by immediate superiors who had lost all sense of perspective and local populations clamoring for war.

Over the years George Pickett has been described as everything from Hubbs's great captain ready to take on the British Empire to Winfield Scott's mediocrity, stumbling through matters of which he had only a modest grasp. Conversely, Geoffrey Phipps Hornby is consistently remembered as a courageous man who would rather disobey orders than start a war.

The record shows George Pickett liberally misinterpreted his orders, then held to a rigid path, refusing to make a commitment without confirmation from his superiors. The prospect of being on the point of U.S. foreign policy must have been a thrilling antidote to dreary frontier duty. However, he was ignorant of even the most rudimentary facts about the Treaty of Oregon, inexcusable for a man poised to shape events on an international scale. Once he grasped the gravity of his acts, his righteous indignation over perceived slights was replaced by high anxiety. After that he sought a peaceful course, despite his posturing for Hornby, his superiors and civilians such as Hubbs. In reality he was not prepared in any fashion to take on the might of the British Empire. George Pickett would much rather have lunched and held forth with Geoff Hornby than fight him.

Hornby sincerely wanted to avoid war. Owing to his family connections, he was familiar with the nuances of foreign policy, and the importance of Great Britain's economic ties to the United States. He also was aware of the Pacific Station policy of nonconfrontation and the views of his superior, Admiral Baynes. To have commenced hostilities without exhausting every avenue—especially checking first with the admiral—would have ended his career.

More than anyone, Admiral Baynes deserves credit that the only casualty of this first stage of The Pig War was a pig. That's why he was knighted the next year.

But the crisis was far from over. While Baynes was attempting to restore calm, William Selby Harney, having had time to digest Pickett's letter, was preparing to send reinforcements.

CHAPTER 12

Reinforcements

The day after the *Shubrick* left with Pickett's dispatch to Harney, Griffin Bay again settled down to uneasy conviviality. Pickett and Hornby stopped posturing and exchanged visits while British sailors and marines and American soldiers – many of them recent expatriate Europeans – mingled, swapped newspapers and cigars, and talked about home. Tourists continued to pour off the boats from Victoria and all the while a new town was being born.

Pickett's first tent stake was barely hammered when the first liquor establishment rose in a wall tent about twenty-five yards off. This was San Juan Village. Soon, barges appeared with shacks from the abandoned mining camp on Bellingham Bay, followed by rot-gut whisky, cots, dirty curtains, and young Indian women. The women were mostly escaped slaves, or slaves being worked for a profit, or simply hopeless girls cast adrift from their groups. Soldiers, sailors, and marines were ready and willing, much to the chagrin of their respective commanding officers.

The *Victoria Gazette's* reporter (who called himself "Curioso") wrote that "some three or four persons had started little groggeries near the landing from the harbor and several parties had been in a state of drunkenness the night before." Charles Griffin was amazed: "Soldiers, Inds. & Men all been determined to be drunk together. Never saw anything like it."[1]

Such was tension-wrought San Juan Island.

It was not the island William Selby Harney envisioned. In his mind, British ships were lying offshore, guns run out, marines at ready near the boats, waiting for a false move from the gallant Virginian. Pickett had shown pluck, so Harney recommended him for brevet promotion. Soon the army, with the backing of the locals, would come to Pickett's aid. Even the newspaper in Olympia opined that the government had at last done the right thing.[2]

San Juan Island was not Harney's only concern. He was having trouble with his junior officers, a rebellious lot who, in his view, had required whipping into line. In recent weeks they had questioned his judgment in using soldier labor to build a private residence for himself off post. One officer had resigned from the service over it. Inflammatory letters began to appear in the *Pioneer and Democrat*, the *Colonist*, *Gazette* and even the *New York Times.* An anonymous letter, supposedly written by an officer, stated that "General Harney, who is here called 'Goliath'-for two reasons, first, that he is a very large man; and second, that he is all matter and no mind - ought I think to be court-martialed, and dismissed from the service for his conduct in this case." Another officer, who claimed to be stationed at San Juan, proclaimed Harney "one of the weakest officers and most arrogant humbugs in the army, and not at all qualified for his position. He is a laughingstock, wherever he goes; and his administration is a series of blunders and mistakes. He is as callous as a pot-house politician, and insensible, I am afraid, to shame."[3]

The San Juan officers were aghast at this attack and circulated a petition denying any part of the letter. However, Captain Lewis Cass Hunt, commander of Company C, Fourth Infantry, in a letter to a lady friend, boasted about submitting articles detailing Harney's failings (see Chapter 14).

With personal tensions and frustrations building, Harney received Pickett's August 3 letter outlining his encounter with Hornby, and describing British ships "...lying in a menacing attitude in the harbor."[4]

He must have fulminated by the time he got to Douglas's proclamation, which gravely condemned the American occupation and stated that the islands had always been "undeviatingly claimed to in the Crown of Great Britain."

Never one to be surpassed in righteous indignation, Harney replied on August 6, chastising the governor for sending a warship "...to convey the chief factor of the Hudson's Bay Company (Dallas) for the purpose of seizing an American citizen and forcibly transporting him to Vancouver's island to be tried by British laws." Until Harney's government received "proper redress" from Douglas – in what form was not stated – the soldiers would remain. The general did not mention anything about sending more soldiers, which he already decided to do.[5]

The general wrote the War Department the next morning to advise them he was sending Lieutenant Colonel Silas Casey from Fort Steilacoom to San Juan Island with reinforcements. If dispatching Casey with three more companies, plus heavy guns, was not escalation enough, Harney's prose was so incendiary it must have raised President Buchanan right out of his chair. After reiterating Hubbs's view of the pig incident, the general once more complained about how the Royal Navy was intimidating American citizens in collusion with the Hudson's Bay Company; how the HBC "pretended" to own the island, but only had a few shacks to show for it; and how the company had threatened "at different times, to send the northern Indians down upon (American settlers) and drive them for the island." If all of the aforementioned was not enough to generate alarm about his diplomatic skills, Harney confirmed it by declaring, "...It would be well for the British government to know the American people of this coast will never sanction any claim they may assert to any other island in the Puget Sound than that of Vancouver's, south of the 49th parallel, and east of the Canal de Haro; any attempt at possession by them will be followed by a collision."

Harney might have raised the president's hopes in the next paragraph by stating "...no one is more desirous than myself for an amicable settlement..." But he dashed them again by concluding that the British had forfeited their rights to the island for being so "perfidious." The president could rest assured that Harney would "use all the means" at his command to hold on to the San Juans.[6]

Harney's letter may have been laced with gross exaggerations and a couple of outright lies, but the underlying truth was that Douglas *had* claimed the San Juan Islands for Great Britain. Moreover, he had been attempting to enforce British jurisdiction for more than eight years going back to the Cussans lumber incident on Lopez Island. He had dispatched John DeCourcy to San Juan to eject American "trespassers." This was the solid ground upon which Harney could have built a case. It would have satisfied even the President of the United States. Acting Secretary of War William Drinkard said as much a few weeks later.

After finishing off the Douglas reply, Harney told Pleasonton to write Pickett and endorse his actions on San Juan. Pickett was to continue to reject a joint military occupation and stop the British Magistrate from enforcing civil law-even over British subjects. "...No joint occupation nor any civil jurisdiction will be permitted on San Juan island by the British authorities under any circumstances," Pleasonton wrote. This placed Harney precisely in accord with Baynes, but for entirely different reasons. Pleasonton completed the missive by advising Pickett that Casey was on the way with reinforcements...and would assume command.[7]

Casey's orders were to reinforce Pickett and take command on San Juan Island, leaving only one officer and a detachment to mind "public property" at Fort Steilacoom. He was to take all of his ammunition and field guns and leave promptly aboard private steamers as "British authorities threaten to force Pickett's position." If need be, Casey was authorized to call out the "Volunteers," presumably the American settlers, to defend San Juan Island. "...This authority the General is confident you will exercise with judgment and discretion," Pleasonton cautioned. No regular officer relished attempting to control armed civilians with a thirst for real estate.

To impress the British that the Americans intended to remain in force, Casey was to remove the *Massachusetts's* eight, 32-pound naval guns and place them in position to protect the harbor. Pickett would turn over his instructions to Casey: "Their substance may be stated: in not allowing any joint occupation of San Juan Island, either civil or military and that the right of our citizens on the Island will be respected as on American soil." [8]

Still another mail pouch was dispatched on August 8 with letters explaining Harney's actions to the Adjutant General of the U.S. Army, Colonel Samuel Cooper in Washington City, and Department of California commander Brigadier General Newman S. Clarke in San Francisco.

The Clarke letter included an enclosure addressed to the "Senior Officer of the United States Navy, Commanding Squadron on the Pacific Coast. "This was a plea for naval support in the San Juan Islands. While Harney did not think the British would attack his soldiers, he expressed hoped for something better than the slow-moving and soon-to-be toothless *Massachusetts* to observe the Brits. [9]

Harney's letter to Cooper (which, by army protocol, was really intended for Lieutenant General Winfield Scott), though brief, contained more half-truths and exaggerations to justify sending reinforcements. According to Harney, the islands had been under Whatcom County jurisdiction for "months" and taxes had been paid to the county by "foreigners" as well as by Americans living on the islands. (He neglected to mention that the only taxes ever paid by "foreigners" had four legs and had been wrestled into canoes in the dead of night.) Because Whatcom County was clearly in charge, the British never attempted to "exercise authority" over the island except clandestinely, as in the case of the pig. This changed when Magistrate DeCourcy and other "civil authorities" were commissioned and sent in a warship to enforce British laws after learning of Pickett's landing. [10]

At Fort Steilacoom, Casey wasted no time, setting off the next day aboard the requisitioned sternwheeler *Julia* bound for Port Townsend. He barely cleared the Tacoma Narrows on his way to Townsend when he was hailed by the survey steamer *Active*, chugging full throttle in search of him. The captain, James Alden, breathlessly reported that if Casey attempted to land his troops and guns the *Tribune*, anchored in Griffin Bay, would open fire[11]. This information came from Pickett who—unaware that the British had decided not to oppose reinforcements and that Hornby had decided not to press the issue of a joint occupation—believed a landing near the HBC wharf would be "interfered with." Casey weighed Pickett's passion for drama with what he knew of the Royal Navy, or as he termed it, the "quasi enemy" in the Pacific Northwest, and decided to continue. [12]

He called that evening at Port Townsend where he ran into Archibald Campbell, who seemed to be continuing his career as a key government official specializing in being the "last to know." The sight of 180 fully equipped infantry with a hundred more soldiers, plus eight guns on the way, troubled him enough to accept Casey's invitation to come along and observe the landing. Campbell's presence was expected to lend weight to the negotiations the colonel hoped to set in motion. Little did Casey know that Campbell had become persona non grata in Victoria.

A heavy fog rolled up the strait and smothered the island, which made negotiating Cattle Point on the southern end almost impossible. The *Julia*'s captain told Casey that, by his reckoning, they were just off a long pebble beach not far from Pickett's camp. He suggested Casey land the troops and the howitzers (small cannon that hurled long, looping rounds) on the beach and unload the freight in Griffin Bay when the fog burned off. Being a sternwheeler, the *Julia* could nudge her bows right on to the beach. Casey thought it was a splendid idea and ordered it done, while the *Active* and *Shubrick* stood by. The troops trudged through the heavy sand and rock and up a low bluff, beyond which Pickett's camp occupied the level prairie. Pickett's soldiers told their newly arrived mates that where the prairie faded into the fog was Griffin Bay and the British warships.

While his troops were settling, Casey and the *Julia* rounded the point and steamed into the harbor as the fog lifted. The *Tribune* was anchored several hundred yards out, broadside to shore, with gun ports open, just as Alden had described her. The *Julia* dropped anchor and the crew and several soldiers left behind unloaded Casey's stores, including ammunition for the howitzers, food, tents and other provisions. Contrary to Pickett's warning, the British "did not interfere with the landing of our freight. Whether they would have interfered with the landing of the troops I cannot say. It is Captain Pickett's opinion that they would." [13]

Indeed. While the *Julia* exhaled her last and lowered her boats not far from the *Tribune*, another warship was steaming toward South Beach from the direction of Victoria. Despite several days of amicable relations with British officials, Pickett's imagination was again generating catastrophe. He sent a messenger to the *Julia* with an urgent message for Casey to come ashore at once and proceed immediately to Pickett's camp at South Beach. The ship (later identified as the *Satellite*) was adjacent to his camp and appeared to be ready to open fire! Once it did, the marines and sailors from the *Tribune* would likely land on the harbor side and assault the American position. If so attacked, they should fire the howitzers, spike the guns, loose a volley of musketry and high-tail it for the woods.

Hubbs vividly recalled the strategy. Soldiers from the Ninth and Fourth Infantry and Third Artillery dotted the hills east of the camp (rather than emerging from the beach) in their "blue coats and brass buttons" while Casey's howitzers joined Pickett's on the crest of the hill overlooking Griffin Bay. Casey sought out Hubbs when he came ashore and told him that he hoped to avoid bloodshed. At the first shot Hubbs was to mount his horse and guide Casey "across the retreating grounds. "This did not set well with Hubbs, who thirty-three years on, professed that while the British outnumbered the Americans two to one, the Americans could have held them off if the "Hero of Gettysburg" had remained in command:

> Things looked very different since Pickett had been superseded in command, and from what we afterward experienced the British forces would have been allowed to land unmolested, for a little fever and ague struck the new officers now in command. [14]

Casey actually was hesitant to countermand Pickett's orders, having so recently arrived. However the *Tribune* had not reacted when he unloaded his stores. This prompted Casey to ask Hornby for a meeting. Several hours later Hornby came ashore with the respective commissioners, Prevost and Campbell. Casey later claimed that he admonished Hornby for threatening Pickett with deadly force. When he asked Hornby from whom he received his instructions, Hornby replied Admiral Baynes. If Casey wanted to meet him he would have to go to Esquimalt Harbor.

Changing to dress uniform, replete with plums and epaulets, Casey and Pickett, joined by Campbell, departed the next morning aboard the *Shubrick*. The meeting fell through over protocol. Casey insisted Baynes leave his eighty-four-gun ship-of-the-line, *Ganges*, to meet with him aboard the *Shubrick*, a lighthouse tender with a twenty-four-pound cannon mounted in the bow. Baynes had shown forbearance in leaving the island to the U.S. Army until diplomats settled the question. But he would not call upon a lower ranking officer aboard a tin-pot steamer a third the size of his own ship. Several hours went by as they haggled over the venue – Pickett serving as messenger boy – until Casey finally gave up and returned to San Juan Island.

The following day in a report to Harney, Casey explained that he went to Esquimalt on his own volition to avoid a collision. If Baynes had promised not to threaten Pickett, Casey would have recommended withdrawal of reinforcements in anticipation of a diplomatic solution. Casey went on to explain the protocol flap, which may explain why he had not spoken to any Royal Navy officers since. The chilly response spurred him to seek four more companies of soldiers, plus a detachment of engineers to build fortifications. It was not pleasant "...to be at the mercy of anyone who is liable at any moment to become your enemy." Casey also thought of contacting the U.S. Navy in San Francisco Bay. In the meantime, he promised to "resist any attack they may make upon my position." [15]

Casey's requests for more troops and heavy guns were approved, along with brief instructions to build semipermanent fortifications that included entrenchments and gun platforms. Pleasonton relayed Harney's displeasure with Casey for his attempt at international diplomacy, but commended him for making the peaceful gesture and urged him to treat British subjects with the same courtesy as American citizens. [16]

Douglas also was unhappy with Casey over the blown meeting. He was on board the *Ganges* during one of Pickett's shuttles and asked the captain why it had been Baynes and not himself to whom Casey applied for negotiations. Pickett at first said Casey was unaware the governor was there. In the very next breath he squandered his diplomatic points by stating that Casey wanted to speak to Baynes, not Douglas. Pickett had a way with the governor.

Using measured words, Douglas chose to go to the source and vent his ever-growing frustration on Harney, whose letter he had received two days before. On August 12 Douglas wrote Lord Lytton:

> It has now been clearly established that the Military occupation of San Juan Island has been under-

> taken without the knowledge or authority of the government of the United States, and upon grounds that are entirely false, both in fact and in principle...[17]

Douglas felt certain that once the American government did find out, Harney's actions would be rejected.

The governor next wrote Harney, hoping to convince him that the HBC had no jurisdiction over the islands, even to the point of claiming the company had no influence with the government on Vancouver Island. He gave an "unhesitating and unqualified" denial to the charges of threatening Cutlar with arrest, though he did not mention the pig incident. He asserted that no ship of war had "ever been sent to convey the chief factor or any other officer of Hudson's Bay Company to San Juan for the purpose of seizing an American Citizen." [18] He referred Harney to an enclosed copy of the Marcy letter, contending that his government had never deviated from the spirit of the document. He claimed to have dismissed accounts of a depredation committed against HBC property, stressed that had he decided to act, he would have first applied to the authorities in Olympia. And finally, if Harney knew of the "fancied grievance" when he visited Victoria, he should asked the governor about it before he dispatched Pickett from Fort Bellingham. In closing, Douglas asked that the troops be withdrawn. [19]

Two days later Archibald Campbell finally posted his own letter of inquiry to Harney. The commissioner mainly wanted to know why he had not known beforehand that Pickett's landing was something more than chasing Indians. Judging from Pickett's orders, he initially thought Washington had issued fresh instructions to Harney, so he decided not to interfere, despite Prevost's urgings. While he agreed the San Juan Islands rightfully belonged to the United States, he no longer believed the dispute had been resolved, and that meant trouble. Unless the general had:

> ...some intimation from the War Department

> which has governed your action, I fear that the decided action that you have taken in declaring the island American territory may somewhat embarrass the question. I will be greatly relieved to learn that you have some authority from the government for the decisive step you have taken, though I do not pretend to ask or desire the information in my official capacity... [20]

Harney apologized to Campbell for the briefing oversight. He thought the commissioner already had left for Washington City (which does not explain the Pleasonton briefing about "northern Indians.") His actions had nothing to do with the boundary dispute, Harney claimed. The British were attempting to enforce their laws over American citizens. He closed by wishing Campbell well in the commission's work and pledged to support it. [21]

A mollified Campbell wrote back excusing himself for being presumptuous. He then defended the general in a September 3 report to Secretary of State Lewis Cass, taking the opportunity to castigate Prevost and his government once more for obfuscating and delaying the boundary settlement. It was clear the British government had ordered the Vancouver Island government to treat the islands as "British dominions," in violation of the standing agreement. The HBC had long coveted the island; therefore was it any wonder that they would contest a military occupation by the rightful owners? [22]

On San Juan Island, two capital class warships were aiming their guns at Casey, who did not know Baynes had decided not to attack. He acted on his instructions to entrench his camp in a secure spot and build an earthwork for the heavy guns that would give the British pause. Over the next several days more than 300,000 board feet of lumber was landed, enough for several gun platforms, barracks and other structures. Casey also managed to land the *Massachusetts's* guns on the beach but did not have the means to move or place them. To underscore his alarm he itemized the British forces available to blow him off the island: five ships, 167 guns and 1,940 sailors, marines, and sappers. 23

The guns eventually were manhandled to the top of the ridge overlooking the Hudson's Bay dock and Griffin Bay. On August 17, Casey's reinforcements arrived, including four batteries (companies) of the Third Artillery, who disembarked on the Hudson's Bay Company wharf, marched up Charles Griffin's road and over the ridge to the prairie camp, accompanied by a patchwork military band. The new arrivals boosted Casey's forces to 15 officers and 424 enlisted men, plus 50 civilian laborers engaged to build the new camp.

Hornby reacted with alarm and probably cursed himself for assuring the governor and admiral that no American reinforcements were forthcoming. "Six of their heavy guns are placed on the ridge of the hill overlooking the harbour; and by throwing up a parapet (the guns) would command the harbor; even in their present condition they would be difficult to silence," he wrote Baynes. "The other two heavy guns and field pieces are placed to defend their camp." This did not appear to be a force designed to repel raiding Indians. Rather, "they seemed not only prepared to defend themselves, but to threaten us."

The captain wondered what would happen when the Whatcom County Sheriff returned and tried to collect taxes from the HBC? And worse, rumor had it that Harney himself was coming with 400 more soldiers. "They are continually landing supplies of all sorts, and have now on the beach large quantities of lumber for gun platforms. Scantling of Barracks, etc., so that there is every symptom of their occupation being permanent." As matters stood, Hornby could neither protect the magistrate nor enforce British laws. The Americans had demonstrated to him that they would take what they wanted when they wanted, regardless of prior agreement or international law. If they forced the magistrate to strike his flag and stopped him from doing his duty, Hornby, by previous instructions, would evacuate the magistrate.

He would then fire on the American camp to "resent the insult to the flag and...this I should do unless I hear from you to the contrary." [24]

Baynes was so alarmed at Hornby's state of mind that his reply of August 16 was swift, specific, and firm:

> In my memorandum to you of the 13th of August I desired you by every means in your power to avoid a collision with the troops of the United States. It is now my positive order that you do not, on any account whatever, take the initiative in commencing hostilities by firing on them or any work they may have thrown up...Should the troops of the United States commit any aggressive act by firing on the Tribune or any of Her Majesty's ships or boats, you are at full liberty to resent the insult by adopting such measures as you think [desirable?] informing me of the circumstances as quickly as possible. [25.]

Baynes' remarkable calm and forbearance in the face of bluff and bluster (from both sides) quelled the initial excitement of the occupation, and the standoff began to wane by mid-August.

The respective magistrates, Crosbie and DeCourcy, presaged the eventual joint occupation by acting jointly in banning the sale of liquor on the island. The soldiers may have been Americans, but a good many rabble rousers were venturing over from Victoria to get in on the fun.

Cooperation between the two peace officers almost came to naught when Deputy Collector of Customs Hubbs refused to allow ashore passengers from Victoria, and then required all ships to clear customs at Port Townsend before landing at San Juan. His growing appetite for power peaked when he quarantined John DeCourcy's baggage. In his memoir, Hubbs recalled DeCourcy, James Forsyth, and a U.S. Mail agent, Captain John Scranton, returning from a shopping trip to Victoria, at which time Hubbs ordered everyone to pay duty. All three men refused, but Forysth and Scranton were allowed to land anyway. Hubbs refused to budge on DeCourcy's property. The Irishman, at least according to Hubbs, blustered that he would unload his gear under the *Satellite's* guns and signaled the ship to send a boat. That's when Pickett interceded at Casey's direction and DeCourcy finally was permitted to bring his baggage ashore. Far from being grateful, Hubbs believed this demonstrated that the U.S. Army was next to useless with Silas Casey (and not Pickett) in command. [26]

By Sunday, August 21, all was quiet. Casey attended services aboard the *Satellite* and posted general orders that soldiers were not to disturb the Hudson's Bay Company farm. This was probably in response to a letter of complaint to Douglas written two weeks earlier by Dallas.

"Our sheep, cattle and horses are disturbed at their pasturage, and driven from their drinking springs, in the vicinity of which the troops are encamped," Dallas wrote. "Much of the pasturage has been destroyed. In a future day I shall be prepared to bring forward a claim against the United States Government..." In the near term Dallas wanted to know what Douglas was going about providing protection for stock farm "...of which we have had till now, almost undisturbed possession during the last six years." [27]

No question. Times had changed for Belle Vue Farm, and more changes were coming. Casey intended to move next door. If the colonel wondered how an articulate, urbane gentleman such as Pickett could graduate last in his West Point class he knew after spending several nights at the Spring Camp site. It may have been out of range of British guns (if they remained anchored on Griffin Bay), but it certainly did not escape the fury of mother nature. "We are encamped in rather exposed situation with regard to the wind, being at the entrance of the Straits of Fuca," Casey wrote. "The weather at times is already quite inclement." Gale force winds two nights running nearly blew the old colonel out of his tent. [28]

On August 22, Casey ordered his growing force (now about 450 men) to move camp to the north slope of the ridge near the HBC barns – once home to the errant pig that started the whole mess. Large, conical Sibley tents were shipped from Fort Steilacoom to the new site, which he considered "a very good position for an entrenched camp." The tents would supplement the clapboard buildings Pickett had already brought from Fort Bellingham, among these the hospital, barracks, laundress and officers' quarters.

Casey also saw to camp defenses, outlined in a letter to acting adjutant Alfred Pleasonton: "I shall put my heavy guns in position to bear on the harbor, and also on vessels that might take a position on the other side. Shells from the shipping might be able to reach us, and we may not be able to protect the camp from there; but I shall try." [29]

On the 23rd, a combat engineering team (or sappers), led by Corps of Engineers Second Lieutenant Henry Martyn Robert, arrived to design and supervise construction of an earthen fortification on a rise east of the new camp. The site had a commanding view of both strait and bay.

Throughout the work, William A. Peck, Jr., a private soldier on the team, kept a diary of his experiences on San Juan Island and in the Pacific Northwest. On disembarking from the *Massachusetts* at San Juan, he had his first taste of British humor: "While they were shoving off in their boats, the men pulled directly under the guns of the H.B.M. Sloop of War *Satellite* and the musicians played 'Yankee Doodle' for dear life." By the August 25 Peck recorded that his team was engaged in "laying out the works for a fort all day." Because no teams of dray horses or oxen were available, the team supervised infantry and artillery troops not engaged in drilling. [30]

All of the work was done by pick and shovel, as per Alfred Pleasonton's instructions:

> ...Have platforms made for your heavy guns, and cover your camp as much as possible by entrenchment, placing your heavy guns in battery on the most exposed approaches...select your position with the greatest care to avoid fire from the British ship(s). [31]

The redoubt site could not have been more ideal and Robert took advantage of it, laying out his platforms with a precision still evident today. The British officers were impressed. They especially knew how a formal fieldwork could alter the situation on San Juan Island.A fortress not only provided a means of last-ditch defense, but properly sited, would permit a smaller force – even with inferior troops – to resist a larger one until help arrived. "(Casey's camp) is very strongly placed in the most commanding position at this end of the island, well sheltered in the rear and one side by the Forest and on the other side by a Commanding eminence," wrote Prevost. [32]

While the soldiers dug, guests arrived, among them Washington Territorial Governor Richard D. Gholson. The governor held his hat over his heart while nine companies, led by Colonel Casey on horseback, passed in review for him at the old spring campsite on the prairie. Not to be outdone, the British invited the governor to witness gun drills and have tea aboard the *Satellite.* Another visitor was former Governor Isaac Stevens, the newly elected Delegate for Washington Territory to the U.S. Congress. [33]

Others from all walks of life came as well. Some, such as Matthew Macfie, a British subject, relied on the eloquence of facts rather than bombast to describe what they saw. Macfie visited San Juan at the height of the crisis, catching the *Shubrick* over from Port Townsend. His ship dropped anchor at 6 p.m. in Griffin Bay.

> ...H.M.S. *Satellite* was lying off with guns shotted, and pointed in the direction of the American camp,

> which was about a mile and a half from the beach. A boat came to us from the British man-of-war for letters, and I was introduced to the midshipman in charge as a 'clergyman' from England. This term, in British parlance, having a technical meaning – which it has not in America – and not being applied by my host in the British sense, the young officer was pleased to draw gratuitous conclusions, by which I seemed likely to be placed-innocently-in a position as false as it was delicate.

Macfie tabulated about 500 men and was not far off. With the arrival of Robert and his team the U.S. force had grown to 461 officers and men. He described the earthworks under construction and mounted with cannon, which moved him to remark: "Judging from appearances, I am not sure that our nation has ever been so nearly precipitated into a war with 'Brother Jonathan' since 1812." He casually visited the tents of American officers, who "spoke freely of the international 'difficulty' that had arisen, and confessed that while convinced of the justice of their cause, they occupied their present position reluctantly. There was none of that thirst for war with England manifested by them which characterizes the less cultivated portion of American citizens."

He was next invited to Casey's tent:

> ...The venerable colonel, a man of about 65, seemed more concerned if possible than his brother officers that harmony should be maintained between the two countries, and assured me that he was using all his influence on the side of peace. He regarded it, he said, as the greatest calamity that could befall the cause of civilization all over the world, that two nations, allied by community of race, language, laws, and religion, should be plunged into hostilities. This

> was saying a great deal of a man whose fortune was war. Little then did my excellent friend apprehend the melancholy consequences of civil tumult with which his own country was so soon to be visited. I must express the surprise and gratification I felt at seeing one in the colonel's station having a reputation for sober and reflective piety. He told me he was in the habit of repairing to the British ship of war to attend divine service every Sunday, and I learned that by a pleasing coincidence, Captain Prevost of the *Satellite* was a man of the same character.

No matter. Casey promised that if "a single shot" was fired from a British vessel his troops would shoot back. "...'It is almost certain,' said he, 'that in that case your ships would blow our handful of men here to atoms, but 300,000 men would instantly pour in from the states to take our place.'"

No wonder Macfie expressed relief when Admiral Baynes returned from Valparaiso. "I have no hesitation in saying that but for the timely arrival of Admiral Baynes, war was inevitable." Had Douglas remained in charge, Macfie was certain that burial parties would be working under flags of truce. Douglas was still bitter over the loss of Oregon and "...from that moment imbibed inimical prejudices toward them that only wanted a suitable occasion for its manifestation." [34]

Those prejudices were still at work in the governor's mind and his exasperation was growing thanks to a stinging article in the *Colonist* on August 17. Following the usual wordy opening, the editor got to the lead: "An error has been committed by somebody." The government – civil and naval arms alike – was being wishy-washy in response to the American landing. Douglas must have choked when he read:

> Either the Administration should have been sat-

> isfied with a pacific policy, manifested by serving the United States authorities with a formal protest or an assertion of our sovereignty in the first place, and to have allowed the matter to rest until despatches (sic) were received from the imperial government, or it should have at once landed troops on the island without making such a display of force or asking permission. We confess that we are not disposed to accept peace at any price; for if that were the case cowardice would be the safest policy. [35]

Douglas decided to again vent his anger on Hornby. On August 17 he wrote Baynes that a "passive" and "retrograde" policy would not work with Americans. He was familiar with the "American Character" after his many years in the Pacific Northwest. As such he believed that if the naval officers had obeyed his original instructions no bloodshed would have ensued. Now the Americans were dug in and there would be the devil to pay getting them out. "Had that (joint) occupation been effected as I intended, I feel confident in my own mind that no further reinforcements of American troops would have been landed, no fortifications would have been thrown up, and all of the action in the case would have been in perfect accordance with our national character and feeling," Douglas wrote. He reminded Baynes of his "clear and definite instruction" from the Commonwealth office about treating the San Juans as British dominions. Compromise now would only imperil British rights here just as it had on the Columbia River. The British were in a "complicated and humiliating " position, which by no means guaranteed peace. He concluded his letter by advising the admiral that he was going to complain to the home government about the Royal Navy. [36]

Baynes was unmoved. If Douglas wanted San Juan to remain British he should not have allowed the American squatters to settle on the island in the first place, the admiral countered in an August 19 letter to the Admiralty. (He did not bother to reply to

Douglas.) Several paragraphs were devoted to Douglas's bluster over embattled British "subjects," observing that British subjects on the island were largely in the employ of the Hudson's Bay Company. He blamed the scarcity of British settlers on the "confined and narrow views of the Hudson's Bay Company. A few American squatters, as before-mentioned, have established themselves from the opposite coast." Baynes also questioned Douglas's judgement during the pig affair, when he sent a Justice of the Peace (Magistrate DeCourcy) with the dubious mission of arresting the officer in command of the U.S. troops. Even worse, if the officer resisted, DeCourcy was to seek assistance from the Royal Navy:

> The officer was summoned, but fortunately no further proceedings took place, the Governor having revoked the order...had this been carried out, I fear the result would have been a serious collision, as an officer in command of a company of soldiers was not likely to surrender himself without resistance. [37]

How could Douglas treat the islands as British when their possession was under review by both governments? This gave the British the perfect excuse to demonstrate restraint, for

> ...it cannot be said we have withdrawn from San Juan Island, consequently there has been no compromise of dignity or honor...if the authorities of the United States have taken a false step, it renders it all the more necessary that we should avoid doing so, and endeavor, if possible, not to complicate the boundary question still more and embroil the two nations.

Baynes saw two courses open to him. He could eject the

Americans from the island by force and risk war; or protest the occupation and leave a ship of war in the harbor to oversee British interests, pending on decision on the boundary. "Had they been filibusters and not Federal troops, the case would be very different...I was decidedly adverse to a joint military occupation, which could in no way strengthen our claim, and was very likely, from various causes, to bring about a collision." [38]

Simple arithmetic moved Baynes not only to avoid challenging the Americans militarily on land, but to discourage a joint occupation. As stated above, most of the British numbers were sailors, who could not hope to contend with infantry, of which the U.S. had ample supply. And these soldiers were "ready to embark."

It was the views of Baynes, not Douglas, that the British government accepted in the end. On October 21, these instructions to Douglas from the Duke of Newcastle of the colonial office:

> ...in consequence of the opposite views to which your despatch refers as being entertained by Admiral Baynes and yourself in regard to the policy which you think ought to have been pursued toward the Americans, I must point out to you that the fact of overwhelming force of the British Navy, which was so rapidly summoned to the spot, as compared with the force of the United States, removed any possibility of misunderstanding the reasons of Her Majesty's Government for adopting the moderate course of remonstrance instead of violent measures. [39]

Harney was drafting his own letters of justification, including one to Douglas on August 24 after a delay of more than ten days from the receipt of the governor's last, and to Adjutant General Cooper in New York City.

To Douglas, he again vehemently denied having prior knowledge of the pig incident before visiting the governor in July. The general was willing to accept that Douglas had no knowledge of the acts toward Cutlar, but he was not convinced that the British would do anything to head off another such occurrence. The warships in the harbor provided little reassurance in the minds of most Americans that Americans' rights would be protected. That's why his soldiers had to stay.[40]

The general revealed his ignorance of San Juan background when he confessed to Cooper that Douglas's enclosure was the first he had seen of the famous Marcy letter. It was in this same correspondence that Harney seriously began to twist the truth, relaying every xenophobic sentiment at work among American settlers in the young territory to justify his acts. He must have known that he had miscalculated in dispatching close to 500 men, plus heavy guns to an island one could cross on foot in an afternoon. But he could not admit it. He pressed on.

He had reviewed the Marcy letter's provisos and of course they were sound. He had not beefed up the American military presence in Puget Sound until this unfortunate incident. The British, in the guise of the Hudson's Bay Company, had taken a page from the Revolutionary War and War of 1812 and set the Indians upon American settlers.

> Time and again our lighthouses were attacked, and the wives and children of our settlers on that coast were brutally murdered by British Indians. Reports reached me that these Indians had been instigated toward these acts by the Hudson's Bay Company in order to drive them from the lands which this immense establishment covet for their own purpose. I am well aware of the extent and power of this great commercial monopoly, second only to the East India Company which has crushed out the liberties and existence of so many nations in Asia, committed barbarities and atrocities for which the annals of crime have no parallel.[41]

More Northerners were on the way, Harney claimed, because he had it on good authority that A.G. Dallas was threatening to set them upon the Americans. This jelled with what he had been told by Captain James Alden of the *Active*, that "in the event of a collision between the forces of the two countries, he would not be able to prevent the northern Indians from driving our people from the island."

Harney offered to include affidavits from witnesses (mainly American citizens) offering proof of this grasping, aggressive, and inhumane behavior. But he neglected to include the petition from the San Juan settlers that incited the incident – the one that lauds the HBC for saving them from northern Indians.

Clearly these acts were contrived to grab the islands, while Harney was standing on the defensive and had been "influenced by no other motives in placing troops upon the islands." In fact, the British were so impressed by the island's strategic virtues that they were now calling it the "Cronstadt of the Pacific," of which Harney was in complete accord. That's why the British were after them. But he had investigated the Treaty of Oregon, and there was no doubt in his mind that these critical islands clearly belonged to the United States. [42]

The very next day Harney sent yet another report to Cooper stating he had heard a rumor that Admiral Baynes had countermanded Douglas's orders and that the British would not land troops. He quickly added that "nothing official on the subject has reached me."

By the end of August, San Juan Island slipped into limbo. The soldiers labored to create a formal camp, while British sailors watched through spyglasses. The ten-man sapper team, under Lieutenant Robert, did its best to supervise the line infantry and artillery troops, who grudgingly sweated with pick and shovel on the redoubt. One William Moore, a British subject caught selling liquor to the enlisted men, also was dragooned into laboring on the redoubt. And "private property owners," the so-called squatters whom Pickett had come to protect, already were agitating against the incursion of the federal government. [43]

During a lull in the redoubt work – on one of those San Juan evenings when the shorebirds come to rest on quiet silver colored waters – a visitor named Angus MacDonald, late of Scotland and now a resident of Victoria, happened upon an American sentry walking guard on the ramparts. The following conversation seemed to sum up all that had come to pass and still might possibly be.

> "The Americans had only three unsheltered guns that could reach the frigates. As the troops started to parade, I went to look at the guns about a half mile from the parade. They were sentineled by one man. Curious to know how he felt and believing him to be an Irishman, I said a word or two in Gaelic, then said:
>
> 'You are an Irishman.'
>
> 'Yes I am.'
>
> 'Are they going to fight about this little island?'
>
> 'I do not know.'
>
> 'How would you like to fight against the flag of your own country?'
>
> The man with a quick lift of his rifle, and a more advanced lift of his foot, said:
>
> 'I would like to see old England catch a good drubbing anyhow.'
>
> Leaving him loading his pipe and bidding him good day in the ancient Celtic of Scotland, I went my way thinking that there is some account between Erin and England that never was squared." [44]

The same could be said for the Anglo-American border. That would be remedied in Washington City. Word of the pig incident was soon to arrive.

CHAPTER 13

Washington and London

While Harney and Douglas were squaring off, oblivious British and American officials in Washington, D.C., were offering proposals and counterproposals for a water boundary. Such were the realities of transcontinental time and distance at mid-nineteenth century. Violence could flare and pull the two nations into war without the knowledge of their respective governments.

The telegraph had been functioning regionally since Samuel Morse and others hatched the idea in the 1840s. But in 1859 it ran only as far west as Fort Leavenworth, Kansas, and as far east as Carson City, Nevada. Spanning the distance was a stagecoach, aptly described by Mark Twain in *Roughing It*. Theoretically the trip was three weeks each way, but six weeks was the rule, or, judging by human remains bleaching along the trail, it could take forever. Throughout the crisis both nations would dutifully send telegrams. Some made it under schedule, in just over two weeks. Others lagged by more than a month. It was still more reliable to send a courier aboard the steamer.

The Panama Railroad, founded by shipping magnate William

Aspinwall, had been running since January 1855, carrying freight and passengers the forty-seven miles across the isthmus in just over three hours. Modern side-wheeler steamers with names such as *Northerner*, *Cortez*, *Constitution* and *Sonora* waited at either end with boilers fired to cut passengers' exposure to yellow fever or the vomito, as it was called then. Competition was hot and time was money. Depending on seas, a courier with a dispatch pouch could carry word from Victoria to New York City on the average of six weeks.[1]

That is almost exactly how long it took Harney's July 19 dispatch to reach Lieutenant General Winfield Scott's headquarters. The old general quickly relayed it to Washington, D.C., where it arrived on September 3, 1859. But it still wasn't fast enough to beat newspaper reports that had miraculously made it first by telegraph via St. Louis.

So President James Buchanan experienced the timeless nightmare of all government officials -- being the last to know. Buchanan already was familiar with the San Juan Islands. As the peacemaking secretary of state under Polk, he had helped complete the Treaty of Oregon. He also was one of the few to predict that issue of ownership of the islands might one day cause trouble. Now the nation was boiling over as the sections looked ahead to the presidential race in 1860; a race the mild Buchanan had no wish to enter because the result, either way, was bound to result in civil war. Unbeknownst to the president or anyone in the capital, a homicidal abolitionist named John Brown was planning to ignite a slave insurrection in the south. His troops would be armed with weapons he intended to steal from the federal arsenal at Harper's Ferry, Virginia.

Buchanan was not unaware of the irony at work. As a career Democrat, he was acquainted with the shenanigans of William Selby Harney. He especially remembered Harney's ill-fated thrust into Mexico without orders early in the war. He remembered the rank insubordination to Winfield Scott and the messy charges and countercharges in its wake. He remembered counseling President Polk then to be firm with Harney, but Harney had been Andrew Jackson's pet...and Polk was known as "Young Hickory." Buchanan remembered it all. Now Harney was his problem.

The President could not have Harney stepping all over the British with the nation in such a vulnerable state. The Royal Navy could blow anything the Americans had out of the water in any ocean. But Buchanan also was politically astute enough to know he could not now back away from the San Juan Islands like a kicked dog just because the British were angry – and they were going to be angry, that much was certain.

A reply was drafted to Harney that same day by Acting Secretary of War William Drinkard. Its tone left no doubt about Buchanan's feelings on the matter:

> The President was not prepared to learn that you had ordered military possession to be taken of the island of San Juan or Bellevue. Although he believes the Straits of Haro to be the true boundary between Great Britain and the United States, under the treaty of June 15, 1846, and that, consequently, this island belongs to us, yet he had not anticipated that so decided a step would have been resorted to without instructions.
>
> Nevertheless,
>
> ...if you had good reason to believe that the colonial authorities of Great Britain were about to disturb the status, by taking possession of the island and assuming jurisdiction over it, you were right to anticipate their action. It has been too much the practice of the British Government to seize first and negotiate afterwards. [2]

Meanwhile in the British embassy, the ambassador, Lord Lyons, also read the morning papers. Only two weeks before he had been instructed by London that in any water boundary settlement he was to hold on to San Juan Island at all costs. He dashed off a note to Secretary of State Lewis Cass that led with the standard questions: Had it really happened? And, if so, had the U.S. Government been aware of Harney's act? Lyons was "...extremely anxious that this statement should not reach Her Majesty's Government without such information respecting its truth or falsehood, and such explanations concerning it as the Government of the United States may be disposed to afford." [3]

The ambassador also reminded Cass that as recently as May 12 he had sent an official letter, warning that if the water boundary was not settled, and if the United States did not formally agree to restrain its citizens on the island from acts of violence, a "local collision" might occur, which would "embitter" any further discussion. For more than three months, Her Majesty's Government had been awaiting a response to this letter. Were the silence and Harney's act connected? When the two diplomats met two days later, Cass assured Lyons that the U.S. Government already had written Harney directing him to maintain joint occupation status on the island. While the U.S. was not to assume jurisdiction over the island, the troops were to remain on San Juan to protect American citizens from northern Indians... or whatever. [4]

If Cass restored Lyons' calm, it disintegrated two days later with the arrival of the evening newspapers. More details and "full intelligence" about Pickett's landing came with the day's mails, the papers announced, including Forsyth's proclamation, which was published verbatim. Lyons wrote Cass immediately, demanding information and not double-talk. He wanted to relay a full account of the incident to Lord John Russell, the British Foreign Secretary in London, and the more details the better.

In light of the news, the Englishman also took the opportunity to review Cass's comments of the fifth. Lyons was particularly concerned by the word "status" which he thought meant that soldiers would occupy the island, but not enforce the law; a fact that he already had passed on to Russell.

"I am rendered particularly anxious upon this subject, by observing among the news inserted in the evening journals the following document purporting to be an order issued by Captain Pickett, commanding the party of United States troops which has landed on the island," Lyons wrote. The proclamation was attached along a postscript assuring Cass that all communication with London was handled in code, so the information would remain confidential.[5]

Cass replied by begging the question. Instead of offering more information or explaining the proclamation, he tweaked Lyons for misinterpreting their conversation. How could more than sixty armed soldiers occupy an island barely bigger than the city limits of Washington and not exercise some jurisdiction? Two more exchanges followed between the diplomats, whereupon Lyons wrote Russell with a correction, accompanied by a rather windy explanation.[6]

Although an attempt had been made in 1858 to lay an Atlantic cable, it had been unsuccessful, so instant communication between Great Britain and the United States was still seven years off. Telegrams to London went by wire to Halifax, Nova Scotia, thence by steam mail packet to Liverpool, where they were relayed by wire to London. The whole process, including deciphering, took about 10 days, weather permitting.

Russell learned of Pickett's landing when Lyon's telegram arrived on September 21. It was not the reply he had expected, especially after writing thousands of words on August 24 proposing, as James Prevost had, the Middle Channel (President's and San Juan channels) as an excellent compromise boundary through the islands. The Americans should, to Russell's mind, appreciate that they would have three islands – Shaw, Orcas and Lopez – to the British one, San Juan.[7]

He replied to Lyons the next day, in briefer fashion, stating that he too believed Harney had acted independently. But he also wanted an official reply to the May 12 note. Lyons was to request that instructions be sent to U.S. officers not to use military force on the disputed territory without direct authority from the president "...for if these acts are to take place by the sole direction of subordinate officers, and the president does not disavow them, the consequences must be as evil as if the president had authorized them from the beginning." [8]

While Russell was reading and dealing with these dispatches, more were on the way from Lyons. On September 12, Lyons relayed the contents of Drinkard's September 3 letter to Harney., which did not include the passage, *"...it has been too much the practice of the British Government to seize first and negotiate afterwards."* Even with note in hand, Lyons was growing more troubled, especially after receiving a direct report from Lieutenant Colonel Hawkins, who had arrived in Washington on the 13th from Vancouver Island, bearing newspapers and dispatches from Douglas. Hawkins's bundle of correspondence, combined with his firsthand observations, alarmed the British. Northern Indian raids apparently were only ancillary to Harney's true reasons for landing troops. Pickett's proclamation made it clear that the real intent was to make a grab for the island.[9]

This time Lyons did not bother writing. Instead, he marched into Cass's office, demanding an explanation. He could not believe a general in the United States Army could act on the most flimsy of pretexts, and he wanted to know if the U.S. Government really knew what was going on. Cass replied that he had heard nothing since Harney's first letter, but he assured Lyons that the presence of U.S. troops did not mean the U.S. would not leave the island if it was eventually declared British. Newspaper claims that U.S. guns on San Juan could reach the Victoria harbor were preposterous, he added.

Once pressing matters had been discussed, the diplomats reverted to the by-now tiresome question of the boundary line. Lyons offered Russell's August 24 Middle Channel proposal, which would award San Juan Island to the British and leave the remainder of the islands to the Americans.

The withdrawal by U.S. troops or an arrangement

> for joint occupation....would provide for the immediate difficulty...but the course most conducive to permanent friendship between the two countries would be the acceptance by the United States of the fair and equitable proposal contained in the dispatch from Lord Russell.

Cass responded by waving Campbell's proposal at Lyons, citing verbiage from Lord Aberdeen in 1846 that proposed the British would keep all of Vancouver Island and leave the rest south of the 49th parallel to the United States.[10]

Russell pondered the dispatch covering this meeting and replied on Sept. 26, that the current situation made it even more essential that the United States settle the boundary immediately with the Middle Channel as the line demarcation. San Juan Island absolutely had to remain British. Furthermore, Lyons was to press for immediate reply.[11]

If Buchanan was uncertain about his course, decisiveness came in a rush with Harney's August 7 dispatch declaring that Casey had landed with reinforcements. The president was especially alarmed by the passages, "...Any attempts at possession (of the islands) by them will be followed by a collision... " and that any rights the British had to the archipelago had been "...forfeited by the overbearing, insulting, and aggressive conduct of Her Majesty's officers." No wonder Cass decided to rely on time and distance to plead ignorance when asked by Lyons if there was more information from Harney.

Right then the president decided to turn to Lieutenant General Winfield Scott. Three times in Buchanan government experience, the "Hero of Lundy's Lane" had been sent to border communities to defuse crises between local governments over national boundaries and three times he had done it. He would have to go to Washington Territory and temporarily take command. It was true that Scott was seventy-three and so corpulent he could barely walk. On top of that he recently had been thrown from his horse. But at this point half a Scott was better than a whole Harney.

Buchanan notified Scott by telegram on September 14 and followed up with formal instructions through Acting Secretary of War Drinkard on the 16th. The orders outlined the boundary dispute going back to Francis Drake, but stressed that this was a swamp that Scott should avoid. Instead, the general was to focus on making immediate peace and leave the specifics of boundaries to the commissions, under whom both nations would have to build large fires. Scott was to ensure that representatives from both nations could not "...exclude the other by force, or exercise complete and exclusive sovereign rights within the fairly disputed limits," as was stated by Marcy four years before. This gave Scott complete latitude to settle the crisis, so long as he did not back off from the claims of the United States.

The president had reason to be optimistic about Scott's mission. He had learned, through Cass, that the British would be willing to accept a joint military occupation as proposed to Pickett by Hornby on August 3, thereby "correcting a wrong done by Pickett in not permitting this course." This peaceful overture stood in bold contrast to the vengeful screed emanating from Harney. Scott was to do his best to implement Hornby's plan, reducing the American force to Pickett's company and permitting the British to land an equal number of Royal Marines. Scott also was to ensure that the rights of U.S. citizens were on equal footing with those of British subjects. However, if the crisis already had flared into armed conflict, which, in Drinkard's words, "...would vastly complicate the case," Scott was to instigate an immediate truce and arrange for a temporary joint occupation until matters cooled. He then stated the obvious: "It would be a shocking event if the two nations should be precipitated into war respecting the possession of a small island." However: "If we must be forced into war by the violence of the British authorities, which is not anticipated, we shall abide the issue as best we may without apprehension as to the result."[12]

The general departed New York City on September 20 aboard the steamer *Star of the West*, accompanied by aids Lieutenant Colonel George W. Lay and Lieutenant Colonel Lorenzo Thomas and Assistant Surgeon Charles H. Crane. They were scheduled to arrive in Puget Sound on October 16. [13]

Lyons was called to Cass's office on the 14th, where he was "confidentially" told of Scott's mission, specifically that Scott "had been officially informed that the President considered that Captain Pickett had done wrong in not acceding to the proposal made by the British authorities for a joint occupation of the island." Although relieved the highly respected Scott was being sent to resolve the crisis, Lyons suspected the Americans knew more than they were letting on. Not only that, his superiors in London were still screaming for an "official" explanation of Harney's act, not to mention an "official" assurance that the U.S. abided by the spirit of his May 12 letter. [14]

> ...I await with some impatience a more formal and explicit communication from you...because I am persuaded that such a communication would be the most effectual means of displaying in their true light the just and friendly sentiments of the cabinet of Washington. [15]

While more inflammatory newspaper accounts trickled in by wire from New Orleans and St. Louis, Lord Russell in London had digested all that had crossed his desk thus far, plus examined a firsthand report from Hawkins. He wrote Lyons on October 6 that "...the more the irruption of the United States troops into the island of San Juan is examined, the worse the case appears." His research produced these conclusions: Campbell had probably been in cahoots with Harney; Baynes had attempted an amicable solution, only to be insulted by Casey in Victoria Harbor; and Pickett had posted his proclamation in "defiance of the subsisting relations between the two countries." Therefore: U.S.

troops should be withdrawn from the island, which meant U.S. laws could not be enforced; the troops could return only if an Indian emergency arose, and only then in a joint effort with the Royal Marines; and foremost, the U.S. should accept his Middle Channel proposal.

The steamer carrying Russell's missive had yet to dock when Cass finally sent an "official" response to Lyons on October 22. The secretary merely disgorged on paper all that had happened, then reiterated the United States' commitment to the Marcy letter of July 14, 1855. He also included a formal copy of Scott's instructions, in which Scott had been directed to enforce the spirit of that letter. Meanwhile the U.S. still claimed the islands, but were anxious to realize their claim by peaceful purposes. [16]

The home governments had done all they could do to keep the peace. Neither wanted war, yet neither was willing to give up an island sixteen miles long and six and half miles wide. National honor was at stake, a serious matter among nations in 1859 when the scramble for colonies had not yet abated. But business also was important. The British had invested millions of dollars by now in the American industrial infrastructure. A war would be crippling on both sides of the Atlantic. With the question still a long way from being decided—and after all, the Pacific Northwest was still the end of the world – a Band-Aid was required and that was going to be Winfield Scott, the one and only "Great Pacificator."

It all rested on him now.

CHAPTER 14

Stand Down

Winfield Scott loved New York.

This hardly places him in exclusive company. But it is significant in terms of how the U.S. Army functioned at mid-nineteenth century. In 1859, Army headquarters were in New York because Winfield Scott, its commanding general, wanted to live there. At that time, hard though it is to recall now, the United States was a nation with a profound mistrust of large standing armies. The regular army, with barely 16,000 men in uniform, was left to fend for itself, and that included the location of headquarters. Scott liked the parties, during which he would hold forth like a big Buddha in a corner of the room. He liked going to the theater and eating in the best restaurants. He liked traveling up the Hudson to spend several weeks at his beloved West Point. But most of all he liked being as far as possible from Washington, D.C., which, to his mind, had for too many years been overrun with Democrats.

Born and raised near Dinwiddie Courthouse, Virginia, Scott gave up a fledgling law practice in May 1808 to join an army that was expanding to contend with British aggression on the U.S. coastline during the Napoleonic Wars. A strapping six and half feet tall with a probing intellect and an abundance of courage,

Scott made such a mark during the War of 1812 that he emerged a major general with a reputation in Europe as well as North America. His leadership at the Battle of Chippewa in 1814, when his brigade of regulars met British regulars on even terms and won, helped stave off secession talk among representatives of New England states.

Thirty-two years would pass before he was involved in another major war, but he did not disappoint. In what would amount to a second phase of the Mexican War, Scott emulated Cortez by marching his army over the Rio Frio Mountains into the Valley of Mexico. With a highly skilled officer corps—including George E. Pickett, Granville Haller, Silas Casey and William Selby Harney—and a blend of regular army and volunteer soldiers, Scott took the city and ended the war in a matter of months.

Scott's career was not all success. He had been recalled from Mexico to answer charges hurled at him by disloyal subordinates, mainly Democrats and especially Harney. Almost as if in reaction he assumed the leadership of the Whig party and ran for President in 1852 and was soundly thrashed by Franklin Pierce, who had served under him during the Mexican War. The latter blow spurred the move to New York, where he slipped into the routine of arriving at work each morning in full dress uniform, full of spit and polish, only to eat an enormous lunch and spend the afternoon snoozing in his shirtsleeves. His diet and advancing age brought on a nasty case of gout, for which the treatment, then as now, was exercise and avoidance of rich food. He could not bear to give up the latter, so he opted for the former in the form of horseback riding. By then he was nearly as wide as he was tall, which did not make for a solid seat. He was thrown just before his trip to Washington Territory, and his injuries coupled with the undefeated gout meant he could barely move. He was literally stuffed into his carriage and carried aboard his Panama-bound steamer.

Sending an infirm and immobile old man thousands of miles to stop a war was a gamble James Buchanan believed was worth the risk. Scott's prodigious skill and reputation as a warrior, combined with a lawyer's logic, had made him an ideal mediator in crises that flared along the Canadian border between 1837 and 1839. Who better to calm the winds of war than a warrior respected on both sides of the line? Who better than the "Great Pacificator?" Canadian-American border flare-ups were characterized by local citizens succumbing to nationalist passions, driven by an ever-constant lust for real estate or commodities such as fish or timber. Respective national governments were expected to give nothing less than full support, especially the army and navy. Scott's peacemaking came in 1837 in the Buffalo-Niagara Falls area. And the next year later in Aroostook, Maine. In each case the general was summoned by President Martin Van Buren to negotiate with his British opposites. Scott's object was not to attempt to mediate a long-term peace. That was up to the diplomats in Washington and London. His goal in peacemaking missions was to restore calm and seek common ground among the antagonists. Despite the agitation of rabble-rousers, Scott succeeded in both instances, though not without displaying a little passion of his own. At Niagara Falls he confronted a mob, much as a Hollywood sheriff . "I tell you then, except it be over my very body, you shall not pass this line—you shall not embark," he shouted, after which this "revolution" died a slow, grumbling death.[1]

After a bracing voyage and smooth Isthmus crossing, Scott and party left San Francisco on October 17 aboard the Northerner, crossed the Columbia River bar, and arrived at Fort Vancouver on October 20. Scott did not go ashore. Instead, he ordered Harney to come to him the next day. It was in the Northerner's cabin that Scott first told Harney that he was taking command of the department during his stay and then ordered him to accompany him to Portland.[2]

Their time together was strained, owing as much to the bad blood from the Mexican war and its political aftermath as to the recent deposal. How it must have pained Harney to witness the revision or outright cancellation of most, if not all, of his command decisions. To his mind he had operated well within his parameters as department commander, and he had correspondence to prove it. Among these were his blustery exchanges with Douglas, a September 14 dispatch to Scott, and an October 10 diatribe sent over Scott's head to Secretary of War John B. Floyd (an old political crony of Harney's later to become a mediocre Confederate general). Aside from any light they shed on Harney's competence in dealing with an international crisis, the letters gave Scott a revealing look at what was going on in Harney's mind. It was clear by now that Harney knew his government was alarmed by his actions and that he was beginning to worry about the size of the political bite he had taken. For example:

Harney continued to portray the Hudson's Bay Company as a paramilitary organization—with better cannon than U.S. Army forts, and steamers that could quickly be converted into potent warships—bent on dominating the Pacific Northwest. This charge was not entirely unwarranted, coming as it did in response to Douglas's disingenuous claim that the HBC did not exercise any power or authority on Vancouver's Island, and that its officers had no more pull with the government than any other citizen.[3]

He strayed into international boundary negotiations by justifying his acts based on Campbell's irritation with his British counterparts. Because everyone knew Prevost and Campbell were at an impasse, it must have seemed an ideal way to demonstrate the duplicity and aggressiveness of British colonial officials. Harney then stretched the truth when he wrote that Campbell, after reading Pickett's orders, offered the captain assistance and approved of the landing. Campbell initially recorded alarm at Pickett's actions. It was only after Harney assured the commissioner that the army had no intention of taking possession of the island that Campbell responded with relief more than tacit approval.

In response to Drinkard's question as to whether he consulted boundary commissioner Campbell before occupying San Juan Island, Harney replied that he last saw Campbell on July 7, during his inspection tour of the territory's northwestern military posts. At that time neither of them had the slightest notion Douglas was assuming jurisdiction over the island. Harney was careful to raise the issue of "jurisdiction," believing the government would condone rather than condemn his actions on that basis. The president had said as much in his September 3 letter through Acting Secretary of War Drinkard. [4]

A review of the correspondence and Harney's own words convinced Scott to dismiss Harney's perceptions and opinions about the San Juan situation. Additionally, he reversed the disciplinary measures Harney took against his recalcitrant officer corps, then implored Harney to step down as commander of the Department of Oregon and take command of the Department of the West in St. Louis, Missouri. This was a face-saving overture on Scott's part as that command was considerably larger and nominally held sway over Harney's current position.

Paranoia, duplicity and intrigue were common among the officer corps of the old army. Scott could forgive or at the very least stand above that. What he could not abide was amateurism. This made him especially miffed at Harney and Pickett—who was at Fort Vancouver for court martial duty—for their lack of delicacy and precipitous actions over San Juan. The old general could expect such behavior from foolhardy volunteer officers and irate citizens from the north woods of Maine. But Harney and Pickett were professional officers who should have known better than to intrigue in areas best left to the civilian governments.

It was a mortified and much chastened Pickett—a fellow Virginian, from a good family no less – who reported that, thankfully, all had been quiet on San Juan when he left to join a court martial board convened to try one of Fort Vancouver's junior officers.

Scott recrossed the Columbia River bar and by October 24 steamed around the peninsula and up-sound to an anchorage about three miles north of Olympia. Again, he chose not to disembark and did not call on Governor Gholson as directed, likely because in previous peacemaking missions, local officials had been a trial. Scott either wanted to avoid local frictions, or was physically unable to go ashore. The insulted Gholson, in a letter to Secretary Cass, complained that the general's ship never came to Olympia, nor did Scott share with him his instructions from the president. [5]

Gholson used Scott's slight to absolve himself of any responsibility for what might take place. This may have contributed to the civilian versus military discord that was to flare up time and again throughout the crisis and the entire twelve-year joint occupation to follow.

If Harney was displeased to see Scott, the English were delighted. The October 25 edition of the *London Times* informed its readers of Harney's actions but assured them, "England, with its armies and navies is not likely to shrink before such a power as General Harney is likely to bring into action." President Buchanan restored reason by sending "... General Scott to take command, and the temper of this aged soldier [was] likely to be more under control than that of his predecessor."

The editor of the *Pioneer* and *Democrat* also lavished praise on Scott on his arrival, trusting the general to "uphold American rights" in the dispute. It was to be a trust misplaced, at least in the editor's eyes.

By October 26 Scott was in Port Townsend, where he decided to transfer his headquarters to the *Massachusetts*, his flagship during the siege of Veracruz in the Mexican War. A reporter from San Francisco's *Daily Alta California*, who accompanied Scott on the initial stage of his journey, recorded his impressions of conditions aboard the vessel, which changed considerably with a VIP aboard: "The *Massachusetts* proved a very comfortable and convenient conveyance. The general had fine and roomy quarters and a glorious *cuisine* [original italics]."

The general's larder was supplemented by deer, duck, goose, and even a stray seal, all bagged by the ship's master, William

Fauntleroy, and Scott's personal physician. En route to Bellingham Bay, soldiers standing guard on the growing redoubt spotted Scott's ship and excitement rippled through the camp at the prospect of a visit from the great man. But it was not to be. The general again never left the ship, nor his cabin for that matter, throughout his negotiations with Douglas.[6]

Scott directed the ship to ply the waters in question—from Port Townsend to Semiahmoo Spit— while dispatching the revenue cutters *Jefferson Davis* and *Joseph Lane* from all points with instructions for Colonel Lay, who had been sent to Victoria on the 26th to handle the negotiations with Douglas on his behalf. Unlike Casey, who had been snubbed aboard the *Shubrick*, Lay was visited on board the *Davis* by Baynes himself, who even saluted the colonel on his departure. Furthermore, Douglas welcomed Lay to his home and opened his letter book to the American, allowing him to freely peruse correspondence between the British government and General Harney.

Once settled, Lay sent a message to Scott via the *Northerner*, which, on attempting to close with the *Massachusetts*, carried away the old steamer's flying jib boom and lost her own flagstaff with ensign. The flag was retrieved before the ship got up steam to return to California.[7]

On the island, the Americans continued to dig in under the watchful eye of Hornby. Several eye-witness accounts exist of the fortification period, among them the *Daily Alta California* reporter, Peck's diary, and various accounts by island pioneers, such as Hubbs, written or dictated some twenty or even forty years later.

Peck's diary offers some wonderful glimpses of the redoubt under construction. He describe the torrents of rain that plunged the soldiers into gloom, the hordes of Indian prostitutes overrunning the camps, the drunken misadventures of the Irish Sergeant McEneny and included a daily weather report. When Scott arrived off Port Townsend weeks of rain gave onto a gloriously sunny morning, a trend that continued until November 1. The first heavy frost appeared two days later. Peck also noted the latest camp rumors and expressed the soldiers' universal disappointment that General Scott had not called at the island.[8]

The *Daily Alta California* account offers a more objective but no less descriptive view. The reporter booked passage aboard a small sailing ship, the *Ebey,* in Port Townsend. The ship was bound for San Juan with a "deck load of heavy plank for gun platforms for the redoubt on the island" as well as provisions for the troops from the *Massachusetts*, which General Scott had requisitioned for his "migratory headquarters." The *Ebey* was caught in the tides that rip through the islands, and when the fog lifted the next morning the ship was in the Rosario Strait just off Bellingham Bay. It took another three hours to tack to Griffin Bay, where the reporter observed "Love Rock" (near the mouth of Fish Creek) serving as a target for the guns of the *Satellite*.

The *Massachusetts*, even with her armaments stripped, had worse luck with the fog. After leaving Bellingham Bay bound for Port Townsend on the 29th she became lost in the soup and ran aground on the spit that tails away from Smith Island. She remained "with her bows high out of the water for twenty-four hours."[9]

The reporter's descriptions of the prairie and forest on the Cattle Point peninsula could be taken from a later twentieth-century travel guide, but not so the description of San Juan Village:

> ...the main street, which runs westwardly, consists of some twenty odd buildings and huts. Some of these were floated down from Whatcom, Bellingham Bay, and other localities. and give the embryo town quite a stable appearance. The town possesses a bakery, a butchery, three or four barrooms, one aristocratic "two-bit" house, a fruit stand, grocery etc., etc., all of which are liberally patronized.

The soldiers had taken over the Hudson's Bay dock, which

meant that Paul K. Hubbs, Jr., could erect a tent nearby from which to harass British subjects. A road commenced from the town's only street to the top of the ridge, and thence to the Hudson's Bay farm and the camp, by now located just north of it. Preemption farms were "dotting the bay line of the shore," most of their owners continuing to dispute title in the town, while other more hearty souls were actually engaged in sowing winter crops. The soil is described as a "mixture of clay, sand and gravel and said to be great in the production of potatoes."

At the apex of the ridge was the redoubt, on which Lieutenant Robert and his troops continued to labor. The redoubt, dubbed "Fort Harney" in Peck's diary, was:

> ...admirably located as to the Canal de Haro side; it presents a steep precipice, and its guns when mounted, will command the prairie slope to the bay, the view on the canal side, as well as the slopes from the high headlands, some mile and half distant. The work is just beginning its outline and a fair portion is complete, only three gun platforms being planted. The work at the ditch is arduous, as the soil consisting of heavy gravel, intermixed with large granite boulders. A few days more and the redoubt will make a very formidable appearance." [10]

The *Massachusetts's'* guns lined the road that ran about a quarter-mile from the redoubt to the entrance of Casey's new camp, which he noted was named for George Pickett. At least one gun had been mounted on October 14, according to Peck. The camp was nestled amidst tall trees, which even then were under assault from the soldiers' axes.

There was a semblance of a parade ground, on which the command drilled for the pleasure of a Colonel Nauman, commander of the Third Artillery visiting from Fort Vancouver, while Silas Casey officiated mounted on a fine horse. [11] Observing the review were British sailors and marines, among them a young lieutenant who had his own Daguerreotype camera and developing outfit. His images of the nascent camp nestled among the firs, taken on October 27, reveal a mix of simple wooden structures from Fort Bellingham and the conical Sibley tents that Casey had shipped from Fort Steilacoom. In one photo, several soldiers of the Third Artillery strike a pose next to an 1858 twelve-pound cannon beneath the flagpole (stepped in the same spot as today's replica). Off to the side, a soldier in shirtsleeves and a battered forage cap tucks his hands in the waistband of his trousers. Another sits on a wagon tongue in the foreground, puffing on a corncob pipe. Behind them the parade ground slopes to the northwest, bordered by a thick tree line. The relaxed ambience of the photograph reveals that, even as the redoubt was going up, the British and Americans were continuing to fraternize. [12]

Crushing boredom, a powerful thirst, and lust inspired midnight expeditions to the gin mills and two-bit houses of San Juan Village, causing consternation for officers of both sides. In some cases, the whores slipped by the guards into the encampments. The resulting jealousies, fueled by liquor, resulted in acts of "ruffianism" that were severely punished. The commands were losing patience:

> If liquor selling interferes with the discipline of the army, martial law will be proclaimed - which will noticeably sap the progress of the town of San Juan. At present the vicinity is free from another social evil - gambling; but it is hard to tell how long the knights of the green cloth will permit the army to remain free of their presence. [13]

While officers attempted to hold their men in check, Scott was writing. His first letter proposing a reduction of forces followed by a joint military occupation arrived on Douglas's desk via Lay on October 26. At the same time Scott sent a hasty telegram with a copy of the proposal to Washington via steamer and the overland stage to the commanding officer at Fort Leavenworth, thence via telegraph to Washington. It took twenty-eight days to get there, as did dispatches from Douglas and Baynes to their respective authorities, which underscored the necessity of having local officials who could make critical decisions.

Douglas favored a joint military occupation in July and August, but he was backing off from the proposal. On October 29 he proposed to Scott that armed forces be removed and the island returned to a joint civil occupation, pending approval in any case from his higher-ups in London, which could take more than two months. In the meantime, he hoped the general would reciprocate his peaceful intentions and withdraw all American troops on faith. [14]

As far as Harney was concerned, the British still could not be trusted. On October 28 he relayed a dispatch from Casey, who reported that Admiral Baynes had secretly been aboard the *Tribune* when Casey arrived at Griffin Bay on August 10. His source was Archibald Campbell. Casey cited this apparent duplicity as a valid reason for insisting that Baynes wait upon him aboard the *Shubrick* in Esquimalt Harbor on August 11. Why Casey chose to raise this unsubstantiated slight so long after the fact defies any explanation other than, with Scott making peace in the area, he wanted to pin the entire blame on the British.

Harney robustly followed suit, adding a cover to Casey's letter. He reminded Scott that he had mentioned the case of the hidden Baynes during their interview in Portland, but now he wanted it on the record to demonstrate the "duplicity and bad faith" of the British on the San Juan island issue. And more:

> ...This statement exposes three high officials of Her Britannic Majesty's service, viz: the British commissioner, the admiral, the senior captain of the navy in these waters, to the imputation of having deliberately imposed a willful falsehood upon the authori-

> ties of a friendly nation to advance the sinister designs of the British Government in obtaining territory that rightfully belongs to the United States...Is it too much to suppose they would be guilty of like conduct should they be permitted to assume a position in which it would aid their purposes? [15]

It must have pained Scott that the above came from a regular army officer and not a civilian crazed by real estate. Nonetheless, he would deal with the British focussing on the realities at hand. As always, they seemed eager for peace and business as usual.

On November 2, Scott replied to Douglas that he could not accept the removal of all U.S. forces as a requirement to settlement. This had not been expressed as a condition by Lord Lyons, the British ambassador. If it had, Scott said he would never have left the East Coast. Besides, returning the islands to civil jurisdiction would restore the ambiguities that started the trouble in the first place. The headlines and editorial content of the *Pioneer and Democrat* seemed to reflect a popular belief that the San Juans belonged to Washington Territory. And Governor Gholson already had shown he was "...not to be considered a fit person to be entrusted with matters affecting the peace of two great nations." [16]

Scott believed Americans on the island genuinely needed protection from Indians—marauding bands from Coast Salish groups as well as Northerners. He cited as evidence the August 17 Nooksack raid on Whatcom, which had required the response of Haller's company while still aboard the *Massachusetts*.

The general attached a formal proposal to his letter, which basically offered in detail the proposal outlined in his initial letter: Each nation would be permitted one company of light infantry (about 100 men), with each commander serving as magistrate to keep peace between the soldiers/marines and citizens of the respective nations. [17]

On reading Scott's reply, Douglas wrote Baynes, pointing out that Scott could not back down and remove all of his forces. Not only was national honor at stake, but the Americans on the mainland would be up in arms. Douglas believed the real calamity the islanders, British and American, faced was not northern Indians, but each other. That is why he did not want to post military forces there without instructions from his government. His true desire, he said, was to return the island to the status quo, meaning the situation before Pickett landed. In his view, military forces from both sides should be withdrawn. But he had to reassure Scott that American citizens would not be bothered. [18]

With the admiral's blessing, Douglas plunged ahead and wrote Scott that he could not accept Scott's proposal of a joint military occupation without his government's permission. Nevertheless, he offered to withdraw the naval force if Scott would withdraw Casey's troops. He then reassured Scott that, as per the Marcy agreement, he would not attempt to assume jurisdiction over the island. In view of the outrageous charges leveled by Harney at him, the government, and the HBC, Douglas was particularly sensitive about Indian raids:

> ...Protection could not be afforded to persons, who, by wandering beyond the precincts of the settlements, and the jurisdiction of the Tribunals, voluntarily expose themselves to violence or treachery of Native tribes. [19]

The master of the *Joe Lane* himself rowed a longboat through the islands to bring Douglas's letter to Scott. Convinced of Douglas's sincerity, Scott moved quickly. On November 5, he demonstrated good faith by ordering withdrawal of all U.S. Army reinforcements and artillery from San Juan Island. Haller's company was to return to Fort Townsend; and Companies A and C of the Fourth Infantry, H of the Ninth Infantry to Fort Steilacoom; and the last of the Third Artillery companies to Fort Vancouver. Pickett's company would remain. Colonel Lay already had received a verbal agreement that the British naval forces would be reduced.[20]

On Monday November 7, the *Massachusetts* steamed into Griffin Bay where Colonels Thomas and Lay (Peck had them as "Johnson and Lee" — could he have mistaken Lay for Robert E. Lee?) were dispatched ashore with the orders. The pickets were immediately withdrawn, work stopped on the redoubt, and preparations were made to send the reinforcements home. Again, to the profound disappointment of those on the island—British and American alike—Scott chose not to disembark. The chill winds whipped up the bay, bringing on a bout of sea sickness (or his "splendid" table did not agree with him). He hunkered down in his cabin. One can easily imagine him scanning the island with a spyglass and shaking his head in wonder at the folly of man. The redoubt fired a thirteen-gun salute in his honor—the only time guns were discharged from the work. Scott was then visited by Captain Prevost and his officers, while Colonel Lay and several other U.S. Army officers visited Casey's encampment.

At the order to stop work on the redoubt, the soldiers who had been pressed into the digging and rock lugging details were joyful to a man. Peck recorded:

> There were great rejoicings at the order to suspend work on the fort. The tools were collected quicker than ever on a former occasion and brought to their proper repository, with many shouts and much confusion, and to us it is a sad disappointment, looking for considerable credit, as we did, for our services here.[21]

The stop-work couldn't have come at a better time. In November, northwest Washington and the San Juans are at the mercy of northeast winds that roar down the Fraser River Valley, glazing roads, knocking down trees, and freezing pipes. "The weather grows cold constantly since, and in our cotton houses (tents) we feel the change quite sensibly," Peck reported.

While the Americans were breaking camp the *Tribune*, larger of the two British warships, steamed out of the bay leaving the *Satellite* to observe the American exodus. In addition to the San Juan forces, Scott issued an order to all commanders in the territory, advising them that San Juan island was still in dispute and that British subjects had equal rights with American citizens.

Specifics were relayed to Douglas by Lay, who wrote on behalf of Scott that the Americans would continue to occupy the lower portion of the new camp cleared by Casey just north of the HBC farm. Pickett and Company D would remain in the camp "further back—indeed out of sight—on ground cleared up by his company and with comfortable shelter for the winter erected with labor & expense, it is presumed there can be no local feeling even against his continuance there." [22.]

Douglas was pleased with the result, and reminded the general that the military should not interfere with British subjects. Under private cover, he also attached a letter written by Vancouver Island Colonial Secretary William A. G. Young, asking that Pickett be removed. The governor, still rankled by Pickett's truculence and his proclamation, wanted no part of the Virginian on the island:

> ...You will smile at this and with no doubt with reason too, but the words stand recorded nevertheless, and have never been revoked by word, although undoubtedly by deed...his excellency has been informed (but with what shadow of truth he cannot judge) that Captain Pickett is of somewhat hasty temperament and somewhat punctilious and exacting.

The governor was certain, Young wrote, that Scott would concur to a command that would "ensure a continuation of perfect harmony and tranquillity, until the unfortunate question of title may be forever set at rest." [23]

Scott assured the governor on November 9 that no official from Washington Territory would be permitted to interfere with any British subject. British subjects violating the law would be referred to the proper British authorities. In the matter of the change of station for Pickett, Lay responded that the deed was done. Pickett would return to Fort Bellingham, and Captain Lewis Cass Hunt and Company C, Fourth Infantry would remain. An 1847 graduate of West Point—who also graduated near the bottom of his class—and a relative of Secretary of State Lewis Cass, Hunt had excellent political connections. "You will find him a most agreeable and courteous gentleman," Lay wrote.

Hunt was especially agreeable to Scott. In a November 18 letter to a Mrs. McBlair, Hunt described the "disreputable performances of our silly stupid Commander Harney." He then boastfully noted that his instructions were accompanied by a note from General Scott in which the general expressed "...his entire confidence in the intelligence, discretion and courtesy required in the discharge of the delicate and important duties devolving upon me." Hunt believed Scott's use of italics to stress his confidence in Hunt's *courtesies* "...implied a want of that quality" in George Pickett. He went on to describe Harney as a "dull animal" and "reckless, stupid old goose," Archibald Campbell as "weak" and Pickett as a man possessed of "poor judgement." [24]

Hunt was directed to bivouac his troops in "...that part of the camp near and within sight of the Hudson's Bay Company's buildings is to be broken up. The little clearing in the wood and behind the hill has had comfortable shelter erected upon it where one company will be stationed."

Baynes reviewed all the documents and wrote to Douglas on November 9 that he concurred with the agreement.

The "Great Pacificator" had done it again. The *Massachusetts* steamed to Port Townsend on November 8 to await the return of the *Northerner* for the return trip to San Francisco. After enduring another day of extreme weather, including four and half inches of snow, the *Northerner* arrived. But before taking Scott on board the ship was directed to serve as a dispatch boat hauling Lay and a flurry of letters and attached copies drafted by Scott for Harney, Gholson, and Douglas to Olympia and Victoria respectively.

The letter to Douglas contained further assurances that British subjects on the island would not be harassed and any miscreants would be remanded to British authorities. It also promised Douglas that the case of William Moore—the British subject arrested for selling liquor to soldiers on post and assigned to work on the redoubt as punishment—would be addressed by Colonel Casey. [25]

Harney was sent copies of Scott's correspondence with Douglas, the orders to withdraw reinforcements and replace Pickett with Hunt, plus an admonition not to jeopardize what Scott and Douglas had put in place:

> ...the general-in-chief wishes that it be remembered that the sovereignty of the island is still in dispute between the two governments, and, until definitely settled by them, that British subjects have equal rights with American citizens on the island.[26]

When informed of the agreement by Colonel Lay, Gholson was enraged. He did not like being left out, nor did he appreciate being warned to follow Scott's peaceful course. On November 13, the governor ordered returned all fines collected from British subjects, but he protested to Cass the decision to exclude the territorial jurisdiction over British subjects in the islands. He was backed by the legislature, which resolved against "military rule." Cass later advised him that until the dispute was resolved, British subjects were not to be disturbed.

When word of the settlement, with Gholson's interpretation, reached the *Pioneer and Democrat,* the editor screamed "...never has anything occurred in the history of our Territory which has met with so hearty a condemnation...as has the recent deserting of our rights to the island of San Juan."

Scott's settlement was viewed as a sellout dictated by Douglas. The *Pioneer and Democrat* could only conclude that Scott was a victim of old age and "...out of charity to old age and an enervated body, let us...pardon this his first and only great error —an error unpardonable in one in the enjoyment of more youthful age or mental vigor." [27]

On November 11, the *Northerner* finally came alongside the *Massachusetts,* by then leaking badly from running aground on Smith Island, and the general transferred aboard. If Scott was anticipating relief on a swifter and more commodious vessel he was not to find it. The *Northerner* suffered a "defect in the boiler" and had to beat through a furious storm under sail, which made most of the passengers "right down sick." The ship had to dock to make repairs and take on a fresh load of coal, so it "daringly" battled the Columbia River bar and tied up at St. Helens, Oregon.[28] During the respite, Scott again wrote Harney, urging him to resign as commander of the Department of Oregon and assume command of the Department of the West in St. Louis. Harney had requested this command in the past to be near his home and Scott knew it. Had Scott left it at that Harney might have taken the bait. However, he had to add:

> Another motive has just occurred to me for renewing the subject. I have no doubt that one of the preliminary demands which will be made by the British government upon ours, in connection with your occupation of the island of San Juan, will be your removal from your present command. In such an event it might be a great relief to the President to find you, by your own act, no longer in that command. [29]

Scott further muddied his purpose by suggesting that he was ordering the transfer for "public considerations solely and have not received the slightest hint to that effect from Washington." He then gave Harney "leave to decline (the order)."

This Harney did with relish:

> In reply to this communication of the General-in-Chief, I desire to inform him that I am not disposed to comply with such an order. I do not believe the President of the United States will be embarrassed by any action of the British government in reference to San Juan Island; nor can I suppose the President would be pleased to see me relinquish this command in any manner that does not plainly indicate his intentions towards the public service.[30]

With the successful conclusion of negotiations, Douglas and Scott at once sent word by sea and land, realizing the diplomatic situation could have changed in the time it required to send word. Scott actually carried dispatches for both governments, but there also had been telegrams directed to Leavenworth via the overland stage. Everyone settled in to wait.

On Griffin Bay, Hunt organized his command, the British sailors continued with the monotony of port life, and the reinforcements broke camp. Squabbling broke out between Hunt and Pickett over the wooden buildings Pickett had shipped over from Fort Bellingham. While other companies shivered in tents, Pickett's men stayed relatively warm. In the old army, some of the buildings in frontier outposts were built with company funds, compiled from sales of extra rations and a sutler tax. Pickett was permitted to take what he wanted back to Bellingham Bay, but the Virginian left all to Hunt, which he was soon to regret. His second in command, Lieutenant Forsyth, and a junior officer from another company almost came to blows over livestock. It required Henry Martyn Robert, presumably the officer of the day, to stand between them and threaten arrest if they did not back off.

Once the redoubt work was squared away, the guns, ammunition, and other equipment were hauled from the edifice and lugged back down the prairie slope to South Beach. The equipment may have been gone, but the engineers had forever left their mark on the landscape of San Juan Island.

With nothing left to do, the soldiers watched sheets of rains whip down from sodden skies, day after day:

> These are really halcyon days of our soldiering, utterly idle, a thing unknown to an Engineer Soldier, but we are kept busy at nights in a vain effort to keep warm. [31]

The engineers were gone by November 30, the camp thinning as the various companies returned to points south. Pickett placed his company temporarily under the command of Lieutenant Forsyth while he sat on yet another court martial board at Fort Vancouver. [32] The company departed San Juan on November 28, taking only the bare essentials because of tight quarters aboard ship. These included rifles, knapsacks, twenty days worth of food, a few articles of equipage, and as Forsyth noted in his letterbook, "a very small quantity of private baggage." Virtually all of the company property— cannon, stands of rifles, pistols, two months of provisions, brand-new uniforms, a large quantity of oats, and hospital stores— was left on the Hudson's Bay Company dock in the care of Captain Hunt. The property was loaded aboard the schooner *General Harney* by Hunt's men on the afternoon of December 3.

That's when another northeaster struck.

The ship had just got under sail when the wind caught her and with hurricane force drove her onto the rocks, dragging two anchors. The ship rapidly filled with water while desperate soldiers and crew turned livestock overboard and salvaged as many stores as they could. They eventually gave up, waited for low tide and returned to their labors in the darkness. The storm raged for more than twenty-four hours. "The men suffered intensely from the cold, the captain's feet were frozen," Hunt wrote in a deposition justifying the loss of government property in his care. The little that remained that was not ruined was shipped to Fort Bellingham weeks later aboard the sidewheel steamer *Eliza Anderson.*[33]

Pickett returned to Fort Bellingham to find his men short of provisions and living in a barn in midwinter. He wrote Hunt demanding $300 for the buildings he left behind. Hunt forwarded the request to Fort Vancouver, where Pickett's "good friend" Captain Rufus Ingalls cut the sum to $180 and advised Pickett to make do. Pickett must have cursed himself for being too generous or lazy or both.

> It is discouraging to the men of the command to be moved from comfortable quarters into this empty barn and in addition, to accumulation of malfortune in losing the absolute necessaries for a winter campaign; however, there's no word of complaint - all work with a will. I am lamentably deficient in arms, cannot show more than forty effective rifles (for 74 men).[34]

So much for George Pickett's chance at glory on San Juan Island. Four months after their dramatic landing, the men of Company D had been run off the island like thieves and were living like pigs. It seemed a sorry end to such promise.

CHAPTER 15

Pickett Lands Again

While George Pickett and his company were shivering in a barn on Bellingham Bay that winter of 1859-60, Captain Lewis Cass Hunt was enjoying the table of and making a good impression on Captain James Prevost aboard the *Satellite* on Griffin Bay.

His swift boot back to Bellingham Bay convinced Pickett that he had stumbled onto the bad side of Winfield Scott. The general's official report on the matter had been scathing. In an age when even bitter enemies maintained a degree of decorum, Scott practically called Pickett and Harney idiots for nearly starting a war with the preeminent naval power in the world, not to mention the nation's number one foreign investor.

The stung Virginian soon after wrote a friend, wondering why he was being punished "...without even knowing what has been fault?" Scott had "...cast an implicit censure on me for *Obeying Orders* [his italics]." He also was irritated by stories going around that he had exhibited "obnoxious behavior" in his dealings with British officials. The latter aspersion spurred him to seek a letter from Hornby, who cordially damned him with faint praise, writing that "...our intercourse had been of the most courteous nature, and aside from the official matters of the most pleasant and agreeable kind."[1]

Pickett's sole comfort was a joint resolution issued by the territorial legislature, with the still-peeved Governor Gholson's blessing, praising him and Harney for "the gallant and firm discharge of his duties under the most trying circumstances." Pickett later viewed that day as "one of the proudest of my life." Harney sent the resolution to his superiors in the War Department and another copy to Secretary Cass. The commanding general had rejected his policies and urged him to resign his command, yet Harney took the legislature's petition as an endorsement. He embraced Gholson's claim that the islands were sovereign U.S. territory and, as such, belonged under civil jurisdiction. [2]

He turned north and cast a baleful eye at Hunt. The captain confessed to one of his correspondents, a woman named Mrs. McBlair, that he was placing letters in the various newspapers of the region castigating that "wretched, stupid old goose" Harney for his stumbling at San Juan and other missteps as Department of Oregon commander.

> During the whole time I endeavored through several newspapers, to which I had access, to tone down public opinion. I published one or two squibs to throw ridicule upon the foolish affair ...and when Gen'l Scott arrived I endeavored thro' those papers to give a conservative turn to public opinion and prepare for those measures which I felt sure Gen'l Scott would take.

If that was his purpose, Hunt failed miserably. The territory, throughout the twelve-year military joint occupation that was to come, would never accept it. Scott was labeled a stooge to British and American commercial interests. And justifiably so, according to Hunt. In his view it was the "noble old fellow" – Admiral

Baynes – who "...saved us from a war, a war in which the commercial interests of 50 millions of souls, of the same race, would have been destroyed, not to speak of the horrible consequences in other respects."

Hunts letters resonate with disdain for government by the people: "All this wretched performance of Harney is the legitimate result of popular government. It was to please the dear people that Harney made his coup, and he did please the people, silly, blind fools that they are."[3]

Those "silly fools" were not so blind as to miss a sneer of contempt. The reaction Hunt encountered from the American settlers on San Juan and the territorial officials on the mainland convinced him that his days on San Juan Island were numbered:

> I have a very difficult part to play here, inasmuch as I have the active hostility of General Harney...who is seeking a pretext to remove me, and send back Captain Pickett, his pet, displaced by General Scott.[4]

While Hunt was awaiting his dismissal, Scott arrived in New York on December 12, whereupon he gave his report and sent on the dispatches from Douglas (dated November 9) to Lord Lyons.

In his letter to the colonial office, Douglas not only continued to press for a joint civil occupation, but suggested all of the islands between the Haro and Rosario straits be unoccupied. He again stressed the economic infeasibility of stationing troops upon the island because it would attract more squatters (the old HBC bugaboo). Neither government should promise to protect settlers.[5]

Baynes concurred with Douglas at least on this point.

In a letter to the Admiralty, also dated November 9, Baynes, too, stumped for a joint civil occupation. He was wary at first of Scott's offer because, as yet, Scott had done nothing to reduce his forces on the island. "It was ridiculous to suppose that (the troops) had been placed there to protect a few American squatters from the hostile attack of northern Indians. They were evidently there as a menace to us, and until they were withdrawn, I thought it impossible to treat."

Baynes believed that after Douglas's second dispatch to the *Massachusetts*, Scott felt compelled to make an overture and withdrew Casey's forces. By contrast, Baynes believed that the British landing forces would indicate that British subjects needed protection, which he believed they did not:

> Throughout this untoward affair we have been perfectly passive, exercising a degree of forbearance which their Lordships may not, perhaps, altogether approve, but called for, in my opinion, by the almost certainty of a collision at this distant point causing a rupture between the two nations; and I felt that as long as the dignity and honour of the British flag was in no way compromised, I should be best carrying out the views of Her Majesty's Government, and the interests of these colonies, by avoiding the risk of it...Acts of discourtesy on minor points were, on more than one occasion, shown by the authorities of the United States, though the military behaved with perfect propriety. This was all an irritating matter. [6]

But Douglas and Baynes had no influence in London, where the decision for joint military occupation already had been made, the British being satisfied by American sincerity in sending Scott west. Again, the vast distances and the want of telegraph to the West Coast sowed confusion in everyone's mind, most especially Douglas's. Nevertheless, Douglas was unjustly praised for the restraint shown by Hornby.

> (Her majesty's Government) feel it to be cause of satisfaction that your original intention of send-

> ing British troops to the island for the purpose of a joint occupation was not carried out. Such a measure might have led, at the moment, in question, to further disagreements, or even a collision. [7]

The British change of heart had not come without vinegar. Despite expressions of horror emanating from Washington, Russell wrote Lyons that he believed the American boundary commissioner, Archibald Campbell, must have been fully aware of and condoned Harney's actions. He also lambasted Pickett for his proclamation.

Two points rang clear: Exclusive U.S. jurisdiction could not be allowed; and if the U.S. insisted on keeping troops on the island, then a like number of marines should be landed.

With that, the joint military occupation was sealed. [8]

In January, Baynes reported that the *Satellite* was still on station in Griffin Bay. Echoing Hunt's letters, Baynes noted the "most friendly feeling" existing between Hunt and Prevost, as well as the soldiers and sailors. San Juan Village— "fourteen or fifteen shanties"— was almost deserted while the preemption claims were still occupied by American settlers.

Douglas received Newcastle's joint occupation orders January 16, 1860, and passed them on to Baynes. However, the admiral, believing Newscastle's letter "authorized but did not direct" the occupation, demurred until February, content with having a ship stationed on Griffin Bay. Once he received confirmation, he set plans in motion to place the marines on the island.The problem was finding a suitable site. Five locations were selected for study, including a patch of open ground not far from Belle Vue Farm along today's Eagle Cove; a spot adjacent to the Hudson's Bay Company dock; the clearing on False Bay that was Casey's first choice for the permanent American encampment; and the site of future town of Friday Harbor. Baynes finally opted for still another site: a sheltered bay on the island's northwest coast that had been described by Lieutenant Roche in the log of the *Satel-*

lite two years earlier. The site had water, ample room for maneuvering, and some magnificent oaks. That it was livable was evidenced by the remains of Indians structures dotting the prairie area. [9]

Lieutenant Mayne, who had also been along on that earlier exploration, thought spacing the camps so far apart was ludicrous:

> I can't help thinking this a great mistake after we would not send troops there for the last 9 months, that it was not 'English' etc. etc. to do so to 'cave in' now, but I suppose it is ordered from home, and then sticking them on opposite sides of the island as if they were to eat each other. I should like to see how he (Hunt) will laugh at it. [10]

The marines landed on what became known as Garrison Bay on March 21, 1860, under the command of Captain George Bazalgette, a thirteen-year veteran who had served in the Crimean and China campaigns and shared a cabin with Hornby on the perilous Pacific crossing. The force consisted of Bazalgette, two subalterns, a surgeon, and eighty-three noncommissioned officers and men.

What they found was jotted down in the journal of Color Sergeant W. Joy:

> ...landed in a bay completely landlocked, our Camping Ground being on a shell bank — the accumulation of "Years", evidently, as it averaged ten feet high, from thirty-five to forty feet through, by 120 yards long, it was the work of Indians, as they live very much on a shellfish called "Clams", and of course deposit the shells just outside their Huts, hence the bank I mentioned, the brush wood grew quite down to the water's edge, in the rear the forest was grow-

ing in undisturbed tranquillity... [11]

As soon as the landing of the marines became a foregone conclusion, John DeCourcy was relieved as magistrate effective March 20.

Hunt dutifully reported to Harney the British landing on March 27, including Baynes's letter to Hunt and a copy of Baynes's instructions to Bazalgette, which Hunt observed were clearer than his own regarding jurisdiction. The British commander had authority to eject miscreant British subjects from the island and full latitude to consult with the U.S. garrison commander about American violators. Hunt complained that since Magistrate D.F. Newsome had resigned the rise of crime in San Juan Village was testing everyone's limits, particularly Hunt's.[12]

However, the captain had not allowed uncertainties concerning martial law to stand in his way. Earlier in the month he'd dispatched three soldiers to the town to ferret out stolen goods at a local whisky establishment, whereupon the soldiers were thrown into the mud—or as noted in the Port Townsend *Register,* "sent into the street on a 'double-quick Shanghie trot'"—by several burly inhabitants. Hunt reevaluated the situation and sought Henry Crosbie for advice. The former magistrate suggested taking the whiskey peddlers to civil court, presumably in Port Townsend. Only two of three charged went to trial and they were acquitted. Another, whom Hunt identified as a "German Jew whose establishment was the greatest nuisance of all," decided himself to get out while the getting was good. Unfortunately for Hunt, the other whisky sellers believed Hunt had run "the Jew" off the island. As a result, several saloon owners and their compatriots wrote Harney on March 7, complaining that Hunt had closed their saloons and evicted them from the island. In response, Harney through Pleasonton on the 21st ordered Hunt "not to interfere with the trade of our citizens" nor molest them in any way and to "forward to the headquarters, a full and complete account of all your actions effecting citizens." [13]

The order must have crossed Hunt's report of the British landing en route. Hunt reacted with fury. It seemed nothing less than a setup. He was being censured by a commanding general who was not familiar with the low quality of the plaintiffs and, most critically, had not even taken the time to hear Hunt's side of the story. Hunt countered by sending Harney a description of the whisky sellers written by Crosbie, plus a petition from the "actual" citizens of the island extolling the merits of military over civil law. For good measure he added his own remarks pointing out that he had, in good faith, applied to civil authorities to enforce the law. This was :

> As salty an epistle as I dared write, conveying by implication and inference my opinion of the conduct of headquarters, and I am now awaiting with some little curiosity the sequel. With Harney all things are possible, and I should not be surprised if he gave his wrath full swing and removed me. [14]

Which is precisely what happened.

On April 10, orders were issued. Forts Bellingham and Townsend were to again be abandoned. Pickett and Company D would return to San Juan and Hunt and Company C, as well as Haller and Company I at Fort Townsend, to Fort Steilacoom.

These were not simply perfunctory missives replacing a recalcitrant officer. Instead they served notice to the British that the Department of Oregon, once again under Harney's control, did not recognize the joint military occupation to which both governments had agreed. Moreover, George Pickett was to ensure that the British did not interfere with U.S. civilian magistrates, who would be enforcing the law, except in cases involving British subjects, which would be referred to Baynes before action was taken. In Harney's view, the islands were part of Whatcom County, Washington Territory and "the General Commanding is satisfied that any attempt to ignore this right of the Territory will be followed by deplorable results, out of his power to prevent or control." [15]

Meaning war.

Contemporaries and historians alike have concluded that Harney's second Pickett landing was ordered to defy Winfield Scott. He had been verbally twitted by Scott, who shoved him aside and cleaned up the mess with the British. But Harney still believed that stationing Pickett on the island had been a logical and legitimate step considering Douglas's proprietary actions toward Americans in the San Juans. Acting Secretary Drinkard had written as much. He also maintained that while he was aware of the interim arrangements made between Scott and Douglas—which did not prescribe a landing of Royal Marines—neither Scott nor the government had advised him that a formal joint military occupation had been approved.

What he had, in hand, was the support of the civil authorities of Washington Territory, who had issued a fine proclamation on his behalf - and his membership in the Democratic party. Harney had been sustained so many times by party patronage that he must have believed that James Buchanan, a Democratic president, would do what James Knox Polk had done during the Mexican War—namely chastise Scott and back Harney.

He as yet had no idea the world had passed him by. [16]

Despite his threat of "deplorable results," Harney ensured Pickett's orders included copies of correspondence between Douglas and Scott, Scott's instructions to Hunt, and copies of orders from Baynes to Bazalgette. Pickett was to relay his instructions to Baynes through Bazalgette.

While Pickett was making preparations to return to San Juan Island, Hunt was writing over Harney's head to Scott, a violation of military protocol in any era, but an action that had become standard behavior in the highly political old army. Harney certainly was no stranger to it. The letter basically reads as a mea culpa, Hunt stating that he had done his best in a delicate situation, despite the "animus" shown to him by department headquarters. Still in all, he believed his removal had nothing to do with that. He believed the change had "long been contemplated." He closed on a homey note:

> The order comes at a most convenient time; gardens just planted; while four companies are sent to a post having accommodations for three only, and excellent quarters left vacant at Fort Townsend. [17]

Pickett landed on April 30 and immediately dispatched a messenger to Garrison Bay with a letter of greeting to Bazalgette with attachments.

Admiral Baynes's reaction to Harney's orders and Pickett's second landing was mild. After consulting with Douglas, he reported to the admiralty that neither of them intended to enter once again into fruitless correspondence with Harney. They were going to wait for developments from Washington, which they were certain would be swift and ultimately satisfactory. Even so, Baynes cancelled a scheduled cruise, opting to "remain in the neighborhood until matters wear a more promising aspect." [18]

Despite his posturing early on in the crisis, Pickett's cordial relations with Hornby, Prevost, and Richards demonstrated that he could be as much the diplomat as Hunt. He also knew where the political winds were blowing after witnessing the fireworks between Harney and Scott. This time the Virginian was eager to get off on the right foot, and from the start his relations with Bazalgette were cordial.

However, like Hunt, Pickett had his troubles with the liquor sellers. On May 21 he wrote:

> ...Matters are proving worse if possible. Whisky sellers without number are here and are still coming. Two-thirds of the Indians on this end of the island are drunk day and night...My hands are tied. I am to assist civil authorities. Where are they? Things

cannot remain in this position...

And again on June 1:

> Ever since knowledge of the joint occupancy, the desperadoes of all countries have fought hither. It has become a depot for murderers, robbers, whisky sellers - in a word all refugees from justice. Openly and boldly they've come and there's no civil law over them. All the Indian tribes in the neighborhood - Lummi, Swinomish, the Skagit and even the Cowichan and the Victoria Indians flock here in quantities to supply themselves with poisonous whiskey. As a result, this is a perfect bedlam day and night. [19]

Pickett grew more alarmed when a Haida Indian was shot dead in the street by "some rascal" and left in the mud, his family forming a cordon around his body and wailing in mourning rites for days on end. Having lived with a Northern woman, with whom he had fathered a child, Pickett presumed that vengeance would be exacted by the Haida family. Hoping to stave off a raid, he made an unsuccessful attempt to ferret out the murderers and in the end preserved the peace by issuing provisions to the widow. His proclivity for exaggerating his position arose again when, by the end of his dispatch, the dead Indian became a "chief." To underscore his concern he reminded his superiors that he had barely forty men left in his company, in contrast to his counterpart Bazalgette, who had a full compliment of eighty-four marines.

As many as 4,000 Northerners had been reported in the vicinity of Victoria. Many were expected to call at the fisheries located along the island's west coast. That had happened the previous fall during the height of the crisis and the Indian shore parties had been run off by Colonel Casey's men. In the meantime Pickett had the Northern women to worry about. Boatloads had been landed for "nefarious purposes" by white traders; one boat was overtaken and boarded by the *Massachusetts*, but most landed with impunity.

Other Northerners sought employment with the Hudson's Bay Company or American settlers, many of the latter recently discharged soldiers from Pickett's company. Pickett wrote in July that if Northerners were to be removed, it would have to apply to all equally. Otherwise he feared reprisal raids on isolated farms that were easy prey for the war canoes. The whiskey sellers were in still in full blast, too numerous and bellicose for the magistrate to handle. As with Hunt, the Justice asked Pickett for help, and Pickett with Hunt's firing fresh in his mind, at first strongly recommended, as per Harney's orders, that civilian matters rest with civilians. In the end, however, Pickett rendered assistance as had Hunt, such as in the case of a Northerner, whom Pickett arrested for robbery.

In one of the first tests of the joint military occupation, Pickett passed with flying colors. When approached by Griffin, who offered to pay the fine in return for the Northerner's release, Pickett refused, but only after consulting with his counterpart, George Bazalgette at English Camp. "I doubt if a northern Indian can be considered a British subject," Pickett sniffed. [20]

By mid-July, the Indian scare had quieted, largely because on Vancouver Island James Douglas had ordered all Northerners disarmed before they entered the city's inner harbor. Thereafter, the only northern Indian problems involved petty theft, drunkenness and prostitution, enterprises primarily financed by whites. One purveyor was arrested for selling liquor at South Beach. His beached boat was found surrounded by canoes, "drunken Indians on board," by a squad of soldiers. Because he was a British subject, Pickett turned him over to his new friend and colleague Bazalgette. The two captains were spending so much time sorting out citizenship that Pickett requested better riding stock to negotiate the thirteen miles of rough road that connected the camps.

While this international cooperation was going on, Winfield Scott was fuming as he read Hunt's letter detailing, with considerable embellishment, the change in command on San Juan Island. He had no way of knowing Pickett was steering clear of William Selby Harney and developing a positive relationship with Bazalgette.

In a May 14 letter to the Secretary of War, Scott made his case: Pickett had offended the British with his ridiculous proclamation and that was why he was replaced with Hunt. "Hunt (as our officers informed me) was remarkable for firmness, discretion and courtesy."

Scott railed at Harney again for recognizing Washington Territory's jurisdiction. He predicted that if trouble did not ensue, it would be because of the forbearance of the British rather than any restraint exercised by Americans, "..for I found both Brigadier General Harney and Captain Pickett proud of their conquest of the island, and quite jealous of any interference therewith on the part of higher authority." [21]

In his autobiography, Scott characterized the incident and Harney thusly:

> ...Brigadier General Harney, who commanded our forces in that quarter, was a great favorite with Five Democratic Presidents. Full of blinded admiration for his patrons, he had before in Florida hung several Indians, under the most doubtful circumstances, in imitation of a like act on the part of General Jackson in the same quarter, and now as that popular hero gained so much applause by wrenching Pensacola and all of Middle Florida from Spain in time of peace, Harney probably thought he might make himself President too, by cutting short all diplomacy and taking possession of the disputed island! Imitations on the part of certain people always begin by copying defects.

His next few words revealed the depth of his disdain for William Selby Harney: "It is not known that the protege, Harney, was even reprimanded for his rashness. He certainly was not recalled although the measure was suggested by the writer." [22]

When Lord Lyons learned of the change in command, he wrote Cass on June 6. The situation was "deplorable," particularly Harney's threat of "deplorable results." [23]

Lyons pointed out the inconsistencies between this correspondence and that of General Scott, not to mention the agreements struck by both governments, and stated that he was confident that the U.S. government would take steps to correct the situation. The mortified Cass and his boss, President Buchanan, once again claimed to be the last to know. However, Scott's letter to the War Department indicates that Cass had been aware of Harney's orders since May 14. No document trail exists on the matter between the War and State departments.

Was Cass feigning surprise because the U.S. was investigating the matter and hoping to have an answer before the Brits found out? Could it have been more Democratic patronage at work on Harney's behalf? Perhaps the War Department staff was on spring break. We'll never know. What we do know is that hard paper rescinding Harney's orders and ordering him back to Washington, D.C., did not leave the capital until June 8. [24]

Finally, Harney had gone too far even for his fellow Democrats.

Colonel George Wright, commander of the Ninth Infantry, was given the Department of Oregon. Wright recognized Scott's agreement but left Pickett in command. They were friends and mess mates dating back to the Mexican War, and it was Wright who in 1855 had rescued Pickett from the tedium of Fort Gates, Texas, to command a company in his new regiment. [25]

Several weeks later, when word of his firing finally reached him, Harney grudgingly packed his things and by mid-July started his journey east via the Cowlitz River landing, thence overland to

Olympia and down Sound. His prospects were not all bad. As per Scott's November offer, he was going to St. Louis and the Department of the West, a command that extended from the Mississippi River to the Continental Divide, from the Canadian to Mexican borders. As Scott observed, Harney's "punishment" for the "San Juan imbroglio," as it came to be called, was a slap on the wrist.

Harney stopped by Victoria on the Express Steamer on July 14. Baynes noted:

> ...received no communication from him and consequently did not feel myself called upon to show him any attention after the coarse and unwarrantable language he made use of in his letter to the Adjutant General of October 29, 1859, with regard to myself, Captains Prevost and Hornby as well as Her Majesty's Government. [26]

Oddly enough, Wright wrote the War Department in late August stating that he too had never been given any specific instructions concerning the joint occupation of San Juan Island. Therefore, he would fall back on Scott's instructions of November 5-9, which were relayed to Harney by Colonel Thomas during Scott's West Coast visit.

Pickett, meanwhile was throwing himself into the role of peacemaker. On receiving from Wright his confirmation of command and directions to abide by Scott's orders – of which he states Bazalgette never received a copy – he wrote Bazalgette, closing with this nugget:

> I do not for a moment imagine that anything would have happened to disturb the perfect understanding which has existed between us, both officially and personally since my arrival on the Island, but I think it due each other in the position we occupy to communicate at once any change of orders

or instructions from our superiors in command.[27]

Those instructions were still taking shape. In January 1861, British officials were still wary of the mixed nature of authority on the island, particularly that the U.S. had on board a magistrate and collector of customs who were not subject to Pickett's orders. But Pickett was doing his best to strike a balance. Both single, Pickett and Bazalgette got on famously not only in matters of jurisdiction, but on trips together to Victoria, where they were observed tipping glasses at the Colonial House.

Thus was the tone set for the spirit of mutual cooperation between the two camps throughout the joint occupation.

CHAPTER 16

Joint Occupation & Settlement

No one believed the joint military occupation would last twelve years. Even Douglas finally concluded that complete withdrawal of civil authority was the way to go, but he assumed like everyone else that with the crisis over, the boundary commissions would finally settle the matter. He wrote as much to the Foreign Office on May 7, 1860. Therefore, on July 20, Russell wrote Lyons to request that the United States withdraw the civil authorities. The U.S. refused, which was to cause nothing but trouble. [1]

Acting Secretary of State Trescot did urge the British and American commissioners to get on with it. The British government was prepared to be accommodating, even if it meant submitting the question to third party arbitration, much as Cutlar had suggested when he and Griffin first squabbled over the pig. Indeed, as early as 1858 Lord Stanley at the Colonial Office wrote that he believed that the matter should be settled by arbitration, while the Admiralty that same year urged an attempt to negotiate with the Americans on establishing the Middle Channel as the boundary. Failing that, the Admiralty believed the government should settle on Canal de Haro, which would let the Americans have all the islands. [2]

By December 1860, the British formally offered to submit the question to the kings of Norway and Sweden and the Federal Council of Switzerland for binding arbitration. The settlement also would require the Americans to pay $500,000 to the Hudson's Bay Company and Puget Sound Agricultural Company for the properties they had been forced to evacuate in the Cowlitz River Valley and Fort Vancouver as per the Treaty of Oregon. The claims of the companies were still outstanding. [3]

The United States grudgingly approved the arbiters, but balked at paying $500,000 for properties originally valued at $300,000 (although the HBC had reset the value of all properties at $650,000). The new Secretary of State, Jeremiah S. Black, told Lyons the issues would have to be settled separately. [4]

The issue also would have to pass the Senate, and that body, in turmoil over the issue of secession of the Southern states and anticipating the prospect of a Republican administration, was hardly prepared to vote on it. A resolution written by Senator James M. Mason of Virginia passed committee and was submitted to the whole body, but no action was taken.

Negotiations continued during the Lincoln Administration, when in April 1861 the British forwarded an amended draft suggesting arbitration for the HBC claims as well as the water boundary. By then Fort Sumter had been fired upon, and the draft moved to the bottom of the mounting pile on Secretary of State William Seward's desk.

By November, relations between the U.S. and Great Britain nearly collapsed into the shooting war that Lyons, Cass, Scott, and Baynes had so deftly avoided. Former U.S. Senator Mason, now a Confederate envoy, and fellow traveler John Slidell were on their way to London to petition the Court of St. James for recognition, when they were snatched from British steamer *Trent* on the high seas. Their captor was Captain Charles Wilkes of the U.S.S. *San Jacinto*, the same Wilkes who twenty years earlier made the earliest U.S. charts of the San Juan group—charts used by American officials to justify their claims.

The incident prompted the British to put their forces on the eastern seaboard on full alert, precipitating another crisis. San Juan Island vanished on the diplomatic front, although Lyons and Seward did review the HBC claims in 1863. Lyons was directed not to bring up the water boundary, however, and the whole issue was held in abeyance until 1867.

Meanwhile, island residents were not paying taxes or customs duties, which attracted elements with little interest in establishing communities with prosperous farms, churches, and schools. Indeed, on the American side, the old issue of territorial/military jurisdiction still bubbled while San Juan Village floated on a sea of bad whiskey, prostitution, and lawlessness. Still in all, the joint occupation was going its peaceful way, thanks to the cordial relations between Captains Pickett and Bazalgette. Pickett spared no effort to be accommodating, which seems a far cry from the man who is remembered more for his belligerency than anything else on San Juan Island.

Pickett was so cooperative that he ordered Deputy Collector of Customs Paul K. Hubbs, Jr.— who hero-worshipped Pickett forty years on— not to attempt himself or to encourage American citizens to settle on plots within the British military reservation (essentially today's English Camp). He even wrote to Fort Steilacoom requesting maps so that the respective reservations could be properly defined, which earned him points with his British counterparts.

In a letter to Silas Casey, the Virginian offered similar praise for Bazalgette and his men, but in the same letter expressed envy at the efficiency of the British operation and decried the already growing neglect of his camp by Department of the Pacific authorities. His men, he wrote, had not been paid in six months, while the British not only were paid each month, but earned additional "colonial pay or in other words double pay." This difference in the care and feeding of the two forces would prevail until the end of the joint occupation. [5]

Matters of pay soon seemed trivial when the District of Oregon learned that on April 12, 1861, South Carolina's military forces fired on Fort Sumter. On June 11, Colonel George Wright, in acting upon orders to withdraw regular U.S. troops from the Northwest, ordered San Juan Island abandoned and Captain Pickett and company to embark for San Francisco in preparation for subsequent transfer east. As per their agreement in 1860, Pickett advised Bazalgette of the movement and added:

> I cannot take leave without expressing to you both in my own name and that of my officers, the gratification we have experienced from our very pleasant intercourse with you during the passed year, and our sincere regrets at having to break up these associations. [6]

Bazalgette returned the sentiment.

Farewells were premature, however. On June 21, Wright cancelled the orders, which Pickett relayed to Bazalgette on June 25. That same day a troubled Pickett submitted his resignation from the U.S. Army in preparation for heading east and joining the new Confederate Army.

Pickett did not write about himself, so we have to rely on his third wife, LaSalle Corbell Pickett, who made a fifty-year career of being a widow after Pickett's death in 1875. It took about six weeks for word of the rebellion to reach San Juan Island. Then Pickett would have to decide between nation and state. In one of her concoctions, LaSalle includes a letter in which George stated that his state was like a "family," while the nation was a "friend." Citing the homily, "Home is Where the Heart Is," Pickett elected to go with Virginia, even though his West Point appointment was granted him by the state of Illinois. [7]

Although he decided to resign in June, relief would not come for a month. As a gentleman, Pickett decided he could not just up and leave, so he was still on the island, wearing the uniform of a U.S. Army captain on July 21 when the first Battle of Bull Run (or Manassas) was fought—a battle that involved many of his West

Point classmates, now colonels or higher, in both armies, including Thomas "Stonewall" Jackson.

Finally, on July 25, Pickett was relieved by Captain Tom English of Company H, Ninth Infantry, with two officers and forty-nine soldiers. Pickett steamed up-sound to Fort Steilacoom, where he left his company, signed over his stores, and departed via horseback for Vancouver Barracks. He stopped in Olympia briefly to give his friend James Tilton $100 for the care of his son, Jimmy, still living with the Collins family a few miles south in Grand Mound. Although the Collins homestead was on his way, he did not stop to see the boy and rode on out of his life. In Vancouver Pickett presumably caught a lumber schooner for San Francisco, where he hoped to anonymously disembark and book passage on a Panama-bound vessel.

An unofficial grace period apparently operated in some quarters to allow Southern officers to get their affairs in order. Department of the Pacific commander, Brigadier General Edwin V. Sumner granted Pickett an "official leave of absence" pending acceptance of his resignation. However, the Virginian already was a celebrity from his Mexican War days and the pig incident, and was taking no chances. On the steamer from San Francisco he traveled under the name of "Edward Eldridge," even though Hugh Fleming, his friend and former second in command at Fort Bellingham, also was aboard. [8]

When Pickett arrived in New York City the grace period was over and he had to sneak through the city to launch the career that would bring him lasting fame at Gettysburg, followed by physical and financial ruin and an early grave. [9]

On San Juan Island the joint occupation proceeded peacefully, as civil jurisdiction on both sides had been suspended. As such it had to be continually redefined for each commanding officer. For example, early in 1863 American Camp commandant Captain Lyman Bissell stopped Whatcom County Justice of the Peace E.T. Hamblett from ejecting a British subject from a claim on the island. Bissell then suspended Hamblett "as a functionary of Washington Territory." On reading Bissell's report, Major General George Wright, now commander of the reconstituted Department of the Pacific, wrote Bissell through District of Oregon commander Brigadier General Benjamin Alvord. Wright approved Bissell actions by citing Winfield Scott's original orders that territorial officials were not to interfere with British subjects.

To void future conflicts, Alvord directed Bissell to confine jurisdiction of American civil authorities to the southern end of the island. The northern end should be under British law.

The new Department of Pacific commander, Major General Irvin McDowell, saw it differently after visiting San Juan Island in September 1864. Americans and British were scattered throughout the island, thus making geographical boundaries moot and impractical, he wrote Alvord. From here on out, McDowell ordered, civilians, would submit to civil authority only if they chose to do so; and joint military rule should continue. [10.]

Washington Territory next petitioned Secretary of State Seward to grant civil jurisdiction in 1866, the territory believing the rule of a single military officer arbitrary and unacceptable. Officers had been urged only to advise in squabbles, but some in sheer desperation had acted and this caused trouble.

Such was the case in September 1866 when a complaint was filed against post commandant Captain Thomas Grey and his deputy First Lieutenant William Preston Graves, both Second Artillery, by Deputy U.S. Marshall Jared C. Brown.

Grey and Graves tore down 150 feet of paling fence that had been erected by Isaac Higgins, whose San Juan Island history predated Pickett's landing. His fence blocked the road from the military post to the Hudson's Bay Company landing on Griffin Bay. Higgins had been warned to remove the fence but responded with threats and verbal abuse, according to Grey. When he refused to remove the barrier, Grey ordered Higgins expelled from the island, advising headquarters that Higgins was "one of the most disreputable vagabonds in Washington Territory."

Grey's action gave the territory the excuse it needed to enforce its claim to jurisdiction. Here was a clear case of abuse of power by federal officers. Higgins filed a grievance and an indictment for "malicious trespass" was sworn out on September 7, 1866, against the officers in United States District Court, Third Judicial District at Port Townsend. A warrant was issued, but efforts to arrest the officers were unsuccessful. Consequently, another indictment was filed for obstruction of legal process, and another for assault and battery, which also named four enlisted soldiers.

Warrants were issued again in March and April 1868. Higgins also sued Grey for $10,300 for arrest, confinement and expulsion from his property. Grey again refused to appear, but it mattered little. The court ordered Grey to pay Higgins $5,000 on September 12, 1866, after which the two officers finally hired a Steilacoom attorney. A Pierce County judge threw out the ruling. The territory's trespass indictment also was thrown out in 1868.

The Grey-Higgins incident prompted Major General Henry W. Halleck, now Department of the Pacific commander, in November 1867 to write the War Department. The only way to end the tension between military and civil authorities on San Juan Island was to take decisive action one way or another. His suggestions included placing the entire territory under martial law or changing the boundaries of the territory to exclude the San Juan Islands. He then took a page from William Selby Harney's book and cited the pig incident and the attendant folly in questioning whether the British had the wherewithal to colonize British Columbia. The U.S. should put a stop to the mess and make a treaty with the British to take over the whole thing. [11]

On January 9 and 15, 1868, the Territorial legislature passed another memorial to the U.S. Congress to end the military occupation of the island, listing all previous grievances. The climate had seemed right for the move because the U.S. Senate recently questioned whether the occupation was feasible. But the Johnson and Grant administrations held firm to the end. — much to the relief of the British, not to mention the Canadians, who had achieved dominion, or self-government, in 1867 but remained under the yoke of British foreign policy.

Grant's ambassador to Court of St. James, Reverdy Johnson, concluded an agreement with Britain in 1869 that would submit to a third-party commission the San Juan water boundary, as well as several other pressing issues including a major disagreement over the activities of the C.S.S. *Alabama.*

The *Alabama, Shennandoah* and other Confederate commerce raiders devastated the U.S. whaling and merchant fleets during the Civil War. What was not sunk was either sold off or transferred to foreign registry, which sent insurance rates skyrocketing and tax revenues plummeting. That the British government never formally recognized the Confederacy as an independent nation—and considered the commerce raiders with their Southern officers and British crews scarcely more than pirates—did not matter. She did recognize the South as a belligerent, remained neutral and colonial ports had given succor to the vessels throughout the war. U.S. shipping magnates had lost money and someone had to pay.

This made it all the more intriguing when Michigan Senator Zacharia Chandler, speaking in support of Massachusetts Senator Charles Sumner in 1868, rose from his seat and thundered that if the British did not wish to pay up for the shipping sunk by the *Alabama*, then she should cede Canada to the United States. The issue became known as the "*Alabama* Claims" and would contribute to the delay in the San Juan boundary settlement. Unfortunately, President Grant was still bitter over the tons of British weapons shipped to the Confederacy and he firmly believed the commerce raiders contributed to prolonging the war. While Grant was no friend of Sumner, he went along with the bombastic senator, even to the point of endorsing the acquisition of Canada. This whipped up war fever in the popular press, but not on Wall Street, where conventional wisdom had it that war with Britain would bring economic collapse. Not only had British capital fueled American industry from the start, but British loans were settling the war debt and establishing the nation on a peacetime footing again. [12]

Someone finally explained these facts to Grant. Soon negotiations over the *Alabama* Claims, fishing rights, Fenian raids in Canada, and yes, even the San Juan Boundary Dispute, once more took a peaceful course toward arbitration.

Finally on May 8, 1871, the Treaty of Washington was signed by the British and Americans and ratified by Congress the following month. Kaiser Wilhelm (Emporer William) I of the newly constituted German Empire was named arbiter, due to the influence of George Bancroft, the U.S. ambassador in Berlin. The Kaiser selected a three-man commission, which was directed to meet in Geneva where it would review evidence from both nations as to whether the boundary should be the Haro or Rosario straits. Three men. How ironic. That is precisely the number of men Lyman Cutlar suggested review the true value of the pig all those years ago. [13]

The commissioners — Professor Heinrich Kiepert, a geography teacher at the University of Berlin, Councillor Levin Goldschmidt of the Imperial High Court of Commerce and Dr. Ferdinand Grimm, vice president of the High Court — deliberated for more than a year and had their share of disagreements. Dr. Goldschmidt in particular was dismayed at the choice of channels from which they were to make their selection. He believed the obvious choice was missing from the table: the Middle Channel (President's and San Juan channels) that runs between San Juan, Orcas and Shaw islands. He felt so strongly about it that he had suggested amending the treaty. [14]

However, the British, wanting the issue settled at long last, backed off on their 1859-vintage proposal of the Middle Channel, largely because of the stubbornness of U.S. Secretary of State Hamilton Fish. The New Yorker never wavered from Archibald Campbell's conclusion: If one traced the boundary to the middle of the Strait of Georgia, then took a straight edge and drew another line directly south, the line would run through the Haro

Strait. As far as he was concerned it made the question moot. No objective commission could possibly rule otherwise. The commission would adhere to the letter of the treaty or the U.S. would back out.

The commission finally voted two to one to award the islands to the United States, with Goldschimidt writing a lengthy dissenting opinion. The Haro Strait had to be the "southerly" channel dividing Vancouver Island from the mainland cited in the Treaty of 1846. As Dr. Grimm pointed out, the Haro Strait touches Vancouver Island. The Rosario Strait does not. Also, the Haro Strait is deeper, wider and certainly more amenable to international shipping. It was truly "...most in accordance with the true interpretation of the Treaty concluded..." [15]

The judgement was endorsed by the emperor and a ruling was issued on October 21, 1872, staring out with the royal, "We, William, by the grace of God, German Emperor...", of course.

Messages were sent to both posts via telegraph and the British Captain William Delacombe made immediate plans for departure. On November 22, 1872, the Royal Marines packed up their gear and left their tidy camp of 27 structures, plus a formal garden to the Americans. Had cannon existed on the island salutes would have been exchanged. U.S. officers—including the commander of the Department of the Pacific, Brigadier General Edward Canby—exchanged worried missives over the matter, but let it drop. A simple good-bye with kind letters would suffice. A small contingent, led by First Lieutenant James Haughey traveled to the camp to say good-bye. Haughey's men brought a large U.S. flag to run up the pole soon after the Union Jack came down. But to their surprise the pole had been chopped down. Evidently it was to be used to replace a spar lost by a British ship on a rough Pacific crossing. Old Glory instead went up the telegraph pole. The San Juan Boundary Dispute — The Pig War — was finally over.

As with all stories of near misses, "ifs" abound.

If James Douglas had not placed the Hudson's Bay Company

on the island, the Americans might not have responded with customs collectors and county sheriffs. If Lyman Cutlar and Charles Griffin had not both exploded with rage that June morning and settled their differences instead, A.G. Dallas, William Selby Harney and George E. Pickett might never have been involved. Conversely, if the Royal Navy officers had followed Douglas's orders and forced the issue with Pickett, the Pacific Northwest might be shaped differently today.

History ultimately turns on individual choice. If blunders were committed along the way, the right choices were made in the end. Two powerful nations nearly went to war, spent thousands of dollars and pounds and exchanged tons of paper over ownership of an island 16 miles long and six and half miles wide. But honor had been served and the peace kept, the pig being the only casualty.

Some war. Some pig.

Notes

List of Abbreviations

BC	Buswell Collection, Center for Pacific Northwest Studies, Western Washington University, Bellingham, Washington.
FO	British Foreign & Commonwealth Office
NA	National Archives
SAJHA	San Juan Island NHP Archive

Chapter 2

Quest for Wealth

1 Nokes. *Columbia's River,* pp. 179-191.

In writing this brief survey of explorations that resulted in claims and counterclaims to the Oregon Country, I found the following revealing and insightful: Surely there is no better survey of exploration of the Pacific Northwest than David Lavender's *Land of Giants: The Drive to the Pacific Northwest, 1750-1950* (1958); for a wonderfully lucid portrait of how science and commercial opportunism merged in the late 18th century, see William Goetzmann's *New Lands, New Men America and the Second Great Age of Discovery* (1986) or his *The Atlas of North American Exploration From the Norse Voyages to the Race to the Pole* (1992) written with Glyndwr Williams; Enlightenment values and exploration also are probed in *Enlightenment and Exploration in the North Pacific 1741*-1805 (1997), edited by Stephen Haycox, James K. Barnett, and Caedmon A. Liburd (1997); Richard J. Nokes's *Columbia's River The Voyages of Robert Gray, 1787-179* (1991) offers a penetrating study of one of America's most neglected explorers, Robert Gray; and finally Walter A. McDougall's daring *Let The Sea Make A Noise: A History of the North Pacific from Magellan to MacArthur* (1993) takes a step beyond academia and allows the principles to speak for themselves.

Chapter 3

Manifest Destiny and Joint Occupation

1 Mackie, *Trading Beyond the Mountains* , pp. 44-68.

2 Billington, *Westward Expansion*, p. 383, 532-533. Billington's thesis of the westward expansion remains the seminal work on the subject in the historiography of the American West. His view that the passage of Walker Tariff and the repeal of the Corn Laws sped the signing of the Treaty of Oregon is further underscored by fiscal realities. The British then, as they are now, were the largest foreign investors in the fledgling United States—a fact that would overwhelm political jingoism throughout the nineteenth century (See Chapter 16, n. 12.)

3 FO, *Abstract*.

Chapter 4

Treaty of Oregon: Table Set for Trouble

1 FO, *Abstract*, pp. 50-51.

2 FO *Abstract*, "Treaty of Oregon, 1846, Article I."

3 Ibid., p. 108.

4 Goetzmann, *Army Exploration*, pp. 105-107; FO *Abstract*, pp. 118-199. The map cited by the British—*Geographical Memoir upon Upper California in Illustrations of His Map of Oregon and California*, 30th Congress, Ist Sess., Sen. Misc. Doc. 148, 1848—was drawn in 1848 by Charles Preuss as a follow-up to his 1846 Fremont version that traced the Oregon Trail from the mouth of the Kansas River to where the Walla Walla joins the Columbia. Preuss was a German immigrant from St. Louis. This was a map of the entire West and was considered a breakthrough for the times in that it revealed virtually all of the mountains, rivers, and basins. However, according to Goetzmann it lacked accuracy, showing mountains where none existed and, of course, giving the British an excellent basis for their claim of the Rosario Strait. Preuss, like any good cartographer, combined research with firsthand observation and, unfortunately for U.S. diplomats, this included Vancouver's charts but not those of Charles Wilkes, which, in all fairness, would have been relatively recent and perhaps unavailable to Preuss at the time. Wilkes's charts, incidentally, quite clearly show the San Juan Islands situated in the Strait of Georgia. The Haro Strait is labeled Canal de Haro, while Rosario (Vancouver's) Strait is labeled "Ringgold" Strait.

5 FO *Abstract*, pp. 108-109.

Chapter 5

The San Juan Sheep War

1 As quoted in Miller, *San Juan Archipelago*, pp. 15-16.

2 Report of Captain Alden to Prof. A.D. Bache, Superintendent United States Coast Survey, Oct. 31, 1853, *36th Congress*, p.87. James M. Alden was a midshipman on the U.S.S. *Vincennes*, under Capt. Charles Wilkes. This was the famed "Great United States Exploring Expedition," the nau-

tical counterpart to Lewis and Clark, which explored the entire Pacific Basin, nearly pole to pole, making observations and creating charts that have barely been surpassed by modern technology. In the early 1850s he was given command of the U.S.S. *Active*, a sturdy sidewheel steamer, based in San Francisco and later out of Mare Island Naval Shipyard in Vallejo, California. It was at Mare Island that Alden became a good friend and colleague of then-Captain David Glasgow Farragut, the yard commander. Alden became familiar with nearly every feature of the Pacific Coast, which included the inland waterways of Puget Sound. When the water boundary survey was authorized he recruited his nephew, James Madison Alden, to become the official artist. The younger Alden went on to become a renowned landscape painter, whose subjects included Yosemite Valley.

3 Ibid.

4 *Belle Vue Sheep Farm Journal*, May 3, 1854. Griffin's cabin was one of "seven small houses" in the Belle Vue cantonment, just up from Grandma's Cove. Griffin's headquarters also consisted of an outhouse and barn and six acres under cultivation adjoining the dwellings. Another forty acres were planted on the other side of Eagle Cove. The Hudson's Bay Company imported a variety of breeds to the Pacific Northwest, starting with the more numerous California breeds in the 1830s and 1840s. The California sheep probably included the Churro, which was descended from the Spanish Churra brought to the Americas shortly after the conquest. The breed continues today in the Navajo-Churro. In the late 1830s, at the behest of James Douglas, Merino, Leicester, Cheviot and Saxony breeds were imported from Europe to improve the quality of wool. See *Cultural Landscape Report, Vol. II*, Fort Vancouver NHS, Vancouver, Washington.

5 FO, *Abstract*, p. 124-127.

6 *Belle Vue Sheep Farm Journal*, May 6, 1854. "Rum" is an archaic word meaning queer or odd.

7 As quoted in Miller, *San Juan Archipelago*, p. 28.
8 Gough, *The Royal Navy and the Northwest Coast*, p. 90. The policy of

swift reprisals that included mass destruction of property did not sit well with Douglas, who feared a massive Indian uprising. Once he succeeded Blanshard, the Indians on the lower end of Vancouver Island were handled with restraint. However, in dealing with the Northerners the Royal Navy returned to draconian measures.

9 RG76, NA, *Geographical Memoir*, p. 29. If tides were optimum through San Juan Channel between the tip of San Juan Island and Lopez Island, the "beach" may have been Grandma's Cove, situated just below Belle Vue Farm headquarters. The cove is sheltered, the beach sandy and a trail leads to the top of the bluff. When the Cullen/Barnes party moved off to another beach, it could have been one of several coves located along the island's southern coast, or anywhere along South Beach. The Americans also could have driven the rams over the hill to Griffin Bay to a spot near the Hudson's Bay Company dock. But the commandeered canoe was likely beached below the Indian village, which was located between Belle Vue Farm and Grandma's Cove. The author's guess is that the auction site was the large cove directly down the prairie from the redoubt. The American account has the incident taking place at a sheep station on the island's northern end, which seems far fetched considering the time and distances involved. George Gibbs, a geologist with the U.S. Northwest Boundary Survey, in March 1859, described four other sheep stations on the island, each with a "corral" and a cabin. (See note 10.)

10 *Belle Vue Sheep Farm Journal*, April 1, 1855; and Edson, *The Fourth Corner*, p. 98. A healthy ram can weigh from 175 to 200-plus pounds apiece, which underscores that it was no easy task loading the animals into the canoes. No wonder the Americans pulled firearms when Griffin ordered them to release the animals.

11 Roth, *History of Whatcom County*, pp. 77-78 and Edson, *The Fourth Corner*, p.98. Kanakas with knives charging down the hill probably spiced up the account with visions of Captain Cook's demise on a Hawaii beach in the 1770's. If Griffin's Kanakas rowed across the channel to Victoria and the Americans saw the *Beaver* emerge before they could launch their boats, the incident had to have taken place near Belle Vue Farm and the island's southern end. Douglas later wrote that the *Bea-*

ver went after the Americans with an armed posse on board, but was about two hours behind. Native Hawaiians crossed the Pacific to work in the Pacific Northwest starting with the Astorians in 1810 and continued with the Northwest and Hudson's Bay companies. Many married into Northwest Coast Indian groups, which created excellent links for trade and enhanced the labor pool. Several families among the Lummi Nation, located north of Bellingham, have Kanaka ancestors.

12 Miller, *San Juan Archipelago*, pp. 29-31. This came to about $15,000 in American dollars at mid-19th century.

13 Ibid., p. 31

14 The National Guard, State of Washington, *Collection of Official Documents*, p. 2.

15 Ibid., p. 2.

16 FO, *Abstract*, pp. 130-133.

17 As quoted in Miller, *San Juan Archipelago*, p. 46.

18 FO, *Abstract*, pp. 145-146; and RG76, NA, *Geographical Memoir*, p. 29. U.S. geologist Gibbs, again in March 1859, conversed with Griffin as well as C.L. Denman. Denman told him that he had been engaged to lay out claims by a lawyer named Sabatt "in strength of advices and secured from Washington." Twenty-six claims of a quarter section each (160 acres) were staked out, with 27 quarter sections (or 4,000 acres) left to the Hudson's Bay Company. Gibbs observed that only two of the claims had been settled thus far (one by a Scotsman, the other by two Kanakas), which seemed to confirm that "the whole seemed to be a matter of bare speculation."

19 Lyons to Cass, April 27, 1859, *40th Congress*, p. 218.

Chapter 6

The Pig Incident

1 Griffin to Douglas, June 15, 1859, San Juan Island NHP Archive, hereafter SAJHA (copy from BC Archives); and RG76, NA, *Geographical Memoir*, p. 31. One other interesting comment Gibbs makes is that Charles Griffin, who was "very open and unreserved," told him that in his opinion the islands had always belonged to the U.S., and that Prevost had blown the issue by offering the "Middle Channel" as a compromise boundary. Judging by this fuming letter to Douglas, Griffin was paying lip service to Gibbs. Tabulations vary on the number of Americans on the island at the time of the incident. Twenty-two men signed the petition submitted to Harney, but not all were residents as evidenced by the signature of Paul K. Hubbs, Sr., a resident of Port Townsend. Counting families there may have been 25 to 29 Yanks on the island as opposed to seven British subjects.

2 Ibid.

3 *Belle Vue Sheep Farm Journal*, June 15, 1859. The three exclamation points are Griffin's.

4 Ibid.

5 *40th Congress*, pp. 183-184 and Miller, *San Juan Archipelago*, pp. 54-55. The courthouse is purported to be the oldest brick building in Washington State, having been hauled around the horn from Philadelphia in 1858 by an entrepreneur hoping to make a killing selling grubstakes to miners bound for the Fraser River Gold Rush. Unfortunately James Douglas issued a decree that all miners had to report to Victoria before traveling up the Fraser to the diggings. That made Whatcom a ghost town overnight and the brick store soon became public property. It still stands at E and Holly streets in downtown Bellingham, Washington.

6 The Washington State Historical Society in Tacoma has a double-barrel *shotgun* in the collection donated by the Cutlar family. It is complete with pedigree and was included as the weapon of record in the exhibition, "George Pickett and the Frontier Army Experience," which ran at

the Whatcom Museum of History and Art in Bellingham from December 1994 to April 1995. The San Juan County Historical Museum has in its collection a percussion cap, muzzle-loading rifle, which was donated by a local family. The family claims the rifle was given by Cutlar to an ancestor. No paper trail exists for the rifle, which makes it suspect. However, Cutlar used the word "rifle," not "shotgun," in his affidavit. Where does the truth lie? And does it really matter? We do know that the gun was loaded.

7 Jacob was discharged by Griffin on June 28 for "having been beastly drunk all yesterday, & having connived with Clallam "Joe" in stealing liquor." *Belle Vue Sheep Farm Journal*, June 28, 1859.

8 40th Congress, pp. 260-261

9 Dallas, Tolmie and Fraser have streets named for them in Victoria. Mt. Dallas on San Juan island also is named for Dallas. Dallas stressed his travel aboard the *Beaver* in response to Harney's charge that they came aboard the warship, the H.M.S. *Satellite* . See Chapter 15.

10 Hubbs, Jr., "Pickett's Landing on San Juan and the Cutler Incident," *San Juan Islander*, Oct. 22, 1909. This piece also was included in Hubbs's obituary in the same newspaper on Feb. 17, 1910. Hubbs's brush with history ended with the boundary dispute. He remained in the islands for most of his life, working occasionally, living off nature and telling the Pig War story to those willing to listen.

11 Hubbs, Jr., *Seattle Post-Intelligencer*, June 4, 1892.

12 Perhaps there is a Curse of the Pig War. Look at the record: Pickett loses an entire division in one afternoon at Gettysburg; Harney is fired before he sees a single Civil War battle; Granville Haller is drummed out of the army in disgrace during the Civil War; and Forsyth stumbles his way into Wounded Knee. But these events also may explain why there was such a thing as a "Pig War."

13 McKay, Charles, "History of San Juan Island," *Washington Historical Quarterly*, 2:4, 1908, pp. 290-294. Charles McKay claimed to be the last

survivor of Pig War period. Like Cutlar, he established a squatter farm on the island in 1858 on his way back from the Fraser gold fields.

14 Miller, *San Juan Archipelago*, pp. 57-58. The historian David Hunter Miller spent a large chunk of his time in the 1930s and 1940s exploring this incident and then assembled a research trail historians tread to this day. San Juan Archipelago was actually one chapter in a greater diplomatic history. The paperback volume is primarily a recitation of primary sources linked by a spare narrative that includes several lucid conclusions, among them the perception about Dallas's behavior. See Chapter 15 for a passage from his August 5 letter to Douglas.

Chapter 7

William Selby Harney

1 This included the famous march into Florida in 1818. See Chapter 8.

2 Ness, *The Regular Army on the Eve of the Civil War*, p. 27.

3 Clow, "William S. Harney," *Soldier's West*, p. 43.

4 Ibid., p.45. Greyhounds are known for a tight cranial cavity. Kearny had no use for flamboyant officers and did not suffer fools. Following the U.S. conquest of California, he arrested the posturing John C. Fremont and marched him back across the plains in rear of his formation.

5 Murray, *The Pig War*, p. 16. Harney eventually replaced Wool as commander in the Pacific Northwest.

6 Polk, *Diary of a President*, pp. 197-198. Ironically enough the court martial board was urged by Secretary of State James Buchanan, who would one day fire Harney for displaying similar zeal.

7 It is not known if Pickett was aware of Harney's gallows humor, but he employed his own variant of the act on twenty-two North Carolinians during the Civil War, which almost resulted in his own hanging as a

war criminal by U.S. authorities.

8 In another little twist of Pig War lore, Fleming was fired and reassigned as Pickett's second in command at Fort Bellingham. He was reassigned before the Pig War crisis, but in 1861, took the same steamer with Pickett back to the East Coast.

9 This included the famous march into Florida in 1818. See Chapter 8.

Chapter 8

The Petition

1 Tacoma Public Library, *Northwest Ships & Shipping Database*,. This database is available on the Internet. A large number of ships and shipping sources were used in its compilation. The slow-moving warship *U.S.S. Massachusetts* was one-hundred and sixty-one feet long and thirty-one feet abeam, and was listed as anywhere from seven-hundred and forty-nine to seven-hundred and seventy-nine tons. She was built in 1845 by the Samuel Hall shipyard in Boston. The ship plied the Liverpool to New York route as an auxiliary steamer until it was purchased by the war department for the Mexican War, during which she served as Gen. Winfield Scott's flagship in the harbor of Veracruz. The *Massachusetts* steamed on Puget Sound from 1856-57, then again from May 1859 to the outbreak of the Civil War, operated alternately by the navy and army. While on the sound, she carried eight 32-pound guns and a company of soldiers or marines. During the Pig War incident she was under lease to the army's Quartermaster Corps. The *Massachusetts* was one of the first combination sail/steam-powered vessels in the inventory and as such, featured a screw propeller that could be raised with the ship under sail. The screw eventually was left permanently in place, but the ship was so slow under steam, and required so much fuel, that Pleasonton advised Casey to operate the vessel under sail if at all possible. The navy removed the ship's engines in 1861 and converted her into a brigantine.

2 Richards, *Isaac I. Stevens*, pp. 326-327. Harney's harassment of the

HBC was well known to company employees at Fort Vancouver. He'd requisitioned company property without compensation. He also referred to Northerners as "British Indians" even to the extent of referring to their raids as "instigated by the Hudson's Bay Company, in order to drive the Americans from the lands which this immense establishment covet for their own purposes."

3 *Belle Vue Sheep Farm Journal*, July 9, 1859.

4 McKay, "History of San Juan Island," *Washington Historical Quarterly*, 2:4, 1908, p. 291.

5 *Belle Vue Sheep Farm Journal*, July 9, 1859. Perhaps it was here that the "warship" misunderstanding arose and the Americans may have not been telling tall stories. The *Beaver* had once been the only steamer in northern waters, and often had been chartered by the government as a gunboat to deal with marauding Indians and county sheriffs absconding with sheep. Most American citizens in the area were aware of this fact. Perhaps Hubbs decided to stretch the truth just a bit, one ship with guns being as good as another. Or maybe Hubbs did not mention the *Satellite* at all. Maybe he said "gunboat," and Harney, who probably saw the *Satellite* when in Victoria, assumed that was the "warship." McKay wrote: "They (the HBC) had sent a gunboat to take one of our men to Victoria..." Ironically, attorney Paul K. Hubbs, Sr., had the sequence of events and the identity of the ships involved nearly spot-on — except that he identified the humble survey ship *Plumper* as a "frigate" — in his September 3 letter in support of Harney to President James Buchanan. Presumably this information came from his son. A.G. Dallas vigorously disputed the letter, referring to it as "unintelligible."

6 Crosbie to Cass, April, 1860, *36th Congress*, pp. 1—4; and Bancroft, *British Columbia*, p. 617n. U.S. Magistrate Henry Crosbie is generally considered a dispassionate and reliable source on the Pig War. He also pointed out that northern Indian raids were the main reason the British preceded the Americans in settling on San Juan.

7 Hubbs, Jr., *Seattle Post Intelligencer*, June 4, 1892.

8 Harney to Scott, July 19, 1859, *40th Congress*, pp. 147-148. As stated in the narrative, the petition, which Harney attached to his letter, never mentions the Hudson's Bay Company by name. But Americans often looked upon the HBC and British government as one and the same, and actually under Douglas it was generally true. The conflicts between the home government and the HBC—licensing in the gold fields, the secretiveness over the Belle Vue Farm, the anticolonial attitudes of many in the British parliament—were unknown to most Americans.

9 Ibid., pp. 147-148. Harney viewed the existence of the Vancouver Island colony and New Caledonia (soon to be British Columbia) as merely temporary, as not enough British colonists existed to make it viable. Harney undoubtedly read reports of the topological survey in 1854 (Whiting and others) that stressed the military significance of the San Juan Islands.

10. Ibid., pp. 147-148.

11. Miller, *San Juan Archipelago*, p. 64. Dartmoor was an infamous British prison that housed American servicemen during the War of 1812, which ended only 45 years before and was still in the nation's living memory.

12 Ibid., p. 147-148 and Miller, *San Juan Archipelago*, p. 63.

13 Utley, *Frontiersmen in Blue*, p. 188. Haller and two companies of infantry were ambushed and barely escaped massacre by more than 500 Yakamas. Haller lost five killed and seventeen wounded after being besieged for two days on a hilltop, followed by a two-day running retreat that cost him his howitzer and pack train. He went on to serve in the Union Army during the Civil War, but was courtmartialed and dismissed from the army for "disloyal conduct." Congress reinstated Haller and promoted him to colonel in 1879, shortly after which he took command of the newly reopened Fort Townsend. He retired in 1882.

14 Haller, *San Juan and Secession*, pp. 7 and 11; and Thompson, *Historic Resource Study*,. p. 24, n.; *Roder Narrative*, Bancroft Library;

BC, WWU; and Gordon, *Pickett*, pp. 62-63. Haller's argument is based on the way Casey was addressed by Harney in Special Orders 72—as "commander of Fort Steilacoom," a single military installation, rather than the entire "Upper Puget Sound." In Haller's opinion the closure of Forts Bellingham and Townsend and Pickett's subsequent assignment to San Juan Island underscored the demotion. But lacking actual evidence of a conspiracy, Haller suggested that the officers "could read between the lines" in terms of interpreting orders. He prefaces the accusatory paragraph with "...I may be doing injustice, but my candid impression is..." His suspicions were aroused by the homes of record of the officers who gathered that evening at Fort Bellingham on Harney's inspection tour. Pickett, Edmund Fitzhugh, and *Massachusetts* master William H. Fauntleroy were from Virginia, while Harney was from Tennessee. Haller neglected to mention that also at Fort Bellingham that night were Harney's adjutant, Captain Alfred Pleasonton, and quartermaster Captain Rufus Ingalls, who hailed from the District of Columbia and Maine respectively. Both rose to the rank of major general in the Union Army during the Civil War. Roeder (actual spelling) was one of the founders of Whatcom, the precursor of today's Bellingham, Washington. He was in Whatcom the evening Harney and company stayed in Bellingham. The officers stayed with Roeder, Pickett and Fitzhugh in Whatcom. The quarters of each were somewhat more commodious than those of the fort. Fitzhugh was manager of the Bellingham Bay Coal Company and was one of the Americans who joined Cullen and Barnes in pinching Griffin's sheep four years before. Fauntleroy, a civilian, also held an interest in the Bellingham Bay Coal Company. He is not to be confused with Charles M. Fauntleroy, a Confederate naval officer. The intrigue of a Southern cabal to start a war was given further impetus by a letter George Pickett wrote to one of his former officers after the Civil War. In the letter, Pickett mused that the new President (and his prewar buddy) U.S. Grant should start a war with a foreign power to reunite the nation. His wife, LaSalle, actually alleged in one of her works that the San Juan incident was provoked by Pickett and Harney for that very purpose. Historian Lesley Gordon speculates that Pickett might have expressed that wish to her when they were living in poverty after the war.

15 *36th Congress*, p. 117. James W. Forsyth, a native of Maumee, Ohio,

would go on to become a key officer on the staff of Union Maj. Gen. Philip H. Sheridan during the Civil War, eventually rising to the rank of brigadier general of volunteers. In one of the many ironies of the war, it would be Sheridan's corps that pierced the flank of Pickett's Division at Five Forks in the Spring of 1865, opening the door to Lee's surrender at Appomattox. Forsyth would continue in the service after the war mainly as a staff officer under Sheridan, who rose to Army chief of staff. Following Sheridan's retirement in 1885, Forsyth assumed command of the 7th Cavalry in 1886, ten years after the Little Big Horn disaster. He would lead the regiment at the so-called Battle of Wounded Knee in December 1890, in which 150 Sioux men, women and children and 25 soldiers were killed. Even though he was censured for bungling what was to be a simple disarmament of Sioux warriors, he retired a major general in 1897.

16 Miller, *San Juan Archipelago*, p. 59 & 73.

17 John DeCourcy to Douglas, as quoted in Miller, *San Juan Archipelago,* p. 73.

18 *40th Congress*, pp. 183-184. Constable G.T. Gordon would end up fighting for the South during the Civil War and would be a lieutenant colonel in temporary command of a North Carolina brigade at the Battle of Gettysburg. In his classic *Pickett's Charge*, author George Stewart relates how Pickett introduced Gordon to one of his staff officers on the eve of the famous charge: "This is Colonel Gordon, once opposed to me in the San Juan affair, but now on our side." The staff officer recalled that Gordon told Pickett "...my men are not going up today," as they had been heavily involved on the battle's first day

19 Pickett to Pleasonton, July 27, 1859, Letters Received, Adjutant General's Office, RG 94, NA; and Pickett to Pleasonton, July 27, 1859, Letters received, Department of Oregon, RG393, NA. Pleasonton would rise to major general of volunteers in the Union Army during the Civil War, and be instrumental in reorganizing the cavalry of the Army of the Potomac into a single corps, which became a potent striking arm. At the Battle of Brandy Station in June 1863, the Union cavalry "arrived," matching for the first time the cavalry of Confederate General Jeb Stuart. They

went on to win a smashing victory over Stuart at Gettysburg. An inability to keep his opinions to himself got him into trouble with Union Major General George Meade, his commanding officer. He then became the odd man out when Ulysses S. Grant brought Major General Philip Sheridan east to command the cavalry corps. He finished the war in the western theater and bitterly resigned from the army in 1868. He has earned lasting fame among Civil War buffs mainly for promoting twenty-three-year-old George Armstrong Custer from captain to brigadier general. The town of Pleasonton, California is named for him. Some correspondence in RG 94 and RG 393 is not included in either collection of Congressional documents and is more revealing of the personalities. Many thanks to Pickett biographer Lesley Gordon for assistance in obtaining these records.

Chapter 9

George Pickett and the Frontier Army

1 Edson, *The Fourth Corner*, p. 35. Edson's book was first published in the early 1950s. Because she was raised in Whatcom County "before the coming of the railroad," she knew many of the people mentioned in her history.

2 Returns, Fort Bellingham, 1856. BC.

3 For more on George Pickett, see Gordon. Lesley J., *Pickett: General George E. Pickett in Life & Legend*. Chapel Hill, NC: University of North Carolina Press. 1998; Longacre, Edward G. *Pickett: Leader of the Charge*. Shippensburg, PA: White Mane Publishing Company, Inc. 1995; Selcer, Richard F. *Faithfully and Forever Your Soldier: General George E. Pickett, CSA*. Gettysburg, PA: Farnsworth House Military Impressions. 1995; Pickett, LaSalle Corbell. *Pickett and His Men*, Atlanta: Foote & Davis Company. 1889, and *The Heart of a Soldier as Revealed in the Intimate Letters of Genl. George E. Pickett, C.S.A.* New York: Seth Moyle. 1913; and Patterson, Gerard A., "George E. Pickett — A Personality Profile," Civil War Times Illustrated 5, May 1966.

4 Returns, Fort Bellingham, 1856-1857, BC.

5 Utley, *Frontiersmen in Blue*, pp11,. 19. Former National Park Service Chief Historian Robert Utley has set the standard for historians of the army and Indian frontier. Most of the general information about the frontier army comes from this volume and the sequel *Frontier Regulars*.

6 Ibid., p. 29

7 BC.

8 1860 *U.S. Census*, Whatcom County, Washington Territory, SAJHA.

9 Report of Col. Joseph K.F. Mansfield on the U.S. Military Reservation at Bellingham Bay, Washington Territory, Dec. 7-8, 1858; and Port Townsend, Washington Territory, Dec. 3-4, 1858. RG 94, NARS.

10 Ibid.

Chapter 10

Governor Douglas Responds

1 Pioneer and Democrat, July 29, 1859.

2 Pickett to Mackall, Sept. 10, 1857, BC.

3 Thompson, *Historical Resource Report*, p. 42. Douglas's initial orders to Hornby no longer exist.

4 F&CO, U.K., Biographical Sketch of Geoffrey Phipps Hornby, SAJHA.

5 Hornby to DeCourcy, July 30, 1859, as quoted in Miller, *San Juan Archipelago*, p. 71.

6 Gough, *The Royal Navy and the Northwest Coast*, pp. 150-151.

7 Miller, *San Juan Archipelago*, pp. 76-78. Campbell claimed he met with Prevost at Griffin Bay on the 27th and 28th in an In an August 18 letter to Secretary of State Cass.

8 Hubbs, Jr., *Seattle Post Intelligencer*, June 4, 1892.

9 Pickett to Casey, *40th Congress*, p 152.

10 *Pioneer & Democrat*, July 29, 1859.

11 Hornby to his wife, July 31, 1859, Egerton, *Hornby*, p. 64. This same supposition would be offered by Prevost to explain the actions of Harney the Jacksonian. Perhaps both captains got it from Douglas. It has been cited in some works as "British intelligence." Hornby's correspondence comes to us via this only biography of him published in 1896 by his daughter, Mary Augusta Hornby (Mrs. Fred) Egerton.

12 Ibid, pp. 65-66.

13 Pickett to Pleasonton, *40th Congress*, pp. 153-154.

14 Egerton, *Hornby*, pp. 65-66.

15 Casey to Pleasonton, Ibid., pp. 151-152.

16 Haller, *San Juan and Secession*, p. 12.

17 Gough, *The Royal Navy and the Northwest Coast*, p. 161. The account by these officers underscores how time and distance spawned many of the apocryphal stories that characterize the Pig War.

18. Miller, *San Juan Archipelago*, pp. 75-77.

19 Ibid, p. 78. In a follow-up letter to Douglas, Finlayson also observed that the boundary dispute might have been settled but they had yet to receive word. There also was worry of events in Italy. Great Britain

could hardly afford war with the United States.

20 Ibid, p. 75.

Chapter 11

'Tut Tut, no, no, the damn fools.'

1 Douglas to Hornby, Aug. 2, 1859, as quoted in Miller, *San Juan Archipelago,* p. 79.

2 Hornby to M. DeCourcy, Aug. 1, 1859, as quoted in Miller, *San Juan Archipelago*, pp. 78-79.

3 Douglas to Hornby, Aug. 2, 1859 (second letter), San Juan Island NHP Archive (copy from BC Archive).

4 Hornby to Baynes, Aug. 5, 1859, as quoted in Thompson, *Historic Resource Study*, pp. 128-129.

5 Hornby to Douglas, Aug. 4, 1859, *40th Congress*, pp. 155-156. What we know of this conversation comes from letters that were exchanged, at Pickett's request, between Pickett and Hornby; and through correspondence between each officer and his superior. Pickett probably wanted a written record and Hornby was pleased to comply. Paul K. Hubbs, Jr., claimed to have been in the tent for the meeting in his 1892 Seattle *Post-Intelligencer* account. It is unlikely that a civilian would have been allowed in a meeting where martial law was the primary subject of discussion. The letter eventually ended up in the documents of the 36th Congress, to which Hubbs would have had access. He paints a belligerent Pickett, which would have been totally out of character at this point.

6 Selcer, *Faithfully & Forever*, p. 42.

7 Hornby to Pickett, Aug. 3, 1859; and Pickett to Hornby, Aug. 3, 1859, 11 p.m., *40th Congress*, pp. 155-157. A highlight of this exchange is

Hornby's recollection that Pickett told him he "believed" Harney's orders came from Washington. In his reply to Hornby, Pickett corrected Hornby's version by stating that he was on San Juan "under orders from my government."

8 Pickett to Pleasonton,Aug. 3, 1859, *40th Congress*, pp. 153-154; Pickett to Pleasonton,Aug. 3, 1859, RG94, NA.; and Gordon, *Pickett*, p. 59. In an accompanying letter to Pleasonton Pickett fumed over the "miserable subterfuge" of Douglas and how if it wasn't for George Pickett and Company D Lyman Cutlar would be in jail that moment and American settlers would have been run off the island. As biographer Lesley Gordon writes, "Perhaps to quell his anxiety and distrust, he asserted unquestioning belief in the mission." 'We are right,' he announced to Pleasonton, 'tho' we all knew it before.'"

9 Douglas to Legislative Council,Aug. 3, 1859, ibid., p. 174.

10 Hornby to Douglas,Aug. 4, 1859, as quoted in Miller, *San Juan Archipelago,* p. 74-75.

11 Legislative Council to Douglas, *40th Congress*, p. 175-176.

12 *Pioneer and Democrat*, Aug. 5, 1859.

13 Campbell to Harney,Aug. 14, 1859, 40th *Congress*, pp. 120-121.

14 Here's an excerpt from the letters exchanged, as per 40th *Congress*, pp. 108-112. It is a good example of where these two men were taking matters: "...With a sincere desire to extract from your letter of the 27th of May the 'very explicit answer' to my communication of the 7th, which you 'submit when taken as a whole,' it conveys to me, I have again given it most careful perusal and consideration, and with due deference, candor compels me to say that, whether taken as a whole or in part, it only conveys to me a very circumlocutory and evasive answer..."

15 Prevost to Campbell, Aug. 4, 1859, *40th Congress*, p. 114.

16 Campbell to Prevost, ibid., p. 115.

17 Miller, *San Juan Archipelago*, n. 1, p. 72.

18 McDonald, "A Few Items in the West," in *Washington Historical Quarterly*, No. 8, p. 196.

19 Baynes to Hornby, Aug. 13, 1859, as quoted in Miller, *San Juan Archipelago*, p. 87

20 Douglas to Baynes, Aug. 15, 1859, ibid., p. 88

21 Douglas to Lytton, Aug. 17, 1859, ibid., p. 88.

22 Hornby to his wife, Dec. 4, 1859, as quoted in Miller, *San Juan Archipelago*, p. 42

Chapter 12

Reinforcements

1 *Victoria Gazette*, Aug. 11, 1859.

2. Harney to Scott, Aug. 18, 1859, *40th Congress*, pp. 162-163.

3 As quoted in Thompson, *Historic Resource Study*, p. 63.

4 Pickett to Pleasonton, Aug. 3, 1859, *40th Congress*, pp. 153-154.

5 Harney to Assist Adjutant General, Aug. 6, 1859, ibid., pp. 147-148.

6 Harney to Assistant Adjutant General, ibid., pp. 180.

7 Pleasonton to Pickett, Aug. 6, 1859, ibid., p. 158.

8 Pleasonton to Casey, Aug. 6, 1859, as quoted in Miller, *San Juan Archipelago*, p. 97.

9 Harney to Pacific Squadron Commander,Aug. 7, 1859, *40th Congress*, pp. 158-159.

10 Harney to Cooper, Aug. 8, 1859, ibid., p. 160. . This time Harney claimed the warship was the *Plumper*, revealing his unfamiliarity with British shipping in the Pacific Northwest.

11 Faust, *Encyclopedia of the Civil War*, p. 5. Alden had a reputation for being a careful mariner and his record attests to it (he retired a rear admiral). However, his caution made him forever after collaterally famous for his conduct during the Battle of Mobile Bay during the American Civil War. As captain of the U.S.S. *Brooklyn*, he was leading Admiral David Glasgow Farragut's line upriver into the harbor when the ironclad in front of him struck a mine and sank. Alden decided to stop to clear the mines, but when he let off steam the *Brooklyn* drifted sideways down river and began to foul the other ships under blazing Confederate guns. That's when Farragut grabbed a megaphone and scrambled into the rigging, screamed: "Damn the torpedoes!"

12 Pickett's warnings reveal that despite several amicable meetings between August 3-10, the Virginian still believed Hornby would attempt to stop the Americans from landing reinforcements. Hornby may have decided he was not going to press the issue, but he was not adverse to a good bluff.

13 Casey to Pleasonton, ibid., pp. 164-166. Most of what we know about Casey's landing comes from the colonel's report. This thorough document reflects Casey's "Old Army" reputation as a quietly competent and reliable officer although even Casey could not resist such passages as: "Seeing the danger of a collision at any moment, which would inevitably lead to war between two mighty nations connected by so many common bonds, and whichever way it might terminate would be eminently disastrous to the cause of civilization and the interests of humanity, I resolved to make an attempt to prevent so great a calamity." A less self-conscious Casey two weeks earlier wrote that he believed the British were "bluffing a little." The native Rhode Islander also graduated near the bottom of his West Point class, however his grasp of infantry tactics was so formidable that he wrote a book that was carried by

officers on both sides during the Civil War. However, he was not able to transfer his formidable thinking to the battlefield. His only fighting came during the Peninsula when he opposed, of all people, Brigadier General George Pickett. Pickett's men actually took a redoubt from Casey's forces and held it for more than 12 hours at the battle of Fair Oaks. Casey was relegated to commanding a brigade (as a major general of volunteers) in the Washington, D.C. defense works for the remainder of the war. After the war, he reverted to his regular army rank of colonel, retiring in 1868.

14 Hubbs, *Seattle Post Intelligencer*, June 4, 1892.

15 Casey to Pleasonton, Aug. 12, 1859, *40th Congress*, pp. 164-165.

16 Pleasonton to Casey, Aug. 16, 1859, ibid., p. 168.

17 Douglas to Lytton, Aug. 12, 1859, as quoted in Miller, *San Juan Archipelago*, p. 99.

18 Douglas to Harney, Aug. 13, 1859, ibid., pp. 171-172. In Hunter Miller's view, this allowed Harney to press his argument about British warships calling on the island. If a ship did not necessarily call for Cutlar, it did not rule out that it could have brought Dallas.

19 Ibid., p. 172. The question remains: If Douglas was concerned with preserving the peace, why didn't he raise the issue with Harney?

20 Campbell to Harney, Aug. 14, 1859, ibid., p. 187.

21 Harney to Campbell, Aug. 16, 1859, ibid., p. 169. Miller believed this was little more than lip service in view of Harney's other reports and orders.

22 Campbell to Harney, Aug. 30, 1859, ibid., p. 188; and Campbell to Cass, Sept. 3, 1859, ibid., pp. 119-120. The incident caught Campbell by surprise, but he clearly viewed it as Prevost's fault. In Campbell's mind, if the British commissioner had not been so prejudiced against the agreement if the first place, it would have been resolved long before Harney

arrived on the scene.

23 Victoria *Colonist*, Aug. 15, 1859; and Casey to Pleasonton, Aug. 14, 1859, *40th Congress*, pp. 167-168. Along with the naval guns came Granville O. Haller and Company I, finally released from three weeks aboard the ship. Wheezing about the islands aboard the old tub must have made the men feel like they were cursed by the Flying Dutchman, doomed never to see land again. However, their cruise was broken up on August 10 by an excursion up the Nooksack River to apprehend some raiders from the tribe of the same name. The Indians had slipped into the town of Whatcom the night before in an attempt to break one of their number out of jail. Guns were drawn at the corner of today's E and West Holly streets in Bellingham, and three Indians and a white man were killed. Haller quickly rounded up the "war party" and dispatched them to Fort Steilacoom where they were held on the good behavior of the rest of the tribe. Ironically, Haller did what George Pickett never did in Whatcom County: fight Indians.

24 Hornby to Baynes, Aug. 15, 1859, as quoted in Miller, *San Juan Archipelago*, p. 90.

25 Baynes to Hornby, Aug. 16, 1859, ibid., p. 91.

26 Hubbs, *Seattle Post Intelligncer*, June 4, 1892.

27 Dallas to Douglas, Aug. 5, 1859, San Juan Island NHP Archive .

28 Casey to Pleasonton, Aug. 14, 1859, *40th Congress*, p. 167.

29 Casey to Pleasonton, Aug. 22, 1859, ibid., p. 180. The new site actually was Casey's second choice. He had preferred an open area about three and half miles north, near False Bay, but it was too far from the HBC dock, which he believed he needed to control. Griffin left Belle Vue Farm and the island in 1862 and was replaced by Robert Firth, Sr. The HBC leased the site to Firth a year later and backed out altogether by the late 1860s.

30 Peck, *The Pig War*, pp. 98-101. Henry Martyn Robert, described as

"sickly" by William Peck, enjoyed a long career in the Corps of Engineers, retiring as a brigadier general in command of the corps, in 1903. However, he is most renowned for writing *Robert's Rules of Order*, a primer on parliamentary procedure still in use throughout the world. Largely because of this book, he is the only individual to be honored with a plaque in the national park.

31 Pleasonton to Casey, Aug. 16, 1859, *40th Congress*, p. 168.

32 Prevost to "Dear Sir," Aug. 22, 1859, as quoted in Thompson, *Historic Resource Report*, p. 132.

33 Victoria *Gazette*, Aug. 24, 1859. Stevens had landed and had a look around within days of Pickett's landing. While calling out the army was not something he had been prepared to do as governor—therefore it is doubtful that he counseled Harney to do it—he was nevertheless full of support for his old Mexican War comrades.

34 Macfie, *Vancouver Island and British Columbia,* pp.29-33.

35 Victoria *Colonist*, Aug. 17, 1859, 40th Congress, 176-177.

36 Douglas to Baynes, Aug. 17, 1859, as quoted in Miller, *San Juan Archipelago*, p. 89.

37 Baynes to Admiralty, Aug. 19, 1859, San Juan Island NHP Archive (copy from BC Archives). Here again lies the disparity between Capt. Michael DeCourcy's and Douglas's versions of when and for what purpose Magistrate John DeCourcy received his commission. True, rumors of the landing were circulating throughout the Puget Sound and Strait of Juan de Fuca, as evidenced by the newspaper articles. But Douglas was genuinely floored by the information that came to him from John DeCourcy via the *Satellite* on July 28.

38 Ibid. In the nineteenth century filibusters were defined as armed adventurers attempting to foment revolution in a foreign country, mainly Latin America. The most famous was William Walker, another Tennessean, who in 1856 took over the government of Nicaragua, introduced

slavery and was formerly recognized by U.S. President Franklin Pierce. He was deposed and deported back to the United States but twice returned. His career came to an end in 1860 when he was captured in Honduras by the Royal Navy, who handed him over to Honduran officials, who marched him in front of a firing squad.

39 Newcastle to Douglas, Sept. 20, 1859, as quoted in Miller, *San Juan Archipelago*, p. 95.

40 Harney to Douglas, Aug. 24, 1859, *40th Congress*, pp. 171-172.

41 Harney to Cooper, Aug. 29, 1859, ibid., pp, 177-178; and Miller, *San Juan Archipelago*, p. 101. Harney mistakenly referred to the body of water around the San Juan Islands as Puget Sound. Actually several bodies of water surround the island, including the Haro, Rosario, Georgia and Juan de Fuca straits, collectively called the "Salish Sea" by anthropologists. Puget Sound begins at Admiralty Inlet near Port Townsend, about 20 miles southeast of San Juan Island. Harney's comments about the HBC's treatment of native populations seem hypocritical, when one considers his central strategy in the Brule Sioux War was attacking winter encampments occupied by women and children.

42 Harney to Cooper, Aug. 30, 1859, ibid., p. 179. Cronstadt, or Kronstadt, was a Russian fortress city near St. Petersburg that the British unsuccessfully shelled during the Crimean War in 1855.

43 For more on William Moore, see Chapter 14, n. 25. Mistrust of the federal government remains a constant to this day among some on San Juan Island.

44 McDonald, "A Few Items from the West," *Washington Historical Quarterly*, July 1917.

Chapter 13

Washington and London

1 Kendall, *The Panama Route*, pp. 179-199

2 Drinkard to Harney, Sept. 3, 1859, *40th Congress*, pp. 148-149.

3 Lyons to Cass, Sept. 3, 1859, FO *Abstract*, pp. 159-160.

4 Ibid., p. 160.

5 Lyons to Cass, Sept. 7, 1859, *40th Congress*, pp. 225-226.

6 Cass to Lyons, Sept. 9, 1859, ibid., pp. 226-227.

7 Russell to Lyons, Aug. 24, 1859, FO *Abstract*, p. 153.

8 Russell to Lyons, Sept. 22, 1859, ibid., p.161.

9 Lyons to Russell, Sept. 12, 1858 and Sept. 13, 1859, ibid., pp. 169-174. According to Hunter Miller, this passage appears in the original letters, but was omitted in the version sent to the U.S. Government Printing Office for inclusion in the Congressional Record. Hawkins left Victoria again on the 8th, catching a mail packet from San Francisco on the 20th. He arrived in New York on Sept.12 and Washington D.C., the next day where he reported to Lyons and also met with Cass. He left for London on the 14th and arrived there on the 23rd.

10 Lyons to Russell, Sept. 13, 1859, ibid., pp. 172-174.

11 Russell to Lyons, Sept. 26, 1859, ibid., p. 174

12 Drinkard to Scott, Sept. 16, 1859, 40th Congress, pp. 160-161.

13 Lay would be a solid asset to Scott during the San Juan crisis, as the smooth Virginian established amicable relations with Douglas. He resigned his commission and joined the Confederacy in 1861, serving obscurely in an administrative capacity. Thomas had been Scott's chief of staff since 1853. During the Civil War he served for a time as adjutant general for the Army of the Potomac, but ran afoul of Secretary of War

Edmund Stanton and was banished to the West to organize Negro regiments. After the war he was named Acting Secretary of War by President Andrew Johnson, who also had good reason to despise Stanton. Thomas testified in the president's behalf during Johnson's impeachment proceedings.

14 Lyons to Russell, Sept. 15, 1859, FO *Abstract*, p. 175. In regards to Cass's secrecy, Lyons wrote: "The Secretary of State told me, both yesterday and to-day that he had received no further intelligence respecting the occurrences at San Juan. Despatches as late a date as the 12th instant must, however, in all probability have reached the war department from General Harney; and it is possible that alarming information contained in them respecting the intentions or disposition of the writer may have led to General Scott's being sent to supercede him."

15 Lyons to Cass, Oct. 1, 1859, *40th Congress*, pp. 228-229.

16 Cass to Lyons, Oct. 22, 1859, ibid., pp. 230-231.

Chapter 14

Stand Down

1 As quoted in Eisenhower, *Agent of Destiny,* p. 198. John S.D. Eisenhower's 1997 work is a good source of information on Scott. Edward Mansfield's *Life and Services of General Winfield Scott*, written to coincide with Scott's presidential candidacy in 1852 is another good secondary source. Most of the background on Scott in this work is drawn from both books.

In the Buffalo-Niagara Falls incident in late 1837, Canadian reformers who called themselves "Patriots" decided on armed revolt to throw the British out of Canada. Americans south of the line—led by "General" Rensselaer Van Rensselaer, son of the War of 1812 general— provided money and weapons. When British authorities exerted pressure, the Patriots and their American allies steamed over to Navy Island, north of the line, and issued their own declaration of "independence" of Canada from Britain. Loyal Canadians responded by assaulting the island, capturing the steamer, setting it afire and sending it over Niagara Falls. Unfortunately, an American was killed in the fracas, which prompted an eruption of war fever, never mind the Canadian protest that the steamer was little more than a "pirate ship." With the country mired in a financial crisis, the last thing President Martin Van Buren needed was war with Great Britain. Scott quickly restored calm and disbanded Van Rensselaer's tin-pot military force, but his efforts were nearly unhinged when the British mistakenly set fire to a ship that had recently been placed in the service of the United States.

The Aroostook Controversy was another loose end in the Treaty of Ghent. The area of contention was a forest in which locals from both nations claimed harvest rights. The crisis flared when respective local posses sent to apprehend "timber poachers" collided, each side capturing a man, including the Royal Warden of the Canadian province. Reinforcements were called in and Van Buren once again ordered Scott to do all he could to avoid an "untoward mistake." Scott replied: "Mr. President, if you want war I need only look on in silence. The Maine people will make it for you fast and hot enough. But if peace be your wish, I can give no assurance of success. The difficulties in the way will be formidable." The people of Maine thought Scott came to fight, but were soon disappointed. Scott convinced both governments to return their prisoners, and revert to the status quo, but no Maine politician would go along with the agreement for fear of alienating his constituency. That's when Scott waded in stroking and cajoling, convincing all parties to let him handle it and offering to take the blame if any were to be assigned. He then took advantage of his friendship with the lieutenant general, Major General Sir John Harvey, who had opposed him during the War of 1812. The two came to an amicable settlement and the crisis and war had been averted.

2 Thomas to Cooper, Oct. 22, 1859, *40th Congress*, pp. 188-189.

3 Harney to Scott, Sept. 14, 1859, ibid, pp. 181-182. All of these observations were partially true, but they actually applied to the early years of white settlement, when the Royal Navy called intermittently and Douglas was enforcing his "forest diplomacy" against Indian villages harboring raiders. The *Beaver* and *Otter* were not effective during Sheriff

Barnes's sheep raid, nor against the onslaught of American miners during the Fraser River gold rush. Those days were gone. The Royal Navy's Pacific Station squadron protected British interests and Harney knew it. Harney could have refuted Douglas's remarks by pointing to the recently expired HBC charter to colonize Vancouver Island; to Douglas's long executive tenure with the company, which only ended that spring when he became governor of British Columbia as well as Vancouver Island; and to the fact that A.G Dallas, his son-in-law, was a governor and major power with the company.

4 Harney to Floyd, Oct. 10, 1859; and Campbell to Harney, Aug. 14, 1859, ibid, pp. 184-188.

5 Gholson to Cass, as quoted in Miller, *San Juan Archipelago*, p. 112. Gholson wrote, "...thus declining to give me an opportunity to comply with my instructions 'to cooperate with' him, and also the benefit of whatever information my official position, and residence in the Territory had enabled me to acquire."

6 *Daily Alta California*, Nov. 23, 1859, typewritten copy, San Juan Island NHP Archive.

7 Ibid.

8 Peck, The Pig War, p.

9 *Daily Alta California*, Nov. 23, 1859.

10 Peck, The Pig War, p.

11 Ibid, p. On October 31, Peck reported that the command was drilled in preparation for the ceremony, under the direction of "his Royal Highness Major Haller," who takes much pride and pleasure in the pomp and circumstance of war, albeit, he has been court martialed for cruelty to enlisted men within the last twelve months."

12 The photographs are in the collections of San Juan Island NHP, the Provincial Archives in Victoria, B.C., and the Whatcom Museum of His-

tory and Art in Bellingham, WA. Photos of the camp, including a photo-mural of the artillery men, were on view in the American Camp visitor center in 1999.

13 *Daily Alta California*, Nov. 23, 1859.

14 Douglas to Scott, Oct. 29, 1859, *40th Congress*, pp. 193-194.

15 Harney to Scott, Oct. 29, 1859 with inclosure, ibid, pp. 190-191.

16 Scott to Douglas, Nov. 2, 1859, ibid, pp. 194-195.

17 Ibid, p. 196.

18 Miller, *San Juan Archipelago*, p. 114.

19 Douglas to Scott, Nov. 3, 1859, *40th Congress*, pp. 196-197. This conformed to the old HBC charter that discouraged expansion that would require the company to pay for the maintenance of troops (See Chapter 5). On the other hand, Douglas also had insisted heretofore that San Juan Island was a sovereign dependency of the Vancouver island colony.

20 Scott to Douglas, Nov. 5, 1859, ibid, pp. 197-198.

21 Peck, *The Pig War*, p.

22 Lay to Douglas, Nov. 7, 1859, as quoted in Miller, *San Juan Archipelago*, pp. 115-116.

23 Young to Scott, Nov. 7, 1959, ibid, pp. 116-117. This letter and Lay's (above) are not included in the official correspondence relating to the matter in the 40th Congress. Moreover, a postscript concerning Pickett's removal was added to Scott's letter of the 5th for official purposes and Thomas's order removing all reinforcements from the island also was backdated to the 5th.

24 Hunt to McBlair, date unknown, ibid, p. 20.

25 Casey to Young, Nov. 21, 1859, p. 205; Crosbie to Gholson, Nov. 30, 1859, p. 205-206; and Douglas to Scott, Nov. 7, 1859, with enclosures, pp. 199-200, 40th Congress. Moore, who claimed to be a British subject, contended he was unjustly punished for selling liquor. He was arrested on September 16 by Magistrate Crosbie for selling a bottle of rum to a soldier named "Crow." Moore claimed he never sold liquor to any soldier, but was judged guilty, deprived of his purse, which contained $160 in cash, and thrown into a tent jail with seven miscreant soldiers. He was ordered to work the next morning with the others on the redoubt, which involved "rolling stones and shoveling earth." Late in the afternoon the constable, none other than Lyman Cutlar, took him from his duties and brought him before Crosbie again. Cutlar removed $75 from Moore's purse, which Crosbie pronounced as Moore's fine. Moore was then released. According to Crosbie, Moore had been "sick and destitute" in Whatcom and cared for at the public expense of $300 not 16 months before. At that time he claimed American citizenship. Back on his feet again Moore had, in fact, sold large quantities of liquor to all persons on the island, Crosbie wrote. The matter was dropped.

26 Thomas to Harney, Nov. 9, 1859, ibid, pp. 202-203. Thomas's letter arrived with enclosures including Scott's November 5 and 9 letters to Scott establishing that no U.S. territorial official would interfere with British subjects nor claim exclusive jurisdiction over the island until the boundary dispute was settled. Miscreant British subjects were to be turned over to British authorities and vice versa. The other enclosure was the order sending Casey's reinforcements back to Forts Bellingham, Townsend and Steilacoom and replacing Pickett with Hunt.

27 *Pioneer and Democrat*, Dec. 2, 1859.

28 Tacoma Public Library, *Northwest Ships & Shipping Database*. Scott was lucky to make it. The *Northerner*, a twelve-year-old side-wheeler, was wrecked two months later in a similar storm off northern California. Forty people were killed. Considered old and worn for her day, the *Northerner* had been on the San Francisco-Columbia River-Puget Sound route at irregular intervals for several years, most of the time in command of either William or Chris Dall. She left San Francisco on her last

trip January 4 at 4:30 p.m., bound for the Columbia River and Puget Sound ports. At 4 p.m. the next day, when about two miles off shore, she struck Blunt's Reef near Cape Mendocino.The captain ran for shore and grounded the vessel on the reef, about twenty miles south of Humboldt Bay. Passengers and crew died when lifeboats overturned in the heavy seas.

29 Scott to Harney, Nov. 15, 1859, *40th Congress*, p. 203.

30 Harney to Scott, Nov. 17, 1859, ibid, p. 204.

31 Peck, *The Pig War*, pp.

32 Throughout his army career, U.S. and Confederate, George Pickett could somehow find a reason to be absent from his post. Army leaves in those days could extend to six months or more. He also was frequently appointed to court martial boards, which, because of the low quality of antebellum enlisted men, were assembled often. Court martials could only be called on the regimental level so that meant board members had to travel to the headquarters post. For the Ninth it was Fort Dalles, even though, as with most frontier regiments, the companies were scattered throughout the territory. Pickett was a popular officer in the old army with lots of connections, which in the case of Fort Vancouver, included Rufus Ingalls, the regimental quartermaster, Alfred Pleasonton, the acting adjutant general, and, of course, William Harney himself. James Forsyth was usually in charge as in the case of the *Harney* wreck and the inspection visit in 1858 of Col. Joseph K. F. Mansfield. Forsyth was an extremely capable officer and this did not hurt his career.

33 Camp San Juan island, Fort Bellingham letterbooks, RG 393, NA, San Juan Island NHP Archive.

34 Ibid.

Chapter 15

Pickett Lands Again

1 George E. Pickett to George E. Cullum, Feb. 19, 1860, as quoted in Longacre, *Pickett: Leader of the Charge*, pp. 48-49; Gordon, *Pickett*, p.p. 61-62; and RG94, NA, SAJHA . Pickett requested a court of inquiry in September 1860 "to investigate his conduct while in command at S.J.I., W.T." The request was forwarded by District of Oregon commander Colonel George Wright, but was never acted upon. That Pickett should wonder why he was being censured seems to further demonstrate his ignorance of issues of the day.

2 Resolution, Council of Washington Territory, Jan. 7, 1860, *40th Congress*, pp. 207-208; and Gordon, *Pickett*, pp. 61-62.

3 L.C. Hunt to Mrs. McBlair, Nov. 24, 1859, as quoted in Murray, "Pig War Letters," *Columbia* 1:3, p. 17.

4 Hunt to McBlair, date unknown, ibid., p. 20.

5 As quoted in Miller, *San Juan Archipelago*, pp. 119-121.

6 Ibid., pp. 121-122.

7 Ibid., pp. 127-128.

8 Russell to Lyons, Oct. 6, 1859, FO *Abstract*, pp. 176-178.

9 RG76, NA, *Geographical Memoir* , pp. 115-116. William J. Warren, secretary of the U.S. Northwest Boundary Commission camped at the site on Feb. 7, 1860 and described in his journal the ruins of an "old lodge House" that had been about 500 to 600 feet long and 50 to 60 feet wide. He also describe "immense quantities of clam shells on the shore." Archaeologist Dr. Julie Stein of the University of Washington has suggested that the structure may not have been a ruin as such, but a winter dwelling belonging to Coast Salish Indian clans. It was common in the culture for the villagers to remove the planks and take them along to spring and summer food gathering areas. Dimension lumber even then was at a premium. If Dr. Stein's assumptions are correct,

imagine the surprise of the original inhabitants when they returned to find red-coated infantry raking the shell midden and throwing up barracks. However, there is no known record of such an encounter.

10 As quoted in Thompson, *Historic Resource Study*, p. 98.

11 Joy, W., Journals. Portsmith City Museum, England, U. K., typed copy, SAJHA. Joy did not mention the lodge house ruin described by Warren.

12 Hunt to Pleasonton, with attachments, March 27, 1860, *40th Congress*, pp. 208-209.

13 Petition to Harney, March 7, 1860; Pleasonton to Hunt, March 21, 1860, *40th Congress*, p. 214-215.

14 Hunt to Pleasonton, with attachments, March 30, 1860, *40th Congress*, pp. 215-217; and Hunt to McBlair, date unknown, Murray, "Pig war Letters," *Columbia* 1:3, p. 20.

15 Pleasonton to Pickett, April 10, 1860, *40th Congress*, pp. 210-211,

16 Ironically, when Harney chose to become a peacemaker rather than a fighter in Missouri at the outset of the Civil War, he was fired and put out to pasture by the Lincoln government. He was recalled to duty in 1868 to help negotiate the end of the Red Cloud War.

17 Hunt to Scott, April 24, 1860, *40th Congress*, pp. 213-214.

18 Baynes to Admiralty, May 5, 1860, as quoted in Miller, *San Juan Archipelago*, p. 136.

19 Pickett to Pleasonton, May 21 and June 1, 1860, RG393, NA, SAJHA.

20 Ibid.

21 Scott to Floyd, May 14, 1860, *40th Congress*, pp. 212-213.

22 As quoted in Miller, San Juan Archipelago, p. 122.

23 Lyons to Cass, June 6, 1860, *40th Congress*, pp. 256-257.

24 Miller, *San Juan Archipelago*, n. p 139; and Cooper to Harney, June 8, 1860, *40th Congress*, p. 213.

25 Wright would capably hold the post until he and his wife drowned in a shipwreck off the Pacific Coast in 1865.

26 As quoted in Miller, *San Juan Archipelago*, p.140.

27 Pickett to Bazalgette, Sept. 8, 1860, SAJHA (copy from BC Archives).

Chapter 16

Joint Occupation and Settlement

1 Miller, *San Juan Archipelago*, pp. 142-144.

2 Russell to Lyons, Aug. 24, 1859, FO *Abstract*, pp. 147-156. Before offering arbitration in 1858, the British, however reluctantly, decided to wait for a report from Captain Richards aboard the *Plumper*. Many in the government still believed that San Juan Island was vital to British interests. Richards reported to Prevost in November 1858 that both channels presented problems for sailing vessels, although Rosario tended to be best. Either channel was acceptable for steamers. Ships transiting for Nanaimo—a source for coal and spars—and the Fraser River would find the Haro easier going, he reported, while those going from Port Townsend north would find the Rosario preferable (as they do today). The San Juan Channel, while considerably narrower, offered safe passage for steamers. Next, in an intriguing opinion—at least for an Englishman—Edmund (later Lord) Hammond, the Permanent Undersecretary for Foreign Affairs in February 1858, opted for the Haro Strait as the "best navigable channel." He was probably influenced by General Sir John Fox Burgoyne, who wrote in 1856 that the British

should not insist on Rosario just because Vancouver charted it "if a decidedly more important one in width and depth be found..." The Admiralty once again in March 1859 stated that giving up the islands was hardly critical so long as British shipping had free access to the channel selected. That's when Russell, as earlier noted, proposed the "Middle Channel". This was the compromise Russell proposed in August 1859 when, unbeknownst to him, the crisis was in full swing. And it was this proposal that was rejected by Secretary of State Lewis Cass in October. By then the issue was in such turmoil, so many toes had been stepped upon, that the British considered it a point of honor to hold onto the islands.

3 Lyons to Cass, Dec. 10, 1860, *40th Congress*, pp. 264-265.

4 Lyons to Russell, Feb. 18, 1861, as quoted in Miller, *San Juan Archipelago*, pp. 151-153.

5 RG393, NA, San Island letter books, SAJHA.

6 Pickett to Bazalgette, June 20, 1861, ibid.

7 Inman, Soldier of the South, pp. 1-6. Inman's book features George Pickett's letters to his wife, LaSalle Corbell Pickett. Douglas Southall Freeman, author of *Lee* and *Lee's Lieutenants,* considered these letters unreliable sources (as do most Civil War historians) because she rewrote them. We're teased with a glimpse of the real Pickett through the brief number of letters from Fort Bellingham, during the Pig war crisis and in the *Official Records of the Rebellion*.

8 *Official Records, War of the Rebellion,* Vol. L., Pt. 1., BC. Pickett is not listed on the passenger manifest of the *Sonora*, which sailed from San Francisco to Panama on August 10, 1861. But the manifest does list Sam Barron, a young naval officer and Pickett associate, whom LaSalle wrote traveled east with George. The manifest also lists Edward Eldridge, a close friend from Pickett's Whatcom years who in photographs bears a strong resemblance to the Virginian. Eldridge later would look after the Whatcom County interests of Pickett's son, James, and rise to Pickett's defense after his death in 1875.The author gratefully acknowledges the

work of Mr. George Stammerjohan, a historian for the State of California who found the *Sonora's* manifest while researching ship movements in San Francisco.

9 Arriving in Virginia in September 1861, Pickett was considerably behind his peers in acquiring a general officer's billet. But he was well-connected and by January 1862 he was brigadier general. He fought his brigade in three actions before taking a bullet in the shoulder during the Battle of Gaines Mill. He was promoted to major general and given a division in September 1862. His first real fight with his division was at Gettysburg, where it was destroyed through no fault of his own. Pickett next appears in 1864, when he ordered 22 North Carolinians in Union uniform hanged as deserters following a failed assault at New Berne. U. S. Army Brigadier General John Peck sent Pickett a note claiming the men were Union soldiers and as such should be treated as prisoners of war. Pickett thanked Peck for the men's names, adding that he now knew exactly who to hang. Pickett's Civil War career came to an inglorious end when his division was overwhelmed and again destroyed at Five Forks. After the war, he had to flee to Canada for several months when Secretary of War Edmund Stanton wanted him tried for war crimes for the North Carolina hangings. General Ulysses S. Grant, an old army friend, interceded on his behalf , and Pickett was allowed to return home. However, he could never return to the army so he tried farming for awhile and eventually became an insurance agent in the greater Richmond area. He worked diligently to compile a division history until his death in July 1875 from an "abscess of the liver." He was only 50. He left LaSalle and their surviving son behind. His first son, James Tilton Pickett — whose mother was a northern Indian - remained in the Pacific Northwest where he worked as a newspaper illustrator. LaSalle deeded George's Bellingham property to James, but in the process stated that she and her son, George Junior, were the only legal heirs, essentially declaring James a bastard. James died, childless, at 30 of typhoid fever. George E. Pickett, Jr., had two sons, George E. Pickett III and Christiancy Pickett, whose offspring live throughout the United States. Several Pickett descendents have visited San Juan Island National Historical Park over the years, the first of whom was George E. Pickett III in the 1930s.

10 McDowell to Alvord, Sept. 18, 1864, as quoted in Miller, *San Juan Archipelago*, pp., 169-171. Former Army of Potomac commander McDowell, who lost the first battle of Bull Run, stumbled from one disaster to another in northern Virginia and was finally sent west to replace the drowned Wright. A job without field duties was to his liking and complimented his abilities. He continued to serve on the Pacific Coast until his death in 1882 .

11 *40th Congress*, pp. 266-268.

12 James, *The Rise and Fall of the British Empire*, pp. 172-173. James writes that dividends on British foreign investments rose from L5 million in 1830 to L50 million in 1870.

13. McCabe, *San Juan Water Boundary Question*, p. 10. Bancroft, was the U.S. ambassador to Great Britain during the Polk Administration and was a key player in the Treaty of Oregon negotiations. McCabe writes that Bancroft had opposed the proposal of the Swiss Federation as arbiter in 1869, and was adamant that the "Middle Channel" not be considered as a compromise.

14 Miller, *Northwest Water Boundary*, pp. 31-67.

15. Ibid., pp. 31-67.

Bibliography

Studies

Floyd, Dale. *Comparative Analysis, American Camp Fortifications, San Juan Island National Historical Park.* Washington, D.C.: CEHP Incorporated, 1996

Sprague, Roderick, Ed. *San Juan Archaeology.* Bound MMS, two volumes. Moscow, ID: University of Idaho, 1983.

Thompson, Erwin N. *Historic Resource Study: San Juan Island National Historical Park, Washington*. Denver, CO: Denver Service Center, National Park Service, 1972.

Manuscripts

Haller, Granville O. *The San Juan Imbroglio*. Typewritten MMS, Bancroft Library, University of California, Berkeley. 1889.

Roder (Roeder), Henry. Dictation by Hubert H. Bancroft. Handwritten MMS, Bancroft Library, University of California, Berkeley. 1878.

Vouri, Michael P. *George Pickett and the Frontier Army Experience, Washington Territory 1854-1859*. MMS. San Juan Island National Historical Park Archives (SAJHA), Friday Harbor, Washington. 1994.

Newspapers

Friday Harbor, (Washington), *San Juan Islander*, 1909

London, (England), *Illustrated News*, 1859.

Olympia, (Washington), *Pioneer and Democrat*, 1855-59.

Seattle, (Washington), *Post-Intelligencer*, 1892

Victoria, (B.C.), *Colonist*, 1859-72.

Victoria (B.C.), *Gazette*, 1859.

Documents

Government Documents

National Archives, Washington D. C. 20048.

RG 92, Records of the Office of the Quartermaster General
RG 94, Records of the Office of the Adjutant General
E225, Consolidated Correspondence Files, San Juan Island, Box 985

RG 393, Records of the United States Army Continental Commands, 1821-1920
Post Records, San Juan Island, eight volumes.
Vol. 1: Letters Sent (Camp Pickett Only, August 1859-July 1861)
Vol. 2: Letters Sent (August 1863-July 1867)
Vol. 3: Letters Sent (October 1868-January1872)

Vol. 4: Letters Sent (August 1867-September 1868)
Vol. 5: Orders and Special Orders (August 1859-Decem ber 1861)
Vol. 6: General Orders, Special Orders (January 1861- Sep tember1868)
Vol. 7A: Orders and Special Orders (1868-1874)
Records and Reclaims, Vol. 7 (History and Description of Post)

RG76, E198, Journals of Exploring Surveys. *Geographical Memoir of the Islands between the Continent and Vancouver Island in the Vicinity of the 49th Parallel of North Latitude*, SAJHA. Archibald Campbell with appendices by Dr. C.B.R. Kennerly, George Gibbs, Henry Custer and W.J. Warren. [The memoir, without the appendices, was published as part of the record of the 40th Congress. The appendices were hand-copied by Mr. Greg Lange and kindly provided to the author by Dr. Wayne Suttles].

Microfilm, M617, Returns from U.S. Military Posts, 1800-1916, Roll 1112, San Juan Island, Washington Territory.

Report of Col. Joseph K.F. Mansfield on the U.S. Military Reservation at Bellingham Bay, Washington Territory, Dec. 7-8, 1858.

Government Publications

U.S. Congress. Senate. Executive Document No. 10. 36th Cong., 1st. Sess. *The Northwest Boundary Discussion of the Water Boundary Question: Geographical Memoir of the Islands in Dispute: and History of the Military Occupation of San Juan Island.* Washington, D.C.: 1868.

U.S. Congress. Senate. Executive Document No. 29. 40th Cong., 2nd Sess. *Report of the Secretary of State.* Washington, D.C.: 1867-

1868.

U.S. Navy Department, Office of the Chief of Naval Operations, Naval History Division. *Dictionary of American Naval Fighting Ships*. Washington, D.C.: GPO, 1969.

Fields, Virgil, F., ed., The National Guard, State of Washington, Collection of Official Documents on the San Juan Imbroglio, 1859-1872. (N.D., N.P.)

British Foreign Office. *San Juan Boundary: Abstract of Correspondence Relative to the Disputed Right of Territory Watered by the Oregon, or Columbia River. 1842 to 1869*. December 1871. (Marked "Confidential.") This document is essentially a narrative of correspondence and documents related to the issue compiled by the British Foreign Office.

Other Documents

Howard E. Buswell Collections, Center for Pacific Northwest Studies, Western Washington University, Bellingham, WA 98225. Buswell was a Bellingham historian, who compiled an extensive collection of pamphlets, photographs, maps, journals, historical reference works, newspapers, microfilms and audio-tapes. His primary interest was lower Nooksack Valley history.

Hudson's Bay Company Records, microfilm, *Post Journals, Belle Vue Sheep Farm, 1854-1855 and 1858-1862*. Hudson's Bay Company Archives, Winnipeg, Manitoba, Canada.

Joy, W., *Journals*. Portsmouth City Museum, England, United Kingdom. Copies housed in San Juan Island NHP Archive.

Roder, Henry, Capt. *Narrative*, dictation by Hubert Howe Bancroft,

Port Townsend, Washington, June 22, 1878. H.H. Bancroft Collection, Bancroft Library, University of California, Berkeley, CA.

Internet

Northwest Ships & Shipping Database. Tacoma, WA: Tacoma Public Library. This database is available over the Internet.

Books

Bancroft, Hubert Howe. *The Works of Hubert Howe Bancroft : History of the Pacific States of America* Volume XXVI, *History of Washington, Idaho, and Montana, 1845-1889* . San Francisco: The History Company, Publishers. 1890.

Bancroft, Hubert Howe. *The Works of Hubert Howe Bancroft: History of the Pacific States of North America.* Volume XXVII, *History of British Columbia, 1792-1887.* San Francisco: The History Company, Publishers. 1887.

Barkan, Francis B., ed. *The Wilkes Expedition Puget Sound and the Oregon Country.* Olympia, WA: Washington State Capital Museum, 1987.

Bemis, Samuel Flagg. *A Diplomatic History of the United States.* New York: Henry Holt and Company (3rd ed.), 1950.

Bennett, Robert A., ed. *A Small World of Our Own: Authentic pioneer stories of the Pacific Northwest from the Old Settlers' Contest of 1892.* Walla Walla, WA: Pioneer Press Books, 1985.

Billings, John David. *Hardtack and Coffee: Or the Unwritten Story of Army Life.* Williamstown, MA: Corner House Publishers, 1973.

Billington, Ray Allen. *Westward Expansion: A History of the American Frontier* . 3rd edition. New York: The Macmillan Company, 1967. Billington's thesis of the westward expansion remains the seminal work on the subject in the historiography of the American West. His view that the passage of Walker Tariff and the repeal of the Corn Laws sped the signing of the Oregon Treaty of 1846 is further underscored by fiscal realities. The British then, as now, were the largest foreign investors in the fledgling United States.

Clow, Richmond L. "William S. Harney." In *Soldier's West: Biographies from the Military Frontier*, edited by Paul Andrew Hutton. Lincoln, NE: University of Nebraska Press, 1987.

Coffman, Edward M. *The Old Army: A Portrait of the American Army in Peacetime, 1884-1898*. New York: Oxford University Press, 1986.

Deutsch, Herman J., ed. *Surveying the 49th Parallel, 1858-61*. Tacoma, WA: Washington State Historical Society, 1962.

DeVoto, Bernard. *The Year of Decision 1846*. Boston: Houghton Mifflin Company, 1943.

Duncan, Janice K. *Minority without a Champion Kanakas on the Pacific Coast, 1788-1850*, Portland, OR: Oregon Historical Society, 1972.

Edson, Lelah Jackson. *The Fourth Corner*. Bellingham, WA: The Whatcom Museum of History and Art, 1968.

Eisenhower, John S.D. *Agent of Destiny: The Life and Times of General Winfield Scott*. New York: The Free Press, 1997.

__________________. *So Far From God The U.S. War with Mexico 1846-1848*. New York: Doubleday, 1989.

Elliot, Charles Winslow. *Winfield Scott: The Soldier and the Man*. New York: The MacMillan Company, 1937.

Faust, Patricia L., ed. *Historical Times Illustrated Encyclopedia of the Civil War*. New York: Harper & Row, 1986.

Gardner, Alison F. *James Douglas*. Don Mills, Ontario: Fitzhenry & Whiteside, Ltd., 1976.

Gates, Charles Marvin, ed. "Report of Col. Joseph J.K. Mansfield on the U.S. military reservation at Port Townsend, Washington Territory, Dec. 3-4, 1858." *Readings in Pacific Northwest History, Washington 1790-1895*, Seattle, WA: University Bookstore, 1941.

Goetzmann, William H., and Glyndwr Williams. *The Atlas of North American Exploration From the Norse Voyages to the Race to the Pole*. New York: Prentice Hall General Reference, 1992.

Goetzman, William H. *New Lands, New Men America and the Second Great Age of Discovery*. New York: Viking Penguin Inc., 1986.

____________________, *Army Exploration in the American West, 1803-1863*. Austin: Texas State Historical Association, 1991.

Gordon, Leslie J., *Pickett: General George Pickett in Life & Legend*. Chapel Hill: University of North Carolina Press, 1998.

Gough, Barry M. *The Royal Navy and the Northwest Coast of North America, 1810-1914*. Vancouver: University of British Columbia Press, 1971.

Green, Frank L. *Captains, Curates and Cockneys: The English in the Pacific Northwest*. Tacoma, WA: Washington State Historical Society, 1981.

Haller, Granville, O. *San Juan and Secession*. Seattle: The Shorey Book Store, 1967.

Hart, Herbert M. *Pioneer Forts of the West*. Seattle: Superior Publishing Company, 1967.

Haycox, Stephen; Barnett, James K.; and Liburd, Caedmon A.., eds. *Enlightenment and Exploration in the North Pacific 1741-1805*. Seattle: University of Washington Press, 1997.

Heidler, David S., and Jeanne T. Heidler. *Old Hickory's War Andrew Jackson and the Quest for Empire*. Mechanicsburg, Pennsylvania: Stackpole Books, 1996

Higgins, D.W. *The Mystic Spring and Other Tales of Western Life.* Toronto: William Briggs, 1904.

Howay, Frederick, W. *British Columbia from the Earliest Times to the Present.* Vancouver: The S.J. Clarke Publishing Company, 1914.

Hutchinson, Bruce. *The Struggle for the Border*. New York: Longmans, Green and Co., 1955.

James, Lawrence. *The Rise and Fall of the British Empire*. New York: St. Martin's Griffin, 1997.

Johansen, Dorothy O., and Charles M. Gates. *Empire of the Columbia: a History of the Pacific Northwest*. New York: Harper & Brothers, Publishers, 1957.

Josephy, Alvin M., Jr. *The Civil War in the American West.* New York: Vintage Books, 1991.

Kemble, John Haskell. *The Panama Route, 1848-1869.* Columbia, S.C.: University of South Carolina Press, 1990.

Lavender, David. *Land of Giants: The Drive to the Pacific Northwest, 1750-1950.* Garden City, New York: Doubleday & Company, Inc., 1958.

James, Lawrence. *The Rise and Fall of the British Empire.* New York: St. Martin's Griffin, 1994.

Longacre, Edward G. *Pickett: Leader of the Charge.* Shippensburg, PA: White Mane Publishing Company, Inc., 1995.

Macfie, Matthew. *Vancouver Island and British Columbia, their History, Resources and Prospects.* London: Longman, Green, 1865.

Mackie, Richard Somerset. *Trading Beyond the Mountains: The British Fur Trade on the Pacific 1793-1843.* Vancouver, B.C., Canada: University of British Columbia Press, 1997

McCabe, James O. *The San Juan Water Boundary Question.* Toronto: University of Toronto Press, 1965.

McDougall, Walter A. *Let The Sea Make A Noise: A History of the North Pacific from Magellan to MacArthur.* New York: Basic Books, A Division of HarperCollins Publishers, Inc., 1993.

Miller, David Hunter. *San Juan Archipelago: Study of the Joint Occupation of San Juan Island.* Belows Falls, VT: Wyndam Press, 1943.

________________. *Northwest Water Boundary, Report of the Experts Summoned by the German Emporer as Arbitrator Under Articles 34-42 of the Treaty of Washington of May 8, 1871, Preliminary to His Award dated October 21, 1872*, Seattle: University of Washington, 1942.

Milton, Viscount W. Fitzwilliam, M.P. *A History of the San Juan Water Boundary Question as affecting the Division of Territory Between Great Britain and the United States.* London: Cassell, Peter and Galpin, 1869.

Morgan, Murray. *Puget's Sound: A Narrative of Early Tacoma and the Southern Sound.* Seattle and London: University of Washington Press, 1979.

Mozino, Jose Mariano. *Noticias de Nutka: An Account of Nootka Sound in 1792.* Seattle and London: University of Washington Press, 1970.

Murray, Keith. *The Pig War.* Tacoma: Washington State Historical Society, 1968.

Nokes, J., Richard. *Columbia's River The Voyages of Robert Gray, 1787-1793.* Tacoma: Washington State Historical Society, 1991.

Peck, William A., Jr. (Coulter, C. Brewster and Webber, Bert, eds.). *The Pig War and other Experiences of William Peck, Soldier, 1858-1862,* edited by C. Brewster Coulter and Bert Webb. Medford, OR: Webb Research Group, 1993.

Pethick, Derek. *James Douglas: Servant of Two Empires.* Vancouver: Mitchell Press Limited, 1969.

Pickett, LaSalle Corbell. *Pickett and His Men. Atlanta*: Foote & Davis Company, 1889.

____________________, ed. *The Heart of a Soldier as Revealed in the Intimate Letters of Genl. George E. Pickett, C.S.A.* New York: Seth Moyle, 1913.

Polk, James Knox. *Polk: Diary of a President, 1845-1849*, edited by Allan Nevins. New York: Longman's, Green and Co., 1929.

Richards, Kent D. *Isaac I. Stevens: Young Man in a Hurry*. Pullman, WA: Washington State University Press, 1993.

Richardson, David. *Pig War Islands*. Eastsound, WA: Orcas Publishing Company, 1971.

Roth, Lottie Roder, ed. *History of Whatcom County*. Vol. I. Seattle: Pioneer Historical Publishing Co., 1926.

Scott, James W., and Roland L. DeLorme. *Historical Atlas of Washington*. Norman, OK: University of Oklahoma Press, 1988.

Selcer, Richard F. *Faithfully and Forever Your Soldier: General George E. Pickett, CSA*. Gettysburg, PA: Farnsworth House Military Impressions, 1995.

Stanley, George, F.G., ed. *Mapping the Frontier: Charles Wilson's Diary of the Survey of the 49th Parallel, 1858-1862, While Secretary of the British Boundary Commission*. Toronto: Macmillan of Canada, 1970.

Stewart, George R. *Pickett's Charge: A Microhistory of the final attack at Gettysburg, July 3, 1863.* Boston: Houghton Mifflin Company, 1987.

Swan, James G. *The Northwest Coast: Or Three Year's Residence in Washington Territory*. Seattle: University of Washington Press, 1992.

Utley, Robert M. *Frontiersmen in Blue: The United States Army and the Indian, 1848-1865*. Lincoln and London: University of Nebraska Press, 1967.

______________. *Frontier Regulars: The United States Army and the Indian, 1866-1891*. Bloomington and London: University of Indiana Press, 1973.

Wood, Bryce. *San Juan Island Coastal Place Names and Cartographic Nomenclature*, University Microfilms International, Ann Arbor, Michigan, 1980.

Wright, E.W., ed. *Lewis & Dryden's Marine History of the Pacific Northwest.* New York: Antiquarian Press, Ltd., 1961.

Magazine Articles

Barry, J. Nielson. "San Juan Island and the Civil War." *Washington Historical Quarterly*, 20:2. April 1929.

Clark, Robert Carlton. "The Diplomatic Mission of Sir John Rose, 1871." *Pacific Northwest Quarterly*, 27:3, (July 1936).

Fish, Andrew. "The Last Phase of the Oregon Boundary Question: The Struggle for San Juan Island." *Oregon Historical Quarterly*, XXII: 3, (September 1921).

Hamblett, E.T. "Sovereign Americans on San Juan island." *Washington Historical Quarterly*, 1:1, (October 1906).

Howard, Joseph Kinsey. "Manifest Destiny and the British Empire's Pig." *Montana, The Magazine of History*, 5:4, (Autumn 1955).

Howay, F.W., Lewis, William S., and Meyers, Jacob A.,"Angus McDonald: A Few Items from the West." Washington Historical Quarterly,8:3, (July 1917).

Jordan, Mabel E.,"The British on San Juan Island." *Canadian Geographical Journal,* LIX:1, (July 1959).

Long, John W., "The Origin and development of the San Juan Island Water Boundary Controversy." *The Pacific Northwest Quarterly*, 43:3, (July 1952).

McKay, Charles. "History of San Juan Island." *Washington Historical Quarterly*, 23:1,2,3,4 (January-October 1932): 290-293.

Murray, Keith. "Pig War Letters: A Romantic Account of the San Juan Crisis." *Columbia, The Magazine of Northwest History*, 1:3, (Fall 1987).

Magnuson, Warren G. "One-shot War with England." *American Heritage*, XI:3, (April 1960).

Patterson, Gerard A. "George E. Pickett — A Personality Profile." *Civil War Times Illustrated* , (May 1966).

Selcer, Richard F. "George Pickett:Another Look." *Civil War Times Illustrated*, (July/August 1994).

Smith, Albert Goldwin. "Notes on the problem of San Juan." *Pacific Northwest Quarterly*, 31:2, (April 1940).

Vouri, Michael P. "Raiders from the North: Northern Indians in Washington Territory in the 1850s." *Columbia The Magazine of Northwest History*. (Fall 1997).

Pamphlets

Vouri, Michael, P. "Royal Stand-off in Griffin Bay." San Juan Island National Historical Park, April 1996.

______________. " San Juan Island Civil War Connections." San Juan Island National Historical Park. November 1995.

______________. "American Camp: in war's dark shadow." San Juan Island National Historical Park.Ó May 1996.

______________. "English Camp: half a world from home." San Juan Island National Historical Park.

______________. "American Camp: A Historic Guided Walk." Northwest Interpretive Association, San Juan Island NHP. 1997.

______________. "English Camp: A Historic Guided Walk." Northwest Interpretive Association, San Juan Island NHP. 1998.

Index

(Sub-topics listed in chronological order.)

Michael Vouri

Historian Michael Vouri has worked as a museum curator, a National Park Service ranger/historian and a newspaper reporter and editor. He has written numerous history pieces for *Columbia, the Magazine of Northwest History* and other publications and has appeared on television's *History Channel*. He lives on San Juan Island, Washington, with his partner Susan and three golden retrievers.

L A N D
S H I N G T O N   T E R R I